The Queen City

A History of Denver

by

Lyle W. Dorsett

Volume One in the Western Urban History Series

PRUETT PUBLISHING COMPANY
Boulder, Colorado

Library of Congress Cataloging in Publication Data
Dorsett, Lyle W
    The Queen City: a history of Denver.
    (Western Urban History Series; V.I.)
    Bibliography: p.
    Includes index.
    1. Denver — History. I. Title.
F784.D45D67   978.8′83   77-7327
ISBN 0-87108-098-2

Quotations from Bill Hosokawa, *Thunder
in the Rockies* (1976) courtesy William
Morrow and Co.

All photographs courtesy of State Historical
Society of Colorado unless otherwise
acknowledged.

First Edition

1 2 3 4 5 6 7 8 9

Printed in the United States of America

Contents

For my wife, Mary Ann

Acknowledgments

This acknowledgment is longer than usual because few books owe so much to others. I have borrowed liberally from the writings of historians and journalists. I trust my indebtedness to them is clear in the *Bibliographical Note*.

Although I began researching this history when I moved to Colorado in 1971, Benjamin F. Stapleton, Jr. and the late George Cranmer enabled me to take a fifteen-month leave of absence from the University of Denver to complete the project. Mr. Cranmer wanted to see an up-to-date history done before, as he phrased it, "all the old-timers die or forget everything they know." We agreed that I should be free to write my own book without any censure from them or any foundation that might support the project.

George Cranmer set the proposal in motion, and Ben Stapleton found the grants. Thanks to Stapleton's efforts, the following foundations underwrote part of the project: Boettcher Foundation, Harms C. Fishback Foundation, Gates Foundation, Franklin L. Burns Foundation, Midwest Oil Foundation, Arthur E. Johnson Foundation, The Hill Foundation, and the O'Fallon Foundation. Mr. Alan E. Bussey in the Department of Development at the University of Denver administered these contributions, and his office secured a grant from the Tremont Foundation as well.

Chancellor Maurice Mitchell at the University of Denver agreed to pay my fringe benefits while I was on leave. Two colleagues, Robert C. Amme and Robert D. Richardson, served consecutively as deans of the Graduate School while this project was in progress. I thank them for awarding me faculty research grants so that I could make two out-of-state research trips.

Three colleagues in the History Department deserve mention.

My chairman, Professor Allen D. Breck, found sources for me and at the end of a difficult year came up with money to pay for the typing. Ms. Mary Behner spent hours of her precious time sorting out miles of red tape when my grant money got lost in the bureaucracy, and she always did so with humor and serenity. Special mention goes to Dr. John Livingston—he patiently listened to my woes, took over many of my chores while I was on leave, and critically evaluated many of my ideas on the book.

Several research assistants did yeoman work: Alexandra "Kiki" Happer, Raymond Neal, Peg Dietrich, Barbara Johnson, and Rick Steele. Kiki tracked down dozens of biographical sketches, surveyed the Chamber of Commerce records, investigated the ski industry, and gathered statistics on every imaginable subject. Ray did work on black Denver. Peg uncovered enough material to write her own book on Denver's annexations, and Barbara tracked down every article written on Denver in the periodical literature. Rick plotted the corporate structure of each railroad that came in and out of Denver, computed the miles of track, and organized it all so that I could use it.

Their work was facilitated by the able and cooperative staffs under the direction of Dr. Maxine Benson at the State Historical Society of Colorado, and Ms. Eleanor M. Gehres at the Western History Department of the Denver Public Library.

Dr. Benson deserves still another expression of gratitude. She dug out reams of documents for me and then generously contributed her knowledge of Colorado history to my effort by reading and criticizing the entire manuscript.

A valued friend and colleague is Dr. M. James Kedro. While tending to his own busy schedule, he discovered hundreds of sources for this book which I would have overlooked, and he read and critiqued the entire manuscript.

Professor A. Theodore Brown of the University of Wisconsin—Milwaukee, my former professor who introduced me to urban history, read the manuscript and offered insightful suggestions.

My wife Mary did so much on this manuscript that she really is co-author. She did research, typed the first draft, listened to my obsessive talk about Denver, and rewrote every page. Like the other readers of the manuscript, she significantly improved it. But like them, she will see that I dodged many suggestions. In short, where there are shortcomings, they can say "we told you so."

Much of this book is based on interviews. Everyone I approached gave freely of their time. George Cranmer saw me two afternoons a week for several months. Cris Dobbins gave me a morning of his busy schedule, and Ben Stapleton never turned me down, although I hounded him for weeks. Fay Carey of Colorado Women's College introduced me to Margaret Evans Davis and accompanied me when I visited the Evans Ranch. Thomas J. Noel, a free-lance writer and historian, shared his own research notes with me and introduced me to Benjamin Hooper. The latter granted me a long and candid interview.

Montgomery Dorsey submitted to several mornings of interviews and permitted me to remove photographs from his wall so that I could have them reproduced for this book.

Robert S. Pulcipher let me intrude on his hectic schedule. He answered numerous questions, furnished me books and photographs, and introduced me to Montgomery Dorsey and the Archives of the First of Denver.

Judi and Mark Foster helped more than they know. Judi gathered the data on the First Women's National Bank of Denver, a project in which she has assumed a prominent role. Mark, my longtime friend and colleague who teaches urban history at the University of Colorado-Denver, gave me his own research materials on Denver. He also helped me unravel complicated threads of the Queen City's history.

Several librarians outside of Denver were especially kind. Jack Brennan, who directs the Western History Collection at the University of Colorado's Norlin Library, and his efficient assistant, Cassandra Tiberio, were always pleasant and helpful. Robert W. Lovett at the Baker Library, Harvard University, did more than locate materials I requested. He found sources relating to my book that I did not know existed.

Two delightful couples made my research trips to Harvard extraordinary. Phil and Janet Greco, and Ron and Nancy Weiher all fed and housed me, squired me to some unforgettable entertainment establishments, and kept me from being lonely.

Thanks also goes to my students in the Denver and Colorado history classes at the University of Denver. They served as sounding boards for many of the themes developed here. I especially thank my former student Terri Cordova. She not only sat through my classes, she helped me clarify several parts of chapter ten.

Finally, I am indebted to Ms. Gina Ellis for her speedy typing of the final draft. Her critical comments were useful, too.

Boulder, Colorado   L.W.D.
August, 1976

Preface

Writing this history was a humbling experience. I was faced at once with an abundance and paucity of source material. Stashed away in libraries, archives, attics, and living memories is a record of parts of Denver's past which is so vast that I could not examine and interpret all of it if I chose to devote a lifetime to the efort. For some corners of the Queen City's history no records survive; or, at most, a few scraps of evidence exist which raised more questions than they answered.

In the midst of my work I came upon an observation by Loren Eiseley. One of the most sensitive and insightful men of our generation, the anthropologist-poet-essayist said precisely what I felt while writing this book: "No man could possibly assimilate every lie, half truth, and truth that bewitched the minds of a past century. With the relative clarity of aftervision we can attempt, at best, only some insights, some relative comprehension of ideas which will always be appraised anew by later generations. So great is the lure of documents, however, that it is easy to be lulled into a false sense of omnipotence."

This quotation points to more than the subjectivity surrounding the "facts" of history. It is a reminder that the questions one person asks about the past will not satisfy the curiosity felt by others.

Admittedly, this is a highly selective history. I not only chose sources which seemed relevant to me, I asked only the questions that struck me as fascinating. I assumed that Denver's emergence as the dominant regional metropolis was not inevitable. That distinction could have gone to any one of several other communities. I wanted to know who made the decisions and generated the resources that moved Denver forward. At the same time, I was curious about what happened to the quality of life as Denver grew from a frontier mining-outfitting post to a modern metropolis.

This book is divided into five parts. Each one covers a significant period of the city's development. Within each time period are two chapters. The first chapter for every section focuses on the community leaders who gave the town identity and direction. A companion chapter is devoted to quality of life.

Prologue

Prior to 1858 the region that is now eastern Colorado was ignored by Spaniards and Anglo-Europeans alike. Aside from some trappers, and traders, no one cared to challenge the Cheyenne, Arapahoe, or Ute Indians for the right to use land deemed worthless. Before the nineteenth century, Spanish explorers maintained that nothing of merit existed on the eastern foothills and plains. Their opinions were reinforced by Zebulon M. Pike when he explored the area in 1806. Four years later he wrote of "tracts of many leagues where the wind had thrown up the sand in all the fanciful form of the ocean's rolling waves, and on which not a speck of vegetable matter existed." Pike's observations were substantiated later by explorer Stephen Long. After his Rocky Mountain expedition, Long argued emphatically that the region was "wholly unfit for cultivation, and of course uninhabitable by a people depending upon agriculture for their subsistence."

During the 1830s and 1840s thousands of settlers from east of the Mississippi crossed the high plains and Rocky Mountains on their way to Oregon. Seldom did anyone offer a complimentary word about the "Great American Desert"—that wasteland between the 100th Meridian and the mountains. The forty-niners, as well as later speculators who followed in their wake to California, reinforced the bleak image of the vast region. The only positive talk about the entire area focused on Pike's Peak. Rumors had spread throughout the 1850s that Cherokee Indians en route to California had found gold in streams near Pike's Peak. Suddenly, in summer and fall 1858, rumor became reality. An organized party of thirty Cherokee Indians and several whites, among them William G. and J. Oliver Russell from Georgia and John Beck, a Baptist preacher from Oklahoma, set out for the Rockies to investigate the rumors. In June 1858 they camped where Denver is today. After finding sparse quantities of gold in Cherry Creek, they moved northward in search of richer streambeds.

While the Russells and their friends combed the area, a Lawrence, Kansas butcher, John Easter, organized a group to prospect the Pike's Peak area. Easter had been inspired by Fall Leaf, a Delaware Indian from a reservation near Lawrence. Fall Leaf had discovered nuggets near Pike's Peak while serving as a scout for the U.S. Army. Easter's party rushed to Pike's Peak and explored the streams south of the famous mountain. Having no luck, they moved to Cherry Creek, at which time they learned that the other prospectors were there. By October 1858 several members of Easter's contingent returned to Lawrence with a small amount of gold dust and with stories about their discoveries and those of the Russell Party.

In summer and fall 1858 the eyes of a depression-ridden nation, searching for any hope of recovery and wealth, turned toward the Rocky Mountains. Word of gold strikes spread from Lawrence to every town up and down the Missouri. Soon the stories reached the east coast. Most accounts were vague or inaccurate, reporting that gold was being discovered in the vicinity of Pike's Peak. Stories that placed discoveries elsewhere were equally erroneous. The Leavenworth, Kansas *Weekly Herald* told of yields near Long's Peak on the "South Fork" of the Platte, and the *Boston Journal* reported discoveries about 600 miles west of Topeka, Kansas. Some Missouri newspaper editors, fearful of mass migrations out of their communities, played down the stories as so much humbug. Despite their warnings of "dangerous crossings" to a desolate land, the editor of the Leavenworth *Herald* exclaimed in September 1858 that "the excitement is still on the increase, and spreading in every direction. St. Joseph, Council Bluffs, Nebraska and Omaha cities; Leavenworth, Kansas City, Independence, Westport, and Lawrence, are all preparing to send forward a living stream of emigration to the gold regions."

Beginning in fall 1858, and then gaining momentum with the more favorable traveling weather the following spring and summer, hundreds of fortune seekers set out for the Rocky Mountains. Most of these speculators were men—there were few women in the early months of migration—who intended to exploit the resources of the mountain streams and then return "home" with a fortune. Others hoped to find gold and then push on and build a new home in a productive land with their newly acquired wealth. A minority among the fifty-niners was a small group of men and women who had other ideas. Some had been involved in the California gold rush, and others had followed throngs of unattached men to scores of lumber or railroad boom towns. They were prospectors, too, but they hoped to find their fortunes panning the streams of baser human nature. Their plan was to exploit unbridled, lonely, and temporarily affluent men who were most certainly going to look for diversions from the boredom of prospecting. The one trait all fifty-niners had in common, though, was a desire to make money and move on. Few entertained visions of building a new life in the Rocky Mountains or on the Great American Desert.

Part I

Turnstile Town, 1858-1870

Chapter 1

On Sunday, April 17, 1859, a young man with dust clinging to his beard and clothing rode horseback into the frontier settlement at the junction of Cherry Creek and the South Platte River. He was William N. Byers. Little in the background of this twenty-eight-year-old newcomer distinguished him from hundreds of other immigrants who had recently descended upon the barren high plain which was still half a day's ride from the mountains. Like many of the men already there, he had left a family behind until he could decide if he would be staying or returning. In company with other fortune hunters, he had only the rudiments of formal schooling. Although he had acquired the skills of a surveyor after spending the first twenty years of his life on farms in Ohio and Iowa, he had never found lucrative or meaningful employment. Somewhat the drifter, Byers worked as a surveyor in Iowa and then moved to Oregon territory. After surveying in Oregon, he sold his skills in northern California. A year later he was back in the Midwest surveying land for railroad companies. He moved to Omaha in 1854 when it was little more than a promoter's vision, consisting of one log cabin and a generous quantity of surveying stakes. Byers helped lay out the infant town, he was a member of the first Board of Aldermen, and he was elected to the first Nebraska Territorial Legislative Assembly. While promoting Omaha, he secured a job as Deputy United States Surveyor for Nebraska, but the title was much more impressive than either the responsibility or the pay.

Byers succumbed to gold fever in 1858. He was losing money on Omaha real estate speculations, and when the first prospectors reached Nebraska from the mountains, he was ready to listen to their tales. After hearing every story, and having traversed some of the route

William N. Byers about 1860
*Courtesy Western History Department,
Denver Public Library*

toward the gold region, he put together a "Guide to Pike's Peak." Byer's guide sold well, but no one could have been more inspired by it than the author himself. He planned to leave for the Rockies with two friends during the winter of 1858, publish a newspaper in the new mining country, and do some prospecting. Before Byers could put his newest dream to the test, he got in a row. While trying to save a German immigrant from the hands of several Irish toughs, the gallant visionary received a serious shoulder wound from a shotgun blast. Despite the nearly fatal nature of the wound, Byers determinedly got himself into shape to make the journey in early spring, and reached Cherry Creek on April 17, three days before his partners arrived with a printing press and two wagons full of supplies.

In most ways William Byers typified the men who were pouring in and out of the Cherry Creek settlement. Many had families but had left them behind. Some had jobs, but few had good jobs before coming to the Rockies. They were continually on the move, seeking fortunes or a better life in whatever territory or boom town was in vogue at the moment. Any thought of remaining permanently on that barren plain at the edge of the mountains—or in the mountains with their unpredictable and frequently severe weather—was considered an advanced form of lunacy. Instead, these malcontents and unfortunates were either seeking a quick fortune or running away from debts, marriages or the law. The gold rush seemed as good a place as any to go.

Despite the similarities William Byers shared with the other mining frontiersmen, it was soon apparent that he was a unique fifty-niner. His singularity was evident when he arrived with a printing press and a plan to open a newspaper office. The typical fifty-niner was equipped with flour sacks or leather bags to carry out the gold. But here was a man who came with two partners who possessed printing and editorial experience. They were going to start a business with a commitment to the community.

By its very nature, the newspaper business demanded a faith in a community's future. An editor, especially in a new town, had to boost the town and its hinterland, attract new settlers, and work untiringly for improvement in order to retain those who were already there. To be sure, newspaper editors, especially the new town promotional variety, were often as peripatetic as traveling circus performers. Indeed, one of Byers' partners, John L. Daily, had worked for several journals in would-be future metropolises in Nebraska and Iowa before embarking on the Rocky Mountain venture. Nevertheless, a newspaper editor at least began his work in a community having faith in its future. That was the nature of his enterprise. He was not interested in merely exploiting resources or people and then moving on to the next horizon like a salesman of patented medicines.

Byers clearly had faith in the future of the Cherry Creek settlement. By August 1859 he had decided to make the frontier community his home. He went to Omaha and packed his wife, Elizabeth, and the small children, Mollie and Frank, into a wagon with the family possessions and returned to the future site of Denver. Once he had decided to relocate, the sanguine newspaper editor was determined to build a city. This enterprise became an obsession for Byers. Incredible hardships and severe competition from other communities never discouraged him. Scores of obstacles thrown in the path by nature, Indians, Civil War, economic crises, and fickle politicians—difficulties that sent thousands of newcomers back to the east or on to more promising environments elsewhere in the west—failed to demoralize Byers. He was confident a city could be carved out of the region, and he devoted all of his ingenuity and energy to make that dream a reality.

Discovery of natural resources in the area that is now Colorado made the development of a regional metropolis inevitable. That Denver would emerge as the service center and directive force of the regional economy was by no means a foregone conclusion. The Queen City could have been Colorado City, Golden, Boulder, or any one of a number of other communities that were vying for the title. Denver's victory in the race to become the dominant city was the result of superior leadership. During the first ten years of the city's life, a group of talented men organized the weak and motley community. In this decade, which was the most trying and uncertain, they gave the town a sense of identity and direction, made effective decisions, and found the resources to implement them. In short, they put Denver firmly on the path to regional dominance.

The center of early Denver's power elite was William N. Byers. His ambition to see Denver win the race over its urban rivals was a dynamo that knew no rest. His newspaper became the official organ of Denver's booster campaign, and his own energy and sacrifices inspired others during the most difficult times. Cities are seldom the product of one person's labor and genius, but it is not much of an exaggeration to say that without Byers, Denver might have survived beyond 1870, but it would not have been the Queen City of the Plains and Rockies.

Only one community stood at the junction of Cherry Creek and the South Platte in 1859, but myopic speculators who had preceded

Byers there by a few months were fighting among themselves. As soon as Byers arrived at Cherry Creek, he saw the folly in petty rivalries, and set his course to unite disparate commercial elements for the major struggle ahead. On the west side of Cherry Creek was a crude settlement of tents and sod-plugged log cabins called Auraria. It was named by its promoters after a town in a not-so-productive gold region in Georgia. On the east side of the creek was a similarly crude plot of hastily built dwellings called Denver City. Originally laid out as the St. Charles Town Company by a group of prospectors and promoters from Lawrence, it was renamed Denver for the Kansas territorial governor, General James W. Denver, by General William Larimer, Jr. and a group from Leavenworth, Oskaloosa, and Lecompton. Larimer and his men found the claim guarded by only one man. Outnumbered, the St. Charles representative was "persuaded" to recognize Larimer's claim to the essentially unimproved land.

In 1859 a Vermonter named Libeus Barney wrote that a stranger to Cherry Creek might think Auraria and Denver City to be one town, but a brief stay "would undeceive him, for there exists between them a bitter spirit of rivalry; each striving with no little effort for the superiority . . ." One of Byers' first tasks was to unite the rival town companies so that all the resources of the Cherry Creek settlement could be pooled. Before leaving Omaha, Byers and his partners, Thomas Gibson and John L. Daily, had set type for part of the four-page newspaper. They called it the *Rocky Mountain News*. This name showed no favoritism to either rival town company. Although William N. Byers and Company printed the first edition on the second floor of "Uncle Dick" Wootton's general store, which was in Auraria, the paper listed its place of publications as "Cherry Creek, K.T. [Kansas Territory]." Across the creek in Denver City, John L. Merrick was trying to beat Byers to print with his *Cherry Creek Pioneer*, but when the *News* came out first, Merrick sold his equipment to Byers, and the *Pioneer* never saw a second issue. Thus ended at least one needless rivalry.

Byers moved his enterprise from Wootton's attic to a small cabin on the Denver side of Cherry Creek in fall 1859, and then back to a new frame structure near the creek, but on the Auraria side, in June 1860. These jumps across the usually idle streamlet symbolized the neutrality that Byers urged throughout the early issues of his paper. He changed the masthead to read "Auraria and Denver," but he continually lobbied for a merger.

After a number of unsuccessful attempts during winter 1859-60, formal unification came in April 1860. Several factors conspired to

5

bring the rivals under the umbrella of "Denver." A key figure in unification was General William Larimer, Jr. No newcomer to the town promotion business, Larimer was nearly fifty years old when he arrived at Cherry Creek. Prior to plotting Denver City lots claimed by the St. Charles Town Company (the Larimer group ultimately gave the St. Charles shareholders $250 plus shares in the Denver City Town Company), Larimer had been an active speculator. While holding a commission in the Pennsylvania militia and attaining the rank of Major General, he organized coal and railroad companies in that state and then tried his hand at promotion in Pennsylvania and Nebraska. A dour-looking man with a strong frame and long, bushy beard, Larimer was determined, obstinate, and aggressive. In a style befitting his title, the general occupied the land of the St. Charles Town Company in 1858 and forced the shareholders to merge with him on his terms. Immediately, he and his son, William H. H. Larimer, and other members of the company, mapped out the town of Denver and began promoting, improving, and selling the lots. Determined to out-promote and outdistance his rivals in Auraria, he began talking of attracting a railroad. He even brought in an Episcopalian priest to give the new town an appearance of order and stability.

General Larimer grew amenable to unification because, thanks to Byers' friend and associate, Andrew Sagendorf, the Auraria Town Company gave Larimer four of its lots as a gesture of goodwill. Furthermore, Byers flattered and patronized the general. In October 1859 the editor of the *News* wrote "General Wm. Larimer, Jr., [is] another of our 'old settlers', and a most valued citizen." Consequently, as other towns began making concerted efforts to compete with Cherry Creek for serving the central Rocky Mountain gold mines, Larimer agreed in early 1860 that consolidation was "an absolute necessity for the survival of all." Despite the fact that Auraria's population was larger, Larimer and his associates would only accept Denver as the name of the consolidated city. Auraria finally accepted the Larimer "compromise," but only after much arm-twisting from Byers, Andrew Sagendorf, secretary of the Auraria Town Company, and a young man only twenty years old named David H. Moffat, who had opened a book and stationery business in Auraria.

On April 3, 1860, Aurarians voted to merge with their rival of over one year. Then on the cold, moon-brightened night of April 6, spectators from both sides of Cherry Creek gathered around the symbol of unity—the Larimer Street bridge—which had been built

General William Larimer taken in 1852.

just a few weeks before. They listened to a speech by General Larimer. Denver City was christened amid more speeches, cheers, and much drinking. The first step toward regional dominance had been taken.

The next ten years were difficult ones for Byers and the few men who shared his dream of building a city. Between 1859 and 1870 over $27 million worth of gold was dug out of the streams and mountains. The bonanza brought thousands of prospectors in and out of Denver. Conservative observers estimated that during some years of the 1860s, between one hundred and one hundred and fifty thousand people—mostly unattached men—passed through Denver City. Nevertheless, the population that was permanent enough to be counted for census purposes was only 4,759 in 1870, a mere ten-person gain over the 1860 figure. The transients, to be sure, brought revenue into Denver. They stimulated business and added to the general prosperity enjoyed by careful businessmen and real estate speculators. Indeed, Byers himself had accumulated impressive assets by 1870. Still, the throngs that came into Denver on their way to the diggings, or who made the frontier town their winter residence when the snows prevented work in the mountains, were a mixed blessing. Without them and the mining hinterland there would have been no town at all; yet, their presence obstructed the building of a stable, attractive community. They could not be taxed for street and public facility improvements because they were not property owners. They seldom did anything voluntarily to help the town because they had no vested interest there and never planned to have any. Aside from spending money on outfitting themselves for the mountains, their earnings were spent on gambling, liquor, and prostitutes. Whatever was left over went for room and board. Consequently, Denver's streets were overrun with drunken and disorderly vagrants, as well as bands of toughs who robbed, assaulted, and even murdered innocent victims at will.

By the time Auraria and Denver consolidated, Byers and Larimer were forced to turn valuable time and attention away from business pursuits towards the problem of law and order. The two civic leaders organized vigilance committees in 1859 and again in 1860. Byers also urged the business community to raise $3,000 for a jail, but they refused. He then suggested a "jail raising," similar to the rural house and barn-raising community projects he remembered from his days in the rural Midwest. But once again his cry was met with apathy. Finally, in 1861, the editor of the *News* agreed to rent one of his own buildings to the city for a jail at twenty-five dollars per month, a sum at least fifty dollars per month less than he could have received from other sources. The infant city's councilmen happily accepted the offer because they could squeeze that much out of the business community.

With few exceptions, Denver's early businessmen were looking out for their individual self-interests. Seldom did they identify with the larger community. Few possessed the vision to see that if the town failed, they would, too. But Byers never gave up. On a person-to-person basis, and through the pages of his newspaper, he agitated, pressured, and educated enough entrepreneurs to keep the community alive. Gradually, progress was made toward civic improvement. By early 1862, thanks largely to the untiring efforts of Byers and Larimer, Denver had a jail, a marshall, and six policemen, plus ordinances outlawing crimes against persons and property and a law against discharging firearms in the city limits.

If Byers' optimism for Denver's future never waned, his emotions must have jumped continually from euphoric highs to depressing lows. No sooner did he celebrate his victory in bringing some semblance of law and order to Denver than he was confronted with the departure of his ally, William Larimer. The ambitious, hard-driving general had won several battles on the Rocky Mountain frontier. He made the St. Charles Company's land his own, imposed the name of Denver on the consolidated Cherry Creek settlement, and turned a nice profit on his real estate investments. But in 1861, when Colorado Territory was organized by Congress, Larimer went to Washington and lobbied to get himself appointed governor. Having served the Republican party, indeed, having virtually organized it in the new territory, Larimer believed he had earned a right to the post. But too many influential politicians in Washington, among them Secretary of War Simon Cameron and Senator Benjamin F. Wade of Ohio, counseled President Abraham Lincoln in favor of William Gilpin. Larimer seemed to accept his defeat gracefully. He returned to Denver when Gilpin's appointment was announced and proceeded to campaign for his own election as mayor of Denver the following November. Defeated in this second attempt to launch a political career in Colorado, the blow was too much for the general's commanding personality. Early in the new year he and his sons announced that Denver was too hopelessly rowdy and crude for them. They moved "back east" to Leavenworth, Kansas.

Larimer's departure was a grievous blow to Byers. The man who had promoted towns in Pennsylvania and Nebraska was one of the few businessmen who shared the editor's understanding that community improvement was essential—that businessmen had to pull together and make sacrifices if they hoped to realize long-range profits in business and real estate. Larimer also recognized that if Denver were to survive, it would need an agricultural hinterland. Too much of Denver's food was imported from the east and New Mexico. Food transported such long distances was extremely expensive, leaving the town less attractive to prospective settlers. An agricultural hinterland would not only solve this serious problem, it would encourage broader regional development. Ultimately, Denver would find more growth and prosperity by serving and outfitting farms as well as mines.

Toward this end Larimer had joined Byers in 1860 on a major agricultural promotion campaign. Byers used the pages of the *News* to encourage people to farm in the region, arguing that profits were more certain in agriculture than in prospecting. The two men organized an agricultural society and sponsored an annual fair to advertise and promote agriculture and disseminate valuable information on farming and stock-raising techniques. But once again the promoters were thinking beyond their contemporaries. The few farmers in the region demonstrated little interest in the ideas, and the businessmen were even cooler to enterprises that seemed to be remote from their own interests.

The failure of the agricultural promotion scheme no doubt added to Larimer's pessimism about Denver's future, but it failed to disillusion Byers. Three months after the general returned east, another man arrived in Denver who would prove to be a valuable ally in agricultural promotion and city building. His name was John Evans. Arriving from Illinois in spring 1862, Evans came to Denver as the second territorial governor, replacing William Gilpin, who had been judged a failure by President Lincoln, the national Republican Party, and most Coloradans. If Governor Gilpin proved innocent of common sense when it came to working with people and finances, the new governor was deemed unsuccessful in handling Indian relations in the territory. Regardless, Evans was a more successful administrator than his predecessor. He managed to hold onto the post for three years, whereas Gilpin had to resign after only one.

Evans may have been weighed in the balances and found wanting as a governor, but he was phenomenally successful as a city builder. Next to William Byers, he did more than anyone else during the 1860s to organize Denver's motley community, give it direction, and place it firmly in the network of the nation's regional metropolises. Immediately Byers and Evans worked well together. Like Byers, the new governor was a visionary. He thought no little thoughts. In his first speech, delivered on the night of his arrival, he spoke grandiloquently of the city's future. Never using the word "if," he prophesied greatness for Denver and its hinterland "when the great commercial auxiliary, the railway" reached the community.

Evans had deep lines and wrinkles in his face which made him look much older than his forty-eight years. He already had behind him a distinguished and varied career and possessed qualities and experience important to city building unmatched by anyone in Denver. Unlike most Denverites, he was neither running away from past failures nor seeking a frontier to make his first mark in life's struggle for power, fame, and wealth. Most people who were comfortably established in the early 1860s would have avoided the hardships of the Colorado frontier, but John Evans was not like most people. He was born in Ohio in 1814 to Quaker parents who had a productive farm. They owned a machine shop, a successful general store in Waynesville, and some valuable real estate. Neither hard work nor deprivation were part of Evans' early life. Much of his youth was spent living in a large, handsome two-story house, and he had access to the local school for three or four years. He shunned the hard work on the farm and disliked the duties in the family store and tool shop. With apparent ease he persuaded his father to send him to a Quaker academy in Indiana, but when he decided to pursue a medical degree in college, his father balked. Ultimately, though, the studious young man pressured his father into lending him the money to attend preparatory schools, and finally he entered the Cincinnati College of Medicine, where he graduated in 1837 at the age of twenty-three. Dr. Evans practiced medicine in northern Illinois and Attica, Indiana. In the latter town he established a State Hospital for the Insane and distinguished himself as its superintendent.

By age thirty the young physician was a successful man, but carving out a niche in a community and being outstanding in his profession brought little fulfillment. He craved new challenges. Having demonstrated his command of private practice and hospital administration, in 1845 he moved into academic medicine as a professor at Chicago's Rush Medical College. Once again he distinguished himself. Besides teaching, he conducted path-breaking research in cholera epidemics, became editor of the *Medical and Surgical Journal*, organized the Chicago Medical Society, and invented an instrument for obstetric surgery.

The death of his wife Hannah, followed by the passing of three of their four children, sapped his ambition and energy for several months.

11

In less than a year, though, his depression lifted, and he began devoting fewer hours to his profession and more time to real estate investment. He had dabbled in Chicago real estate in the late 1840s, but during the next decade it became a challenging and profitable vocation. Quickly he branched out into railroad promotion, organizing the Chicago and Fort Wayne Railroad Company. He soon learned that business and politics were inseparable partners in Illinois, and before long he was active in local and state politics. The politician-businessman had converted to Methodism in the 1840s, and during the 1850s he devoted time and money to his newly found church home. Not satisfied with having taught in a university, Evans now determined to build one for the Methodist church. By 1860 he had used his money and prestige to help organize Northwestern University, and to get Abraham Lincoln nominated for the presidency.

These latter ventures helped vault the ambitious institution builder into a new career by 1862. The Methodist church lobby pressured the Lincoln administration to appoint more Methodists to federal offices, and Lincoln and his party owed a debt to the wealthy Chicagoan. Consequently, when Gilpin was pressured out of the territorial governorship, Dr. John Evans sought the position and Lincoln granted the request.

Unquestionably, Evans viewed the territorial governorship as a first step to still another career. That he saw the governorship as a stepping stone to the U.S. Senate is certain. But to win that elective office he realized he must earn the respect and support of the local power elite. Indeed, he must become a part of that inner group of decision makers, if not the leader himself. This pathway to power was by no means new to the governor. He had built a railroad with Chicago mayor and tycoon William Butler Ogden, and he had organized a bank with one of the meat-packing Swifts.

Ingratiating himself in Denver was the easiest task John Evans would face. He was, after all, the governor, a nationally renowned physician, and scholar. Evans was also wealthier than anyone in Colorado Territory. His assets amounted to well over $250,000, whereas, according to an R.G. Dun estimate, no one in Denver was worth more than 10 percent of that figure in 1862. For these reasons, Evans was deferred to and admired. Furthermore, entering Denver's circle of power was not difficult because it scarcely existed. William Byers, Andrew Sagendorf, and General Larimer had represented what there was in the way of leadership. Now that Larimer had deserted the struggling town, Byers was begging men to join him in looking beyond individual self interest toward developing a city and hinterland.

John Evans in the 1860s.

From his first day in Denver and thereafter, John Evans aligned himself with Byers. It is true that the governor was keeping his eye on the U.S. Senate. But when that dream failed to materialize, he did not pack up and leave as Larimer had done. Instead, he grew obsessively occupied with building a major city. In Evans the editor of the *News* found a willing partner for promoting agriculture. With the governor's support, the Colorado Agriculture Society was formed in 1863, and by 1866 it had enough money to purchase forty acres east of Denver for a fairground. However, when Byers called for local businessmen to raise money to construct buildings and a racetrack, he was met with the usual silence. Finally, with the aid of John Evans and Richard Sopris (a fifty-niner who had earned money by prospecting before becoming active in Denver politics), Byers found enough money to build the fairground and hold a grand opening in fall 1866. For the next fifteen years the fair was held each year in Denver. Eventually it became the Colorado Industrial Exposition. More than agricultural products were displayed. Exhibitions of ores and mining equipment were featured. The annual exposition stimulated business in Denver by attracting people from all over the region, and it played a significant role in promoting agriculture and mining.

The enthusiasm Evans displayed for Denver's future eventually spread to other men in the business community. Both Evans and Byers counseled others that the natural resources of the region made the growth of one major city inevitable. That Denver would become that city, they cautioned, was not certain. Leaders in Colorado Springs and Golden were vying for regional dominance, and if Denver's business community remained indolent, the victory surely would go to one of those towns. Unless Denver entrepreneurs were willing to harness all of their resources toward community development, the future would be grim. Gradually the wisdom expressed by Evans and Byers caught on. A group of men regularly met to discuss what could be done to inspire a sense of community and decide what actions were necessary to promote future urban growth.

Among those who became important decision makers in the 1860s was David Holliday Moffat, Jr. Born in New York in 1839, his early life could have inspired one of Horatio Alger's rags-to-riches stories. With very little formal schooling, he left his lower economic class family for New York City at age twelve. He secured a job as messenger boy for the New York Exchange Bank and worked his way up to a clerkship before he was sixteen. Before his seventeenth birthday he was offered a position as teller with a new banking firm in Des Moines, Iowa. Two years later a more western frontier beckoned the young financier. He accepted a teller's post with a new bank in Omaha, Nebraska, a town that the bank owner and other promoters predicted would blossom to the proportions of Chicago in one or two years. In Omaha young Moffat met William Byers, who shared with him lofty dreams about the new town. The two men became friends. In fact, Moffat was with Byers when he was shot while attempting to rescue the German from the hands of several young Irishmen.

The bank that employed Moffat proved to be no more successful than Byers' real estate ventures. In less than one year after Byers deserted the Nebraska city for the Rockies, twenty-year-old Moffat was ready to listen to his friend's prediction that the community on

David H. Moffat, Jr.
soon after his arrival in Denver.

Cherry Creek was on the move, offering unlimited opportunities to business investors. Due to Byers' prompting, Moffat left Omaha (the bank had collapsed a few months earlier) and arrived in Auraria in March 1860. In partnership with C.C. Woolworth, the young man put the last of his assets into a book and stationery store. The business did well in the early 1860s, and Moffat searched for other investment opportunities.

A man fourteen years his senior who looked remarkably like Ulysses S. Grant was speculating in mines. His name was Jerome B. Chaffee. He was born and raised in New York state like Moffat, albeit from a well-off family that had secured for him an academic education far beyond the national average for the time. The two New Yorkers shared memories of the Empire State. They liked and trusted each other immediately, and jointly they invested in general mining and real estate ventures. By the mid-1860s both had realized considerable profits. Chaffee had taught school in Michigan but then moved to St. Joseph, Missouri, in the 1850s. St. Joseph was a young boom town competing with Topeka, Kansas City, and Independence in the struggle to gain preeminence as the regional metropolis in that developing region. It was there that the ex-schoolteacher entered the banking business. Moderately successful in Missouri, he moved across the Missouri River to Kansas, where he and several others carved out the town of Elwood and entered the regional city competition. Very soon it was apparent that Elwood would always be more impressive on paper than in reality. Thus, when "Rocky Mountain fever" reached the Missouri River Valley, Chaffee was off on what turned out to be the last leg of his westward quest for success, a journey that began in New York, with intermittent stops in Michigan, Missouri, and Kansas.

By 1865 Chaffee had made enough money to enter banking again—but this time on a much larger scale. Two days after President Lincoln died, the comptroller of the U.S. Treasury authorized Chaffee to open the First National Bank in Denver. Two years later David Moffat, who was still speculating in real estate and mines with the banker, bought shares in the First National Bank and became its cashier.

The same year that Moffat joined Chaffee in the bank, a fifty-year-old man of position and means from Missouri opened a law office in Denver. Bela M. Hughes was no stranger to Colorado Territory in 1867. He and his cousin, Ben Holliday, had been operating a stage line from the Missouri River into the Rocky Mountains and on to Salt Lake City since 1861. They were not the first stage line speculators to come into the region. In 1859 General Larimer had

Jerome B. Chaffee in the early 1860s before he had such a strong resemblance to General Grant.

Bela M. Hughes

given the Leavenworth and Pike's Peak Express Company twenty-nine shares of stock in the Denver City Town Company in return for the express company making regular runs into the town. By 1860 at least three competing companies were stopping in Denver, cutting rates, bringing mail and supplies, and giving the new town regular contact with the outside world. In 1861 Hughes and Holliday brought the Overland Stage Company to Denver and eventually bought out all competition. Monopolies seldom cut costs, and the Hughes-Holliday operation was no exception. It is true that they lost over $372,000 between 1862 and 1865 from Indian attacks, but they nevertheless made large profits and increased rates to unconsionably high levels.

Holliday and Hughes sold out to Wells, Fargo and Company in 1866 and turned to other interests. Bela Hughes opened a law office in the town that had been so good to his company throughout the 1860s. The antithesis to David Moffat, Hughes was born in Kentucky. At the age of twelve Hughes did not go to work; rather, his father moved him and the rest of the family to Clay County, Missouri, near Liberty and Weston. The elder Hughes became a prosperous lawyer. He kept young Bela off the farms and out of the factories and placed him in the best private schools in northern Missouri. He later sent him back to Kentucky to complete his education at Augusta College. After college and brief service in the Black Hawk War, young Hughes returned to Clay County and studied law in his father's office. After his admission to the Missouri Bar, he entered politics and was elected to the state legislature. In the late 1850s he moved to St. Joseph, continued his law practice, and entered the stage line business with cousin Holliday.

While Hughes and Holliday were building a monopoly in the early transportation business, a bright, serious, lean young man with dark, wavy hair and muttonchop sideburns made his way to Denver. Twenty-one-year-old Luther Kountze arrived in Denver in 1862. From a farm and general storekeeping family in Ohio, Kountze decided to follow his older brothers to Omaha rather than stay in the family business with his younger brother and father. Financially, at least, it proved to be a wise choice. The Kountze brothers survived the most difficult days in early Omaha. They made enough money to send Luther to Denver in 1862 so that he could open a second branch of the family enterprise in what they judged would be the next boom town on the frontier. In December of that year Luther Kountze took his brothers' investment capital, rented quarters in a drugstore, put up a sign advertising Kountze Brothers Bank, and proceeded to trade

18

Luther Kountze in the late 1860s.
*Courtesy Western History Department,
Denver Public Library*

coins and United States Treasury notes for gold dust. The business prospered. Eventually the banking brothers persuaded nineteen-year-old Charles Kountze to leave the family store in their father's care and move to Colorado Territory to aid Luther with the new bank.

In 1866 the Kountzes changed the name of their bank to Colorado National Bank, and a few months later Luther Kountze decided to invest some of the capital in a new enterprise with Amos Steck. Kountze's partner, next to Byers and Evans, was probably the best known man in Denver. Steck went to the region in 1859 just about the time Byers ran off the first issue of the *News*, and he obviously shared the editor's optimism for the town's future. Steck was born into a wealthy Ohio family in 1822. When he was thirteen his parents sent him to live with an uncle in Philadelphia so that he could take advantage of schools superior to those in Ohio. Given every imaginable advantage, young Steck finished school and studied law with

19

Amos Steck

one of the most distinguished attorneys in Pennsylvania. Amos Steck was admitted to the bar, practiced law, and finally moved to California in 1849. Money was never a problem for him, but he had trouble finding a suitable place in which to settle down. After four years he left Sacramento, returned to Pennsylvania, and again practiced law. In 1854 he married Sara McLaughlin, but soon was overcome with wanderlust. He and his bride moved to Wisconsin, but when news of gold strikes in the Rocky Mountains reached him, he moved once again. Arriving at Cherry Creek in spring 1859, he invested in Denver City Town Company land and became a director of that speculative venture.

The climate of Colorado and the challenge of building a city appealed to Steck. He involved himself in nearly everything that was going on and apparently never gave a thought to going back East. For a time he worked as United States mail distributor for the

Overland Express Company and invested heavily in real estate. Steck early dedicated himself to building a city with the kind of foresight that appealed to Byers. This was evident when Steck voted with Larimer to donate two town company lots to a young physician from St. Louis, Drake McDowall, so that he could open the first city hospital along Cherry Creek. Steck not only handled the mail, sold real estate, and donated time to the hospital (he became secretary of the hospital with no pay), but he agreed to aid Byers and Richard Sopris in organizing a city fund for the poor, and he served as mayor from 1863 to 1864.

Steck seldom passed an opportunity to invest, especially if it promised a good return and at the same time boosted the town. Thus, in 1867 he and Luther Kountze, along with several others, obtained a charter from the territorial legislature and incorporated the Denver Horse Railroad Company. Although it did not go into operation until the 1870s under the name of the Denver City Railway Company, Steck was the president of a company which Byers, Evans, and others saw as symbolic of urban progress. If a town was growing enough to need public transportation, it was clearly a future city.

The incorporation of a street railway was done as much for the image of the community as it was for profit. Everyone realized that the money invested ($100,000 was put into the company in 1867) would not yield a return for several years anyway. Nevertheless, the public transportation company was significant. It was the first major venture in which several businessmen risked their own capital on the future of the community. It demonstrated that some men, at least, were looking beyond simple self-interest toward a larger goal called "community."

The supreme test of Denver's emerging power elite came in November 1867. For five years prior to this time, John Evans had confidentially predicted that the Union Pacific Railroad would run its rails through Denver as it moved westward across the Rockies to complete the transcontinental line. The first disappointment came in 1866 when the company announced that it would go north of Denver through Cheyenne, Wyoming. When this decision was confirmed, a number of Denver businessmen moved to Cheyenne, assuming that the Wyoming town would become the dominant metropolis of the region. To curb this exodus, John Evans, Bela Hughes, and a number of other Denver boosters announced that they were by no means giving up their community. Negotiations were underway with the Union Pacific, they said, to build a line from Denver to Cheyenne, thus plugging the town into the transcontinental railroad.

21

The branch line to Cheyenne was scarcely beyond the talking stage when news came that the Kansas Pacific, which had stopped construction in western Kansas, would push into Denver with all haste. But the day of Jubilee had no more than dawned when devastating news arrived from St. Louis. Colonel James Archer, a Kansas Pacific representative, went to Denver from the Missouri metropolis and unshrouded the grim report that the Kansas Pacific had fallen into financial difficulty. The line could only be built if Denverites raised $2 million to cover the cost. The hopes, dreams, and investments of Denver's faithful seemed gone. Without a railroad, the little town of Cherry Creek would remain just that—a little town. Every sign now pointed toward ruin. The transcontinental connection on which everyone had gambled their future was now Cheyenne's lifeline. The Kansas Pacific was stalled in Kansas, and rumor circulated that if it did resume construction it would bypass Denver by swinging southward to the Arkansas River. Further depressing news came. Promoters in Golden were about to build a tributary line to Cheyenne, making it the center of the central Rocky Mountain mining traffic.

If these factors had conspired to Denver's disadvantage two or three years earlier, Byers and Evans would have been forced to pack their trunks, find another town, and begin all over again. But by November 1867 Denver had enough resourceful men to make one more fight. Most of these leaders had hung on after a fire destroyed many of their homes and businesses in 1863. No sooner had they climbed back on their feet than they were knocked down again by a devastating flood the following year. Truly they had been forged and hardened by fire and water. If they had overcome the ravages of nature, surely they could do something about man-made transportation networks.

For the first few days after Archer's pronouncement, John Evans, William Byers, and David Moffat moved frantically in and out of Bela Hughes' law office and the offices of the First National and Colorado National banks. During these meetings it was decided that a railroad would have to be built—somehow, someway—from Denver to Cheyenne. The first step was to convince the public of this need and then figure out how to raise the money. From William Byers' office came notices urging all citizens to attend a meeting on Wednesday night, November 13, at Cole's Hall on Larimer Street. At that meeting the Denver Board of Trade was organized. Identical to boards of trade in such cities as Chicago, St. Louis, and Kansas City, its purpose was to make crucial decisions for the community and be responsible for implementing those decisions.

The following night the Board of Trade held an open meeting, urging the citizens to ratify an emergency plan. Bela Hughes was the primary speaker. In a blunt address he informed the citizenry that if Denver were to survive, it must rally behind the Board of Trade, follow its decision to build a railroad to Cheyenne, and use every available resource to do it as quickly as humanly possible.

Two more night meetings were held in rapid succession, until it was announced on November 18 that arrangements had been made to incorporate the Denver Pacific Railroad and Telegraph Company with capital stock of $2 million. Among the incorporators, the crowd learned, were Luther Kountze, John Evans, Bela Hughes, and David Moffat.

The informal meetings of Denver's business leaders were now formalized. The Board of Trade was established, and the railroad was projected on paper. Now the monumental task of financing the line remained. To John Evans went the assignment of working out the intricate political and economic details. Businessmen were pressed to purchase stock in the new corporation, and less affluent citizens were urged to buy what they could, make pledges for the future, and donate their labor for construction. For months Evans and his partners twisted arms, delivered impassioned speeches, and made exaggerated promises. At times the situation appeared hopeless. Evans tried to raise money from his contacts in Chicago, but to no avail. After rebuffs from Congress for land grants and broken promises from the Union Pacific to pay part of the materials costs, Evans' tenacity finally paid off. Congress agreed to a 900,000-acre grant for the road on the condition that it would connect the Kansas Pacific and the Union Pacific. At the same time Kansas Pacific representatives raised over $6 million from German investors, more than enough to carry their rails to Denver.

By 1869 rails were heading south for Denver from Cheyenne, and they were being pounded in with all possible haste from western Kansas. The labor of Denver's decision-makers was finally coming to fruition. To be sure, they had not toiled unselfishly. Indeed, handsome profits—some said unconscionable profits—were realized by the power elite. Nevertheless, they had fulfilled their own prophecy for the Queen City. The first locomotive from Cheyenne rolled into Denver in June 1870, followed two months later by the first train from Kansas. Denver now had two major rail connections, placing her in uninterrupted contact with both coasts, the Great Lakes, and the Mississippi and Missouri river heartlands. The town at the junc-

Copied from the frontpiece of *New Tracks in North America* (London, 1870) by William A. Bell. An artist's drawing of the Kansas Pacific Railroad being extended into Denver.

tion of Cherry Creek and the South Platte was now destined to become a major city.

Denver's future as a great city was assured by 1870 because a diverse group of men pooled their talents and resources in a herculean effort to build a city. By twentieth-century standards, the effectiveness and cohesiveness of this group was remarkable. Indeed, their efforts were nothing short of incredible because the civic leaders had so little in common except a vision. Their geographic origins spanned half a continent from New York to the Missouri River. Their ages ranged from youngsters in their twenties to life-seasoned men well into their fifties. Some had come from poor families and had been forced to go to work at an early age with no more than a couple of years of formal schooling. Others were from wealthy families who had afforded them the highest levels of education attainable in the first half of the nineteenth century. Their work experience was as varied as their birthplaces, ranging from farmer and shopkeeper to surveyor, banker, lawyer, and physician.

What these men did have in common was the love of a challenge and the excitement of building something new. Their accomplishments were dramatic by any standard. They turned a raw, chaotic community—a crude and disorganized turnstile for transients—into a bona fide little city. They brought law and order, built a hospital, encouraged agricultural enterprise, plotted a public transportation system, tore down log huts and erected frame and brick buildings, and attracted two railroads. If the town only grew by ten souls from the time they began their labors, the population was more stable, and it had for the first time a certain future of growth that had been no more than a dream ten years before.

Chapter 2

Ralph Waldo Emerson wrote that "for everything you gain, you lose something." If the New England transcendentalist had lived in Denver during the 1860s and had been asked to capsulize the human experience there, he probably would not have said anything much different or more insightful. Those who went to Denver in the 1860s and endured long enough to see the railroads penetrate the town and insure its place on the map surely reaped rewards of personal fulfillment and satisfaction. Some even earned money from investments in business and real estate. For these gains, however, a dear price was paid in loss of human comforts and overall living standards.

John Evans, soon after he arrived to assume his gubernatorial duties, summed it up very well when he wrote to his wife that Denver is "really the only tolerable place" to live in the region. Although he found Denver superior to other Rocky Mountain communities (he described Colorado City as similar to "a deserted Nebraska village"), Evans failed to find a more enthusiastic adjective than "tolerable" to label the Cherry Creek community. While Denver was probably more comfortable than most Colorado towns, by any objective standard it was inferior to most human habitations farther east.

Observers by the score, whether they were from new cities such as Evans' Chicago, hopeful towns like Omaha or Leavenworth, or even economically depressed rural Vermont, saw few physical attractions in Denver. Lavina Porter, her husband, and little boy rolled into Denver by ox cart in summer 1860. She remembered the breathtaking beauty of "an almost level plain surrounded on all sides by towering mountains, whose highest peaks were snow covered even in midsummer." But when this family from Hannibal, Missouri, reached Denver, they were stunned. The Porters had envisioned "Denver a thriving, bustling, busy city . . . it was an exceedingly primitive town, consisting of numerous tents and numbers of crude and illy constructed cabins, with nearly as many rum shops and low saloons as cabins [.]" Mrs. Porter observed that "horses, cows, and hogs roamed at will over the greater part of the village."

That same summer Albert Richardson arrived in Denver. A journalist from New York and careful observer of the Trans-Mississippi West, Richardson noted that Denver had two busy streets, many others that were merely staked out with lots overrun by prairie dogs, and a landscape reminiscent of the Sahara. He remarked that "in New York, our one-story house, fourteen feet by twenty with eight feet of shed for a kitchen, would be an indifferent stable; here it is a palace. Walls of rough upright boards, with cracks battened to keep out the rain and dust; . . . a square clapboarded front, three doors, three windows, and a stove-pipe protruding from the kitchen-roof. It cost three hundred dollars, and had 'all the modern improvements' of this longitude - kitchen and cellar." Nevertheless, Richardson occupied "a better house than any of our neighbors," despite its lack of room partitions and plastering. The New Yorker apparently exaggerated little, if at all, because Elizabeth Byers, the editor's wife, complained that their first house was a board-roofed, one-room log cabin complemented by a dirt floor complete with weed roots. Another pioneer woman recalled paying eighty-five dollars per month to rent a four-room house of rough, unpainted boards, with only muslin to cover the windows.

Home furnishings evidently surpassed the dwellings in crudity during the early years when transportation was difficult and expensive. Many homes had floors for beds. Crude wood benches and chairs, and often nothing but buffalo hides, served as seating and lounging accommodations for family and friends. Until the mid-1860s, when house goods were being made in Denver or brought in with regularity from the East, trunks or wall pegs functioned as wardrobes. Those fortunate enough to have a travel-scarred table from Kansas or a rickety desk from Cincinnati boasted of their treasures and treated them with loving care.

Early settlers not only bemoaned Denver's lack of comforts, they universally complained about the Indians in and around the infant town. Lavina Porter found a number of the Arapahoe tribe "in the lower part of the town" near the river. At once repulsed and moved by what she saw, she noted that the "poor, overworked squaws were busily engaged . . .cooking their vile compounds, and making the skins of wild animals into the uncouth garments that they wore. Loafing around in the sand and dirt were the indolent and unemployed braves, while their filthy and vermin covered offspring, played naked in the sand." Libeus Barney was even more graphic in his uncomplimentary description of Indian camp life in Denver. The women "have no sense of shame," he wrote in 1859 "and live a dissolute, licentious and uncivilized life." To elaborate he described an incident observed one day while strolling past some Arapahoe lodges. He claimed to have found "a squaw busily engaged in picking vermin from her lord's head and eating them with marvelous gusto."

Mr. Barney and Mrs. Porter by no means reserved their disparaging remarks for Indians. The Vermonter lamented that "there are but a few *ladies* here," pointing out that "many are of questionable morality." But in Barney's view women held no monopoly on immorality. Indeed, he believed "morals. . .retrograde rather than improve among us. The Sabbath is regarded more as a holiday than as a day of worship." Mrs. Porter shared his view, explaining that her family had moved on to California because Denver was so ugly. "I was so utterly disgusted with Denver and its squalid surroundings. . . with the combined drunkenness and rioting that existed everywhere in this society composed of the roughest class of all states and nations. . ."

To those intolerant of the ways of the flesh, signs of moral decadence abounded. Historian Thomas J. Noel computed thirty-one saloons in the Cherry Creek community by 1859, when no churches, schools, hospitals, libraries, or banks existed. The following year saloons numbered thirty-five, to serve a population of 4,749. Saloons clearly dominated Denver's early business enterprise. Libeus Barney, a saloon keeper himself, estimated that one out of every three buildings was a saloon by the community's first birthday. An English traveller, Isabella Bird, noticed that "the number of 'saloons' in the streets impresses one, [and]. . .whiskey is significant of all evil and violence."

Although census takers and compilers of business directories did not keep records on houses of prostitution like they did on drinking establishments, the local citizenry recognized that, next to saloonkeeping, dens of ill fame represented the largest business in early Denver. Many women who came to the gold rush town in its first one and one-half years of existence were prostitutes. They were commonly seen on the streets and in the saloons and gambling halls. By the early 1860s a red-light district was well established south of Cherry Creek west of Larimer, and the predominantly male population kept well worn the dirt streets which led to a dozen or more notorious log cabins.

Drinking and carousing with loose women were not the only signs—indeed not the worst signs—of moral depravity. Violent crime was rampant in Colorado's future capital. Horace Greeley said that early Denver was overrun with characters "soured in temper, always armed, bristling at a word, ready with the rifle, revolver or bowie knife." He was convinced that there was more fighting, shooting, and general lawlessness "in this log city . . . than any community of no greater number on earth." Until about 1862, the flotsam and jetsam of frontier society roamed the streets and preyed upon the well-meaning and innocent. Gangs of armed toughs would enter restaurants, eat their fill, and then walk out without paying—daring the entrepreneur to challenge them. Individuals and stores were robbed in broad daylight, and people were beaten mercilessly when bored hoodlums looked for excitement.

In an attempt to bring order to the town, a number of businessmen formed a vigilance committee in summer 1859. Only moderately successful, the committee disbanded in December, and W.E. Sisty, a Mexican War veteran, was elected the town's first marshal. The new marshal lasted only five months when he resigned out of frustration. Marshal Sisty had no jail and no deputies, and his life was continually threatened for attempting to maintain order. A rash of homicides which started during Sisty's tenure lasted until after his resignation. At that time Mayor John C. Moore appointed a four-man police corps to cope with the desperate situation. But the homicides continued. One day William Byers was forcibly taken from his newspaper office for printing an attack on the murderer of a black man who had been killed merely for being black. The editor was spirited off to the Criterion saloon, where he managed to escape. When the hoodlums came after him again, he saved his own life by emptying a shotgun into one of his assailants.

The attempt on Byers' life led to the formation of another citizen-supported vigilance committee. It did its work thoroughly if not humanely. Murderers were swiftly apprehended, and public hangings, attended by hundreds of citizens, came quickly in the wake of a short trial. The fact that Denver had six successive marshals between December 1859 and December 1861 testifies to the difficulties inherent in the job. In 1867, looking back on the previous tumultuous years, Byers wrote "that capital punishment had been the salvation of our western communities in their earlier periods, the history of the times proves beyond controversy." To Byers, at least, capital punishment appeared to be the major crime deterrent. Whether the fear of hanging was more effective than the presence of full-time marshals who worked with vigilance committees it is impossible to say. Nevertheless, by 1862 criminals were not running roughshod over the Rocky Mountain community, and a modicum of law and order had been established.

No sooner had the marshals and vigilance committees relieved Denver of its worst criminals than other problems surfaced to keep the town in a state of turmoil. In 1861 General William Gilpin organized the First Colorado Regiment for the Union Army, with headquarters two miles outside Denver at Camp Weld. Despite Gilpin's paranoia— he was convinced that Confederates were all over the territory and ready to strike at any moment—the Union forces had little to do in preserving Colorado Territory for the Union. Consequently, rowdy soldiers were continually walking Denver's streets and patronizing the saloons, gambling houses, and red-light district. For several months, until order was imposed from Camp Weld, the blue coats drank, brawled, and discharged firearms day and night, adding to the general confusion in the infant town.

As if the marshals did not have enough to do quelling crimes of violence and quieting boisterous soldiers, they were constantly criticized for failing to clean up the town. The city council, created in winter 1859, made it the task of the police corps and marshal to rid the city of animal as well as human pests. Mules and hogs walked the streets of Denver at will, leaving unsightly and unfragrant droppings wherever they went. Irate property owners and drunken sharpshooters frequently shot these derelict animals on sight, adding bloated and noxious smelling animal carcasses to the ugliness of the crude community. And when the law enforcement agents were not busy with these unpleasantries, they were badgered by angry citizens and Byers' scathing editorials to corral the scores of begging, and sometimes biting, dogs which often seemed to outnumber the human vagrants lining the streets and alleys.

Denver's quality of life was less than first rate in still other ways. Colorado became noted as a healthful place in which to live by the 1870s and 1880s, but in the first decade of its existence, disease took a high toll. Libeus Barney seemed a bit confounded when he wrote that "the climate at Denver is exceedingly healthy; the air pure; genial days and cold and refreshing nights; yet there is considerable sickness among the miners. The 'mountain fever' a kind of lung fever," he diagnosed, was debilitating and common. A missionary in the mid-1860s noted little, if any, improvement over Barney's earlier observations. "The climate does not meet the representations which have been made of it. Sickness and death," he wrote to the American

Home Missionary Society, "are here as well as elsewhere." Finally, the man of the cloth warned that "consumptives and those who have heart disease should not come here. Rheumatism is common in the mountains and fever and erysipelas [prevail] both here and in Denver. Now I am not saying," he concluded, "that the climate is worse here than in other places, but only that I doubt whether it has that salubrity which has been claimed for it."

Vital statistics were not recorded during the first months of Denver's existence. Throughout much of the 1860s, deaths and causes of deaths often escaped the attention of health officers. It is known, however, that many people complained of illness and that competent physicians and nurses were scarce until the 1870s. Furthermore, Albert Richardson found the size of Denver's cemetery remarkable. For a small town only two years old, Denver had an amazing number of graves filling the bare, prairie dog-infested hill east of town. Most certainly all of those graves were not occupied by victims of homicide and the gallows, because by 1866 between six and seven hundred remains were buried in the graveyard on the northeastern edge of town.

Because Colorado's climate is in fact one of the most healthful in the nation, it is likely that poor diet accounted significantly for the illnesses mentioned so prominently. Those who made the several-week trek from the Missouri River to Cherry Creek were often disappointed to find out that their health failed to improve upon reaching the Colorado boom town. If they travelled by ox team or horseback, they ate dried beef, dried mutton, sausages, or salt pork, along with soda crackers, unleavened bread, or biscuits. These morsels and coffee were heated on an open fire tindered by buffalo chips, scraps of scrub oak, or driftwood. Fresh fruit and vegetables were either inaccessible or extremely costly along the way. When fruit was available it was usually because a farsighted family had packed a barrel of apples in the wagon. These gems sold for twenty-five to fifty cents apiece to someone who had the money to pry them away from their owners.

Until 1866 or 1867, availability of good food, especially produce, was uncertain in Denver. If available, such items were extremely expensive and out of reach of most citizens. In 1858 vegetables and fruit were unobtainable in Denver. By summer 1859 some settlers had vegetable gardens, and several large-scale farmers in southern Colorado were bringing wagon loads of vegetables and melons into Denver. Nevertheless, prices were high, and these items were not always on hand even if people had the money. Vegetables were readily available in 1861 and 1862, but a drouth in 1863 wiped out most of that year's crop, driving prices to an all-time high. Improved weather conditions made produce available at more favorable prices in 1864, but the following spring and summer a grasshopper invasion left the town hurting once more.

Some items were shipped into Denver from the Missouri River Valley and from New Mexico and Utah. But these shipments were irregular and the prices astronomical. In 1863 a box of peaches arrived from Utah, complete with a freight bill of sixty dollars. Selling the peaches for one dollar apiece, the recipient paid the bill and had only a few pieces of fruit left for himself.

Although items such as flour, sugar, cornmeal, potatoes, lard, bacon, and beef were seldom in short supply, these foods varied widely in quality and price. Inferior Mexican flour sold for ten to fifteen dollars per hundred pounds in 1859. Superior quality United States flour cost fourteen to sixteen dollars in the territory. By the following winter, however, good flour cost twenty-five dollars per hundred weight. In spring 1861 it was all the way down to six dollars, but still one and one-half to two dollars above the prices paid in the states. Butter and cheese were usually obtainable, but again, ranging in price from fifty cents to one dollar per pound, and always higher priced than back East, with quality varying according to the price one could afford to pay.

During the first five or six years of Denver's existence, fresh meats such as venison, rabbit, turkey, and prairie hens were plentiful, and the prices were lower than on beef or pork. By the mid-1860s, when wild game was driven out of the immediate region, local settlers raised enough cattle and hogs to supply the growing market at prices on par with eastern and southern states.

Throughout the 1860s local citizens usually had bread, meat, and potatoes, even if the price was high and quality poor compared to what they had found in the East. What early settlers did not have until agriculture expanded in the second half of the decade and until the railroad reached the city in 1870 was a moderately priced, regular supply of fresh produce, which was so essential to good health.

Commodities other than food were scarce or quite expensive during Denver's early years, driving the town's cost of living to heights well above those in the states. Construction materials such as lumber, nails, and glass were priced far higher than the national average. In summer 1859 lumber cost $100 per 1,000 feet, nails $25 for 100 pounds, and window glass $16 per box. While glass and nails remained dear for four or five years, finished lumber prices declined

33

rapidly as the Excelsior Mill Company opened on the edge of town and drove prices down to twenty dollars per 1,000 feet by 1861. While lumber prices at twenty dollars were reasonable by national standards, brick soon became the favorite construction material. Thomas Warren opened a kiln and brickyard in late 1859 and produced a durable and inexpensive material in adequate quantities.

High prices and shortages were taken in stride by many of Denver's early citizens, especially those who had been in boom towns on other frontiers such as California. In July 1860 William Byers, a veteran of both the California and Nebraska frontiers, noted that he was forced to pay $30.10 to have forty-three pounds of newsprint delivered to Denver, but he shrugged it off, saying, "thus it goes in a new country." Seasoned boom town dwellers, of which Denver had its share, accepted such hardships as the temporary price one must pay on the road to growth, stability, and prosperity.

The normal course of inconveniences and deprivations was one thing, but Denver had hard times that were unusual. Conditions frequently drove all but the most dedicated and optimistic to easier locales. The first of a series of disasters, which convinced the more cynical observers that the gods were not happy with the new Rocky Mountain town, came about two o'clock on the morning of April 19, 1863. Most of Denver was quiet and asleep. Little noise could be heard above the high winds that had been sweeping across the plain from the mountains for several days. Along Blake Street near Fifteenth the wind muffled the noise of late tipplers in the drinking establishments. Then a careless reveler kicked over a stove at the Cherokee House, and piercing screams of "fire!" broke the early morning silence. Soon sleepers on both sides of Cherry Creek were awake.

The harsh winds proved to be a mixed blessing as the flames grew brighter in the vicinity of Cherokee House. The wind's eastward direction from the mountains prevented the fire from spreading to the west side of Cherry Creek, but it swirled sparks and burning debris all over the heart of the east Denver community. The hastily constructed frame buildings were quickly consumed by flames, and the more recently constructed brick structures were gutted within a few hours. By daylight most of the eastern half of Denver between Cherry Creek, Wazee, and Sixteenth Street lay in blackened ruins. The two bucket brigades and small hook and ladder company, organized the year before by the city council, proved to be totally inadequate, even with the help of most able-bodied citizens.

The "Great Fire," as it was remembered for years to come, did at

A street scene in Denver in the early 1860s. Notice
the litter in the unpaved street.

least $350,000 worth of damage. Scores of people were homeless, and over two dozen businesses were crippled or ruined. Despite the fact that few people had insurance, there were some things to be thankful for: no one was killed, and bricks and lumber were in plentiful supply for immediate reconstruction. Furthermore, local money was available to loan for the costly task of rebuilding. The Kountze Brothers Bank at Blake and Fifteenth streets, located in Cheesman's Drugstore, burned to the ground. Fortunately, the branch operation of the larger Kountze family enterprise possessed the resources to construct a new two-story brick structure at Fifteenth and Halladay and underwrite loans to re-establish many injured businesses. Luther and Charles Kountze were viewed by many citizens as saviors of the town because they provided loans to get people started again. Certainly the Kountze brothers took some risks, but the fact that they loaned money at 25% interest per annum suggests that their efforts for the community were not simply philanthropic.

Back to Emerson's compensation, Denver also gained from its losses in the "Great Fire." To be sure, reconstruction was costly, but in place of many frame buildings came more durable and aesthetically pleasing brick structures. Prior to the fire the city fathers had pointed with pride to the "Brick Block," a row of nine brick buildings on the west side of Ferry Street between Fourth and Fifth streets. Soon they boasted of numerous brick facilities and bragged that most were "fireproof."

Exactly thirteen months after Denver was struck by fire, another act of God hit the unsuspecting community with even greater ferocity. For several years Indians and mountain men had warned the populace that idle streambeds such as Cherry Creek sometimes behaved violently if heavy rains fell in the mountains. But the greenhorns observed that Cherry Creek seldom carried more than a small rivulet of water, even during the spring when snow melted and rain came with regularity. Ignoring sage warnings, businessmen jammed both banks of Cherry Creek with stores, shops, and warehouses, and some buildings such as city hall and the Trinity Methodist church facility were constructed in the creek bed itself.

For one week prior to Thursday, May 19, 1864, unusually steady and heavy rains poured on the mountains. On the afternoon of the 19th a shower hit the city. When the rain stopped, black clouds engulfed the region. They were so dense that the mountains were obscured for several hours. That evening a few people noticed that Cherry Creek was higher than usual, but no one expressed alarm. Just before midnight most Denverites were snuggled into bed, while

The great flood in 1864.

the pleasure seekers filled the gambling halls, saloons, and red-light district as usual. One insomniac recalled that just as midnight approached he "heard a strange sound in the south like the noise of the wind, which increased to a mighty roar as a great wall of water, bearing on its crest trees and other drift, rushed toward the settlement." Unlike the fire of the previous year, the flood gave no warning as it spread. The banks of the Platte and Cherry Creek overflowed in the wake of the ferocious torrent.

This time Auraria, or west Denver, was not spared as it had been during the fire. Indeed, that area was somewhat lower, and except for the immediate river and creek areas, it took the most water. Buildings in and along Cherry Creek were swept away, including Byers' *Rocky Mountain News* headquarters, the city hall, the building that housed the Trinity Methodist church, and scores of office buildings, warehouses, stables, and outbuildings. Ranches along the Platte River and Plum Creek were wiped out, and as the sun rose the next morning, both sections of Denver on either side of Cherry Creek were inundated with water, reaching levels of several feet on the lower west side.

Because sand, river rock, and mud could eventually be cleaned out, and buildings and goods not in the direct line of the flash flood could be salvaged, the monetary loss was somewhat less than that from the fire—only about $250,000. Nevertheless, the flood was much more disastrous than the fire. Eight men, women, and children were killed in Denver. Several others on ranches and farms outside of town perished. A number of transients probably died, too, but no one ever realized they were missing.

The Byers family narrowly escaped death as floodwaters invaded their ranch outside of town, picked up their cottage, and carried it to rest on a small island. Colonel John Chivington rescued the family by boat and took them into safer quarters in Denver. Elizabeth Byers remembered that they lived with Governor Evans and his wife for ten days and then tried to go back to the ranch. But as the water was still too high, they returned to Denver to live in the new, but still unoccupied, Colorado seminary building on Fourteenth and Arapahoe until they could reclaim their cottage and land. Although these were trying times for the Byers family, losing their home as well as the *Rocky Mountain News* office and printing press, they were more fortunate than many others. No lives were lost, and at least they had a place in which to live. Countless other people lived in tents and wagons with nowhere to go until the reclamation work was finished.

The flood left more than death, dislocation, and debris in its wake: it left contaminated water, sickness, and disease. While no major epidemic broke out as is often the case with a flood, the water destroyed crops and livestock on the nearby ranches and farms, causing food prices to skyrocket.

If Denver's superstitious dwellers were not surprised that disaster came exactly thirteen months after the fire, they should have been prepared for the next debilitating affair. An old wives' tale maintains that misfortune comes in groups of three. Immediately after the flood came a series of incidents that were far-reaching and tragic. Indians, white soldiers, and settlers fell into open warfare, resulting in terror, hunger, and discomfort for Denver citizens—and leading to ultimate disaster for the Plains Indians.

The Indian-white confrontation from summer 1864 to spring 1865 originated in 1851 as the result of white America's voracious appetite for land and gold. Seven years before gold was discovered in the Rockies, the chiefs of the principal tribes of the plains agreed to allow the United States government to build roads and military posts across Indian country. The Fort Laramie treaty also recognized the right of the Cheyenne and Arapahoe tribes to hunt and live off the high plains and eastern slope between the South Platte and Arkansas rivers, unmolested by white settlers. When gold was discovered in

1858, whites ignored the treaty and moved into the mountains in ever-increasing numbers. Not only were towns springing up as if by magic in the gold region, but stage line posts were built across the land on which the Arapahoe and Cheyenne hunted, and farmers and ranchers began settling the South Platte Valley, building permanent

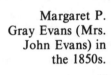

Margaret P.
Gray Evans (Mrs.
John Evans) in
the 1850s.

homes and fencing the land.

Following the historic pattern of white America's treatment of native Americans, the tribesmen were expected to forget previous agreements and move out of the way of white civilization's westward advance. In 1860 federal agents met with representatives of the Arapahoe and Cheyenne, urging them to forfeit the hunting grounds they had been guaranteed in 1851 and to retreat south into a small triangular region between Sand Creek and the Arkansas River. Some Indian leaders agreed to accept the arid reservation, but others refused, claiming the land could not support their people.

After the Civil War started in 1861, Indian leaders grew as

divided as their white counterparts in the states. While some Arapahoe and Cheyenne determined to live peaceably with the encroaching white settlers by remaining on or close to the reservation land, others ventured far beyond to hunt buffalo. The more militant Indians on the high plains obviously shared the thoughts of the Sioux in Minnesota who went on the warpath in 1862. They assumed that the whites were so divided among themselves that the perfect moment was at hand to regain the lands Indians had most recently lost.

During 1862 and 1863 unsurrendering Cheyenne and Arapahoe leaders in Colorado Territory confined their activities to a few cases of stage line and freight wagon raids and incidents of horse stealing and ranch burning. Then in spring 1864 Indian attacks were stepped up as soldiers and civilians harassed scattered bands of Indians. By summer, freight could not get into Denver without great difficulty. When shipments did arrive, prices were astronomical. Necessities such as food and medicine grew scarce during the months following the flood, and a few profiteers who cornered the market on these items extorted money from citizens. Fear of starvation was bad enough, but when rumors reached the suffering little city that Indians were planning to destroy the town, terror and anger overcame the people.

Food supplies continued to dwindle, and fear mounted. Then an incident twenty-five miles outside of Denver hurried the doom of the Plains Indians. Rancher Nathan Hungate, his wife, and two daughters were murdered, scalped and mutilated. When their bodies were brought into Denver, panic and hatred brought demands for action to Governor Evans. The governor, who was assigned the responsibility of overseeing Indian affairs at the same time he was to administer territorial government, acted quickly and cautiously. He called upon all Indians who were not hostile to surrender themselves and their weapons at federal forts. He promised them food and protection. To hostile Indians he promised war.

At this point confusion developed in both armed camps. Some Indians surrendered; others increased the tempo of their attacks. A young career officer, Major Edward Wynkoop, commander at Fort Lyon, emerged as the only white who seriously worked for a peaceful solution to the Indian-white problem. But the well-meaning, humane officer, still in his twenties, was relieved of his command because he was so out of step with white soldiers and civilians who were set on total war. As late as September 1864 Wynkoop tried to bring well-intentioned Indian chiefs together with Governor Evans, but such efforts were futile. The governor succumbed to local pressures to subdue the Indians. He decided to wage all-out war.

A few weeks prior to Major Wynkoop's abortive attempt to arrange peace, Evans received permission from Washington to raise a Colorado regiment of enlistees for 100 days with the expressed purpose of defeating the Indians who were by now playing havoc with the permanently entrenched settlers. To head this force he selected John M. Chivington, the man who rescued the Byers family from the flood the preceeding May. Colonel Chivington was probably the worst man Evans could have selected for the task. Born in Warren County, Ohio, in 1820, Chivington became a Methodist minister. For a quarter centry he was an itinerant preacher, spreading his gospel in Illinois, Missouri, and Nebraska before going to Colorado in 1860. Well over six feet tall, with the build of an ox, Chivington was a fanatical Union supporter who opposed slavery and was anxious to serve President Lincoln in the Union cause. Chivington had an obsessive personality. From his youth he had viewed the world in terms of absolute good and evil. The forces of satan must be conquered and destroyed, he frequently preached; to compromise with the devil was beyond his comprehension.

In 1861 Chivington had told Governor Gilpin that he wanted a "fighting," not a "praying," commission. The South had to be destroyed because of slavery. Now that the "heathen savages" were rumored to be moving toward an alliance with the Confederacy, the Methodist man of God saw Colorado Territory as Armageddon— the decisive battle for the Lord. That Chivington was thinking more of himself as military commander than as an evangelist could be seen by the swaggering posture he maintained in his blue officer's uniform. It is tempting to believe that he deliberately groomed himself with General William T. Sherman in mind. Chivington cropped his hair, beard, and mustache and flashed his belligerent eyes in a fashion identical to the prestigious fighting general. Sherman and Chivington were the same age, and if Sherman had been a few pounds heavier and colonel's epaulets could have been switched for a general's, the potraits of the two warriors could have been interchanged at any time, and only the most careful observer would have noticed the difference.

If the Colorado colonel idolized the Union general, Sherman could never have respected Chivington as a military man. Sherman was a hard, brutal, and determined fighter whose "war is hell" philosophy pushed Union troops through the South and on to the sea, leaving miles of destruction in the wake. Never, however, could Sherman have condoned Chivington's massacre of Indians at Sand

Creek in November 1864. While Governor Evans was out of the territory, Chivington's Third Colorado Regiment surprised the unsuspecting Cheyenne in their reservation lodges. No prisoners were taken despite attempts the Indians made to surrender. One hundred and five women and children, plus twenty-eight men (many of them aged) were shot, scalped, and mutilated on the orders of the fanatical colonel.

After the Sand Creek massacre, Colonel Chivington returned to Denver. He boasted that he and his men had killed between four and five hundred warriors. He felt confident his actions would launch him on a political career. But the blood bath had consequences that neither its architect nor the citizens expected. Irate Indians went on the warpath with unprecedented vengeance. Julesburg was attacked, and nearly every stage stop and ranch between that eastern Colorado town and Denver was overwhelmed. No mail or freight could reach Denver, and the town's stage and telegraph communications with the outside world were severed.

When the details of Chivington's atrocities were learned, he was scorned by all but a few hard-core Indian haters. His hopes for a political career were dashed forever. He was blamed for high prices and near-famine conditions suffered in Denver for the next few weeks. Within eighteen months he left Colorado for California.

The sufferings of Denver's citizens were to a large extent their own making. The territorial climate of hatred for the Plains Indians was spearheaded in the Cherry Creek community. The people goaded Governor Evans into a declaration of war, a position he had been reluctant to take until the political pressure threatened his popularity. Of course, he could have refused to be pushed, but the outcome was inevitable. Had he refused, he would have been removed from office, and someone else would have stepped in and declared war on the Arapahoe and Cheyenne—because by 1864 the white settlers and their government were determined to dispossess the Indians of the high plains and the eastern slope.

Had it not been for the Sand Creek massacre, some historians argue, the Plains Indians might have surrendered peacefully. But that, too, is unlikely. Too many Arapahoe and Cheyenne leaders shared the views of many Sioux. They had been moved, cheated, and betrayed once too often. They had decided to die quickly, fighting for what was by treaty and moral right their land, rather than die slowly while trying to live on arid, gameless land which white civilization— for the moment at least—did not covet.

By March 1865 Denver was liberated from its isolation. A

territorial militia was raised, and it reopened the overland routes to the city. Telegraph and stage operations resumed. The militia saw that they functioned without harassment. After the Civil War ended, more federal troops were sent to Colorado, and the Plains Indians were subdued once and for all.

If Denver's people felt any guilt for their part in the Indian removal policy, they must have believed that their own sufferings during the period of barricaded isolation served as atonement. There was little time to look backward while building a city in a new country. When anyone paused to reflect on the past, it was only to survey his own wounds, never to weep for the Arapahoe and Cheyenne. John Evans' biographer, Harry E. Kelsey, wrote that in late October 1864 the governor had this to say: "We have had a terrible time here during the past summer. The floods first washed us out and then the Indian war interrupted our commerce on the plains so the the Territory has had a severe back set."

Perhaps Denver's city builders reacted much like Francis Parkman did just after shooting an antelope on the Oregon Trail in the 1840s. Parkman recalled, "When I stood by its side, the antelope turned his expiring eye upward. It was like a beautiful woman's dark and bright. 'Fortunate that I am in a hurry,' thought I; 'I might be troubled with remorse, if I had time for it.' " If Denverites were tempted to feel remorse for the dispossessed, they did not feel that way for long. With the Indian war over, they hurried back to the business of building a city, retaining high hopes of attracting a railroad before the decade closed.

Besides working to attract a transcontinental railroad, dedicated citizens looked toward improving the community's quality of life. The 1863 fire had served as an impetus to make physical improvements. By 1865 Denver was more attractive than it had been two years earlier, but it remained a rather ugly, brown place with no trees, no paved streets, and only a few board sidewalks in the business districts. There was too little citizen interest to pave the streets. Money could be raised only to grade thoroughfares and keep the board sidewalks in repair. However, a modest sum was appropriated from property holders to bring water into town for beautification. Trees and lawns had not been planted in the arid town because not enough water was available to keep them alive. In 1865 an irrigation canal named the "city ditch" was dug from the Platte River, with channels flowing to many parts of the community. Upon its completion, residents put in lawns and embarked upon a major tree-planting campaign. The "city ditch" markedly changed the appear-

43

ance of the city. By 1867 a Frenchman, Louis L. Simonin, could note that "Denver had wide streets, quite open, watered [to keep down the dust], planted with trees." This was quite a change from Richardson's 1860 description of Denver as a place that reminded him of the Sahara.

The "city ditch" and the lawn and tree-planting spree it inspired seem insignificant by twentieth-century standards of city beautification. But for Denver in the 1860s it was a remarkable achievement. The turnstile town had thousands of transients who cared nothing about signs of beauty and permanence. Of the minority who shared the power elite's dream of building a city, few were sanguine enough about the town's future to commit money to any venture that would not directly serve their own interests.

Poverty was a serious problem in the Cherry Creek community as early as 1859, but little was done to relieve it. Jerome Smiley, a turn-of-the-century Denver historian, accounted for the lack of concern for the poor by saying, "there were not a great many destitute persons here worthy of aid and attention." In the 1860s few people would have disagreed. This attitude—that most unfortunates were not worthy—was as false as it was insensitive. The truth is that hundreds of men—foolish and shortsighted as they were—went to Colorado with only enough money to reach the mountains. When they failed to find their fortunes, they were stranded, often unable to find employment and without enough money to return home. Many men who had small grubstakes to get started in mining or business ventures became ill and lost everything they had to medical expenses before being strong enough to work. Denver also had countless orphaned and deserted children who walked the streets and begged, with no place to go for food or shelter. There were numerous cases of women—some alone and some with children—who were left behind in Denver while their husbands went into the mountains to prospect. Sometimes these husbands and fathers never returned, or they returned long after the money given to the family had been depleted.

These conditions existed as early as 1859, but they were ignored until 1860. In December of that year the city government, at William Byers' behest, raised an insufficient stipend to aid the poor. In 1861 the territorial legislature authorized the county to levy taxes for aiding the poor. Only $191 was raised in 1862. The next two years the county was more generous, outlaying $702. By 1867 the expenditures for such purposes reached $3,480, but the amount was still not enough to solve the problem.

During the 1860s much time was devoted to arguments between

city and county authorities, each trying to push the burden of poor relief on the other. Finally, with the expense of the flood as an excuse, Denver stopped most aid to the poor, leaving Arapahoe County with the entire task. The county, of course, had a larger tax base upon which to draw, but few officials were disposed to burden residents with taxes to aid indigents when it could be rationalized that most were "unworthy" anyway.

Callousness toward the poor was widespread, but not universal. Elizabeth Byers, who had plenty of hardships of her own, did more to provide relief for the needy than all of the public efforts combined. An attractive, humane woman, she was still in her twenties when she went to Denver in 1859. Within a few weeks of her arrival in the

Elizabeth (Mrs. William N.) Byers in the 1860s.

frontier community, she brought several women into her home to discuss what could be done to help those who were sick or stranded in Denver. In January 1860 she formed the only organization devoted solely to poor relief—the Ladies Union Aid Society. At first dedicated to healing the sick and getting "go backs" home, the Aid Society eventually tried to help deserted children find homes. Elizabeth Byers and her associates also solicited contributions of food, clothing, and money. They sponsored amateur theatrical performances at the Apollo Theater, and all proceeds went to the poor.

The work done by the Aid Society was complemented by some of the local churches. Despite the fact that there were fewer than ten churches, some of which were too impoverished to build their own facilities, they managed to raise money for the poor. Orthodox Jews formed a burial society to assure proper services and resting places for their impoverished dead. Early Roman Catholics, under the leadership of Father J.P. Machebeuf, made what efforts they could in Denver's war on poverty. Most active among the Protestants were members of Trinity Methodist church. In the women's bible class directed by Emma Vincent, a relief society was organized to supplement efforts made by Elizabeth Byers and her supporters.

Religious leaders attempted to care for the sick as well as for the poor. The medical facilities that did exist were crude, crowded, and dirty. There was a city physician in the early years, but his office was abolished in 1864 along with the makeshift city hospital. Indeed, when Dr. John Elsner, an Austrian-born, American-trained physician, arrived in Denver in 1866, he was appalled by the lack of facilities for patients. A Jew who devoted much of his life to aiding the needy and improving Denver's medical resources, he joined Sister Eliza of the Episcopal church in opening a tent hospital. It proved to be a marked improvement over the city jail and saloons which were being used at that time. To their tent Dr. Elsner and Sister Eliza brought patients of all creeds and from all walks of life, asking those who could to pay for their care, to help defray the expenses of treating the poor. Such efforts notwithstanding, Denver was sorely lacking in warm, clean, functional hospitals. As late as 1870, when Dr. Elsner was appointed county physician, he recalled that there was still "no hospital in Denver. I collected patients, who were lying in the hen houses and barns and were heretofore treated for so much a visit, and established a small hospital with 29 beds on Ninth street on the west side of town."

Hospital facilities were not the only trappings of civilization Denver lacked. A paucity of educational and cultural institutions was prevalent. The town had only one tiny circulating library in the 1860s. Opened by A.E. Pierce at the post office in 1859, the facility contained so few books that it hardly deserves the label of "library." Educational opportunities were almost as limited as books. By the end of the decade only two public schools were functioning. One was on Cherry Creek's west side, on Ferry Street, the other on the east side of Larimer. Although the situation improved by the late 1860s, during the first half of the decade, students and teachers labored under the most primitive conditions. Pupils of all ages and educational levels were taught together. Turnover was so great that the teachers seldom knew any student's "3-R" level. To make matters worse, there were few books. Often, the only volumes available for instructional purposes were those brought by settlers from the East and then generously loaned to the schools.

Besides the public educational institutions, two parochial schools were established as alternatives to the inferior public service. In 1864 Father Machebeuf arranged for three Sisters of the Order of Loretto to open St. Mary's Academy south of town at Fifteenth and California. Three years later the Episcopalians opened an academy for girls, Wolfe Hall, at Seventeenth and Champa, on the southern edge of town. These institutions provided the best education available in early Denver because they received ample financial support from tuition and from sources outside of Denver. The classes were better organized and more stable because the families who could pay for these private schools were seldom transients.

Quite obviously, equality of educational opportunity did not exist in early Denver. Many children never had an opportunity to attend school because they went to work at an early age. Orphans and children of the poor were customarily "bound out" to farms or sundry businesses in the city, where they worked long hours for low wages—sometimes for just room and board. The more fortunate youths who were not bound out had access to one of the public schools, but that opportunity was probably inferior to most one-room country schools in the states. Only children from families of means had the chance to attend a parochial academy and obtain an education on par to what existed in other parts of mid-nineteenth century America.

Most Americans in the 1860s did not feel the need or have the money to study in institutions of higher learning. Nevertheless, scholars of such inclination in Denver were deprived unless they could afford to go outside of the territory. In 1862 John Evans decided to change the situation by building a Methodist university for Colorado the same way in which he had built Northwestern University in Illinois. The name Denver University was considered during the planning stages, but when the school was chartered it was called Colorado Seminary. Governor Evans donated the land for the seminary and worked with William Byers, David Moffat, Amos Steck, Jerome Chaffee, and several other prominent men to raise the money for building, construction, and maintenance. The seminary was opened across from the Evans' home on Fourteenth and Arapahoe in 1864, with over fifty students enrolled the first term.

By 1866 Byers proclaimed that education had become up-to-date in Denver with the opening of the Colorado Seminary. He boasted, "there are no superior institutions of learning of the like grade to be found anywhere in America." Educators in Massachusetts or even Missouri might have disagreed with the visionary editor, but there was no time to challenge his statement. The seminary was insolvent the next year, and its doors remained closed until 1880.

Formal educational standards aside, some humanizing experiences were available to Denverites who lived in the city long enough to take advantage of such opportunities. Some citizens—a minority to be sure—wanted more out of Colorado than money and the pleasures it would buy in the game rooms, brothels, and saloons. Early Denver has been depicted as a gathering place for only the crudest, hardest, and most materialistic of the species; however, that representation ignores a small, but important, group of sensitive people. For example, countless opportunities existed for young and old alike to obtain an education in music. Nor did one have to be wealthy. W.H. Watson, a warm and generous man who loved music and children, opened a free children's singing school in 1860, conducting evening classes over a merchant's shop. Trinity Methodist also made free singing classes available to people of all ages during the winter months. There were few private voice and instrument teachers in the early 1860s, but during the closing years of the decade, numerous instructors advertised their services.

If one could quantify entertainment in Denver, such songs as "Sweet Betsy from Pike" and "Old Susannah," banged out on cheap, poorly tuned barroom pianos by bloated maestros and sung by garishly dressed and overpainted chorus girls, would predominate. Still, other forms of live entertainment could be found. The upstairs of the Criterion had minstrel shows, farces, and dance presentations. Ed Chase's Progressive Hall offered variety theater and a stringed orchestra from Chicago. As early as 1859 a troupe from Leavenworth performed "William Tell" and "Richard the Third" to nearly a full house each night at Apollo Hall.

Churches were not to be outdone by the dens of sin. While they provided little public entertainment during the difficult times between 1863 and 1865, the Methodists, Presbyterians, and Episcopalians sponsored horn and organ concerts, quartet singing, and Sunday school songfests during the following years.

Denver was fortunate in attracting well-educated and talented patrons of the arts. Such persons seldom settled raw young cities, but Denver was exceptional because of its climate. Some travellers argued that Denver and its environs were no more healthful than eastern parts of the nation, but medical science begged to differ. The clean, dry air of the Rockies was known to be a tonic for sufferers of pulmonary diseases. Folks stricken by tuberculosis, asthma, and related lung disorders began moving to Colorado in the 1860s. Among them were some well-established easterners who were willing to trade more comfortable and cultured communities for better health.

One of these health seekers was Benjamin F. Woodward. Born into a wealthy Ohio family in 1834, he was given a first-rate education in Rochester, New York. Already a successful merchandiser and telegraph company executive in Illinois by the time of the Civil War, he took a leave of absence in 1862 to aid the Union cause in the Telegraph Corps. When Woodward lost his health during the war, he was advised to move to either California or Colorado. Securing a position with Pacific Overland Telegraph Company in Denver, he became active in business, financial, and civic affairs. In 1867 the mild-mannered, thin, bespectacled war veteran decided to improve the quality of Denver's music. Bringing together talented vocalists who appreciated classical music, he organized the Denver Musical Union. This was not the town's first choral organization, but it became the most important one in the latter part of the first decade. Choral music was dominated by German-born settlers until Woodward became involved. Germans, unlike many other immigrants and most nineteenth-century Americans, loved classical music. The largest foreign-born group in Denver, Germans founded their own societies and performed primarily for themselves. The Germania Glee Club was organized in 1860; and in 1865 several German men introduced the first Turnverein in Denver, complete with a singing group.

Woodward's hope was to involve some of these men, but also non-Germans. He wanted to encourage music appreciation among all groups in the city. In spring 1867 Woodward's union presented the cantata "Daniel." The appreciative audience was not predominantly German, and "Daniel" became the first of a long series of performances supported by the middle and upper economic classes.

Other signs that Denver was losing at least some of the rustic qualities of a mining boom town appeared in the late 1860s. Promoters realized that a predominantly male population was no asset when it came to attracting women or, for that matter, men with wives and children. In 1860 men outnumbered women by a ratio of more than six to one—with too many of the women having vulgar clothes, coarse manners, and questionable morals. As soon as wives and grown daughters of newcomers appeared in measurable numbers, newspapers and other promotional literature played up the presence of attractive, stylishly dressed "ladies." Such emphasis could be made without gross exaggeration after 1865 because women came to Denver in ever-increasing numbers. Some came alone, but many came with families or joined husbands and fathers who had come earlier and decided to stay on. By 1870 men did not even outnumber women two to one. Indeed, by the time the railroad came to Denver there were 2,800 men and nearly 2,000 women.

Promoters seemed to be more concerned about the importance of religion to a growing community than the settlers themselves. Conventional wisdom in the mid-nineteenth century taught that religion brought order and morality and thereby made a growing town more attractive to women and family men. The Reverend William Crawford from Massachusetts, a graduate of Andover and an emissary from the American Home Missionary Society, certainly shared the notion that it was important to get religion into frontier communities. He evangelized throughout Colorado Territory between 1863 and 1868 but found few people who shared his concern for things of the spirit. He disappointingly reported to his superiors that "the excitement is unfavorable to the progress of spiritual religion. Those who live in the quiet towns of New England, do not know what we have to contend with." In Denver, he continued, "all minds are so occupied with the one idea of getting rich, that there is no room for religion."

As late as 1870 saloons still predominated in Denver, outnumbering churches by about eight to one. Nevertheless, for those who felt a need to worship their God there was no paucity of organized religion. By 1866 Jewish services were conducted on a regular basis, and there was Father Machebeuf's Roman Catholic Church. For Protestant Christians a variety of choices existed, including seven churches—Methodist-Episcopal, Protestant-Episcopal, Presbyterian,

Lutheran, Congregational, African Methodist-Episcopal, and African Baptist—all with regular pastors.

Compared to other towns in the territory during the late 1860s, Denver offered a superior quality of life. There were more doctors, dentists, shops, stores, restaurants, and hotels and a wider variety of entertainment and educational opportunities. But in contrast to such cities as St. Louis, Boston, and New York, cities to which Denver's leaders always compared their new town, the Colorado emporium was crude, dirty, disorganized, expensive, and culturally deprived. Why, then, did people make the long and sometimes hazardous journey to Denver City from California and the East? There are many answers to this question. Some came to escape from the law, the Civil War draft, or unhappy family situations. Others came reluctantly because of their health or because a member of the family had chased a dream or an opportunity and had insisted on dragging along a spouse or dependent siblings and parents.

The majority, on the other hand, came seeking that promise of American life called equality of opportunity—and Colorado's frontier promised many opportunities. There was a chance to make money by farming, starting a business, or beginning a trade or profession in a region that others had not already monopolized. There was opportunity to achieve status in a new community in which rigid class lines based on family name or inherited wealth did not yet exist. One of Colorado's first white settlers saw the territory as a place where he could do something for his family. He said, "My wife will be a lady and my children will be educated." Still others went to Denver because the city presented a challenge. It was a place to build new institutions and try something exciting and different. Whether they dreamed of political power, wealth, or social status, the Rocky Mountain frontier was a place where people could build from bedrock—at least that was the promise.

National ideals frequently clash with reality; but when this happens, just enough salvable pieces are left to rebuild the ideal and keep it alive for the next generation. This is precisely what happened in Denver. Thousands came chasing the vision, only to have it escape them once they arrived. There is no other way to account for the throngs who stayed such a short time. For at least some of the most sanguine and determined, modest opportunities existed. By the end of the decade, hundreds were part of the comfortable middle class. They may have been far from wealthy, but they were confident of shelter, food, clothing, and certain luxuries.

The opportunity to make outstanding achievements in business and politics was reserved for a few. This minority was comprised only of white men. Some of them, such as the Kountze brothers, Jerome Chaffee, Bela Hughes, and John Evans had a head start before they came, and that gave them a decided advantage over those who started with nothing. Others, like William Byers and David Moffat, came with little, but through hard work, perseverance, and luck they managed to achieve considerable success.

The most eminently successful men in Denver, who gravitated to the core of the community's power structure, were not only white, they were native Americans and Protestants in religion. Being foreign-born was probably a liability in gaining access to the decision-making circle in the late sixties, but it was no deterrent to making money. A few Germans were remarkably successful businessmen, and several foreign-born professing Jews, among them Hyman and Fred Salomon, Abraham Jacobs, Joel Gottlieb, and David Kline, built mercantile businesses and amassed considerable wealth.

If women tried to get into the business world or power structure—and there is no evidence to suggest that they did in the 1860s—they failed. Most women who worked outside their own homes were domestic servants or laundresses. The few who distinguished themselves and gained notoriety were invariably teachers, philanthropists, church workers, or madames.

Opportunities to build fortunes and gain power were clearly restricted to a few men, although it was obviously possible for many white men and even women to find cozy niches in the middle class. The odds, however, were overwhelming against every black man and woman who came to Denver and dreamed of anything more than subsistence. That most blacks held no illusions about the frontier offering them a better life than they could find in the free states before the war, or in the former slave states after 1865, is evidenced by the few who made a pilgrimage to Colorado. In 1860 only fifteen men and eight women were listed in the census as "colored." Five years after emancipation, that number increased to only 237.

Black residents of Denver in the 1860s were denied opportunities extended to the most vulgar and ignorant whites. Any white child could attend public schools, but black children had no educational facilities until 1867. Blacks paid taxes to support the two public schools but were denied access to them. Not until Frederick Douglass's son, Lewis, came to Denver was a school for blacks established. In 1867 he personally founded a night school for blacks and embarked upon a campaign to get the public schools opened to his people. Joined by Edward Sanderlin and William J. Hardin, young

Douglass finally got the school board to open separate facilities for blacks. Integration did not come until the next decade.

Blacks were not only denied educational opportunities, but the ballot was taken from them as well. There were so few blacks in the territory in 1861 that none of the lawmakers thought to specifically deny black men the right to vote. The law allowed all men twenty-one or older to cast ballots. However, in 1864 this oversight was rectified. An amendment to the law explicitly denying black men the vote was passed. Governor Evans endorsed the amendment and refused to listen to the pleas of Denver's black spokesmen. Evans' successor, Alexander Cummings, was more sympathetic, but he failed to get the amendment changed. Not until the U.S. Congress passed a territorial suffrage law in 1867 were blacks given the ballot.

Blacks were subjected to discrimination in other ways. They had no representatives in the police force, despite the fact that they were beaten and murdered just for being black. Blacks were also ghettoized into the poorest neighborhoods. After the 1864 flood, all persons who could afford it moved their residences from the vicinity of Cherry Creek. Blacks, however, were forced to live in the most threatened dwellings because they were de facto restricted to the first blocks bordering the west side of the unpredictable stream.

No matter how hard they worked, black families failed to climb out of the lowest economic class. According to the 1870 Census, only fourteen black married women were listed as housewives; the majority worked as servants and laundresses. Most of the men found only menial employment as laborers, teamsters, waiters, and cooks. It is true that if the black *people* failed to find opportunities, a few *persons* did manage to build rich estates, live in stylish neighborhoods, and gain respect and prestige in the community. Almost to a man, however, these were mulattoes. By the end of the decade the few nonwhites who were not of the lower economic class were saloon keepers, restauranteurs, barbers, and clergymen. There were three saloon keepers and all were mulattoes; two restauranteurs—both mulattoes; nine barbers—seven were mulattoes; the one clergyman was a mulatto.

With only one exception, every man of African descent who built a successful business, lived outside the ghetto, and actively lobbied for black people's rights, was a mulatto. Entrepreneurs Barney L. Ford, Henry O. Wagoner, and William J. Hardin were all mulattoes—only barber Edward Sanderlin was not. The story here is obvious: the lighter one's skin, the greater the opportunities. The promise of American life in frontier Denver was largely the preserve of white men.

Part II
Youthful City, 1870-1904

Chapter 3

If survival was the major concern of Denver's small leadership corps in the 1860s, growth became the next generation's obsession. The Denver Pacific and Kansas Pacific secured Denver's future, but the prodigious growth of the next thirty years was the result of natural advantages and energetic leadership. Between 1870 and 1900 Denver's population soared from 4,759 to almost 134,000. One reason for the increase was that almost $224 million worth of gold and $541 million in silver was mined in Colorado during those years. But more than precious ore discoveries attracted settlers. Imaginative efforts of community leaders encouraged the boom.

In 1870 Governor Edward McCook called for a program to attract settlers to Denver and its hinterland. He told the territorial legislature that Colorado "needs muscle." William Byers agreed as he echoed the governor's observation in the editorials of the *Rocky Mountain News*. Roger W. Woodbury, the *Denver Tribune*'s editor, joined the crusade. By 1872 scores of entrepreneurs, newspapermen, and politicians were clamoring for a formal promotional campaign to publicize Colorado and its major city. Governor McCook once again went to the legislature. He told the politicians that other states and territories had agencies working to entice foreign and domestic immigrants and it was time Colorado did the same. In response, the legislature created a Board of Immigration and funded it with $6,000.

William Byers and Fred Z. Salomon agreed to coordinate the board's activities without pay so that the small appropriation could be stretched to greatest advantage. Byers, of course, had been a "volunteer" in every promotional cause throughout the 1860s. Although Salomon was not as well known or as experienced in promotional ventures as Byers, he was no newcomer to city boosting.

Fred. Z. Salomon. *Courtesy Western
History Department,
Denver Public Library*

A Jew born in Prussia in 1830, he came to America with his father and began work at an early age. Involved in general merchandising and sales, he traveled the southern part of the United States before the Civil War and then tried his salesmanship in Iowa and Las Vegas. In 1859, when he was in St.Louis buying trade goods, he learned about the gold strikes in the Rocky Mountains. With J.B. Doyle, he purchased several wagon loads of merchandise and took them to Denver. From that year the well-groomed, mustached, and mutton-chopped businessman remained in Denver. He oversaw a general store that advertised "anything from a needle to . . . the biggest grindstone you ever saw," and he soon branched out into the brewery and saloon businesses.

Fred Salomon's business ventures occupied most of his time in the early 1860s, but by 1869 he moved into the inner circle of promoters. He was a member of the Board of Trade, which organized the Union Pacific venture, and he invested much of his own time and money going to Chicago to raise money for Denver's lifeline to Cheyenne. Salomon, like Byers, saw his own business and real estate investments tied to Denver's growth, and he willingly worked with the editor on the Board of Immigration.

These men published three different pamphlets in English and German (Salomon's native language was German) that outlined Colorado's advantages, resources, and opportunities. Through their efforts and those of several legislators, they armed a group of agents with this literature and sent them on recruiting missions. Three agents were dispatched to Europe, one going to London and two to Germany. Nine others were sent east of the Mississippi. Two went to New York City and one to New England, while six others covered an area from the deep south to the Great Lakes.

It is impossible to measure the effectiveness of this campaign (it was phased out in December 1873) because innumerable other promotional programs were going on at the same time. Nevertheless, so many newcomers arrived in Denver by spring 1873 that the city's labor market became glutted. William Byers urged leaders in other communities to keep him posted on employment opportunities. Even after the Board of Immigration was discontinued, the *News* editor was inundated with mail from prospective settlers. He answered each inquiry, suggesting which towns or regions offered the greatest economic opportunities at the moment.

In addition to the Board of Immigration, railroads were extremely effective boosters. When the Union Pacific and Kansas Pacific joined rails in Denver in 1870, Colorado had only 157 miles of track. By 1890 there were 4,176 miles of track in the state, with most lines reaching the bustling new city. The impact of the railroads was more than significant—it was monumental. Construction brought thousands of workers to Colorado, many of whom remained after the rails were laid. Such lines as the Denver, South Park and Pacific and the Denver Rio Grande transformed the little outfitting post into a bustling commercial center, carrying people, supplies, and raw materials in and out daily.

As Denver became the hub of Colorado's rail network, wholesalers, warehousers, and merchandisers congregated there. The city was the most convenient place for receiving goods from the East and directing reshipment to all parts of Colorado. Smelters that originated in the mining towns also moved to Denver. Labor was more plentiful, ores could be brought in by rail from several mining communities, fuel could be hauled there more cheaply, and the refined gold, silver, and copper could be shipped out efficiently. Railroad corporations further stimulated growth by advertising Colorado all over the United States and abroad, urging people to purchase land owned by the companies along the rail routes or to settle infant towns that the companies were trying to develop. Advertising campaigns urged tourists to take advantage of their passenger trains and explore the natural wonders of the Rocky Mountains.

The most imaginative railroad advertising was done by the Denver and Rio Grande Railway. The management employed agents at home and abroad and purchased extensive space in newspapers. The Denver and Rio Grande even hired Stanley Wood, a poet, essayist, and songwriter, to oversee the literary quality of the promotional program. Wood enticed tourists and residents and boosted Denver and the railroad in a variety of ways. In a Durango newspaper, for instance, an advertisement announced that a small investment would buy a round-trip ticket to Denver, where people could avail themselves of the best dental and medical care in the state.

Railroads introduced outside investors to all kinds of Colorado enterprises. Most railroads in Colorado were owned and controlled in part by outside capitalists. The Colorado Central, constructed in the early 1870s, was financed by Coloradans W.A.H. Loveland and Henry M. Teller, along with Bostonians T.J. Carter and F.G. Dexter. In 1880 eastern railroad magnate Jay Gould took over the operation. That same year Gould bought John Evans' controlling interest in the Denver, South Park and Pacific Railway, which had been financed by easterners and Denverites David Moffat, Charles Kountze, W.S. Cheesman, and George Kassler. Gould also began buying stock in

William Jackson Palmer's Denver and Rio Grande. By 1880 he controlled it and several other lines in Colorado.

A complicated series of stock transfers and mergers resulted in the few Colorado lines that were not in outside hands going that way by 1890 or soon thereafter. Out-of-state control was a mixed blessing for Coloradans. Freight rates increased, but once Chicago, Boston, New York, and British capitalists had a stake in the state, they became aware of new investment opportunities. The result was that "outsiders" assumed positions in the inner decision-making circle. But without them and their vast sums of capital, the region could never have developed as fast as it did and Denver's population could not have reached nearly 134,000 by 1900—a feat most businessmen and boosters celebrated with unequivocal enthusiasm.

An outstanding example of an "outsider" who became part of Denver's power elite was a middle-aged Scot, James Duff. Unassuming and unostentatious, yet expensively and impeccably dressed, Duff represented a group of British and American investors in an organization called Colorado Mortgage and Investment Company. Although he speculated in Colorado railroads before leaving the British Isles, operating from a distance was not his idea of wise investing. Before he risked any more of his own or anyone else's capital in Colorado, he decided to study the region personally. In 1877 the enterprising, but wary, Scot arrived in Denver to examine investment opportunities firsthand. Duff provided loans to several railroads, including Palmer's Denver and Rio Grande, and he sat on the boards of other railroads, among them the Denver, Utah and Pacific. The financier speculated Colorado Mortgage and Investment Company funds in Leadville mines, and he provided loans to build irrigation ditches which ultimately carried water to nearly 120,000 acres of arid land in northeastern Colorado. Always diversifying the money in his trust, Duff also put many thousands of dollars into ranching and cattle businesses

Duff was not the only British citizen contributing to regional economic development. Scores of others bet their capital on Colorado's future. Between 1880 and 1900 over 300 cattle companies were incorporated in Colorado, with capitalization exceeding $100 million. Much of this was British money. The same capitalists speculated in Colorado mines. Indeed, by 1890 about two dozen British firms had put over $6 million into local mining stock. Some lost money and liquidated their securities during the depression of 1893-95, but they reinvested once the economy improved. By 1900 more British companies were involved in Colorado's gold, silver, lead, and zinc mines than ever before, with investments exceeding those of a decade earlier.

Metallurgists and mining engineers went to Colorado in increasing numbers by the late 1870s, and they used Denver as their base of exploration. Taking trains into the mountains, they directed mining operations and examined prospective mines for eastern and British capitalists. These experts attracted millions of dollars to most promising enterprises. Besides writing directly to investment companies in England and Germany (most of these scientists were from those countries), they published articles in technical journals, thereby publicizing Colorado's resources with every publication.

In 1882 Hermann Berger, Richard Pearce, Peter H. von Diest, and several other foreign scientists organized the Colorado Scientific Society to encourage technical exploration and promulgate their discoveries. A group of Denver businessmen recognized the utility of this society. In 1884 Denver promoters organized the Chamber of Commerce with the expressed purpose of attracting immigrants, investors, and businesses. One of the chamber's first tasks was to commission the Colorado Scientific Society to do research and publish the results for the advancement of science and the promotion of Denver. An example of this joint enterprise was a little pamphlet titled *The Artesian Wells of Denver*. It explained that an artesian well was a fountain well resulting from water pressure forcing water through a surface hole. The booklet further pointed out that while explorations in 1874 had failed to find such water resources, an artesian well had been discovered in 1883, proving that Denver was not without this important underground asset after all.

The initiative for organizing the Chamber of Commerce and prevailing upon the Colorado Scientific Society for help came from Roger W. Woodbury, the editor and proprietor of the *Denver Tribune* and later *The Times*. A lean, large-eyed, goatee-sporting Civil War veteran, Woodbury was born on a New Hampshire farm in 1841. He toiled both on the family land and in a textile mill until he was seventeen and then apprenticed himself to a printer. He joined the Union Army in 1861 and went to Colorado in 1866. He published the *Tribune* with a partner and quickly joined William N. Byers as a leading editor-booster of Denver. It was Woodbury's idea to organize the Chamber of Commerce once the state legislature stopped funding the Board of Immigration. With support from Charles Kountze, John Evans, H.A.W. Tabor—a newcomer to Denver who had made a fortune in the mines—and a few more similar-minded businessmen, the permanent successor of the old Board of Trade was incorporated.

Captain Roger W. Woodbury in the
New Hampshire Volunteer Infantry in 1863, three
years before he went to Colorado.

One of the promotional purposes of the Chamber of Commerce was to disseminate *honest* information to prospective settlers and investors. During the economic boom of the 1870s (the panic of 1873 had minimal effect on Colorado), swindlers took advantage of investors. To prevent the state and city from gaining an unsavory reputation, the chamber tried to keep outsiders informed of the latest and most reliable information on mining, ranching, and business enterprises.

This drive to give Denver an image of honesty actually began in 1879 when some of the same men who formed the Chamber of Commerce opened the Real Estate Exchange. Its purpose was to screen potential investments for people living outside Colorado. The chamber assumed and enlarged the exchange's function. Another organization later boosted the region with promises of candid advice. The former literary chief of the Denver and Rio Grande Railway, Stanley Wood, in cooperation with Harry H. Tammen of Denver's Tammen Curio Company, began publication of a unique magazine, *The Great Divide.* Wood was a refined, curly haired, mustached man of middle age. A graduate of Oberlin College, he edited *The Great Divide* to promote Colorado and stimulate local literary talent. Wood's magazine featured poems and short stories. Through his journal he hoped to entertain the reader and simultaneously laud Colorado and its people. Less subtle than his literary boosterism were the promotional essays, biographical sketches of successful Coloradans, and testimonials of settlers and tourists.

By 1893 *The Great Divide* was glorifying Colorado all over the world. Circulation offices were located in St. Louis, Chicago, New York, Boston, and London, as well as Denver. Over 32,000 copies were sold on the eve of the depression, some issues going as far away as New Zealand. Stanley Wood's biographer, M. James Kedro, argues that the depression was partly responsible for removing the magazine to Chicago, where it lost its Colorado literary and promotional qualities.

Despite the brief life of this singular periodical, it served a useful purpose. Wood undoubtedly attracted settlers, tourists, and investors to the Rocky Mountains with his creative journalism. Furthermore, he personally offered inducements to prospective settlers by urging them to come to his Arapahoe Street office in Denver, where they could get honest advice on where to farm, prospect, or buy real estate. Stanley Wood, like the directors of the Chamber of Commerce, urged people to let him advise and protect them from swindlers.

Agencies such as the Real Estate Board, the Chamber of Commerce, and Wood and Tammen's *Great Divide* no doubt attracted individual settlers and small investors. Nevertheless, it was the big money—the large investments from insurance companies, banks, and investment corporations—that was vital to the expansion of Denver and its environs. The large investors, of course, were concerned about the safety of their ventures and had their own means of scrutinizing opportunities. Confidential investigators were hired in Colorado for making recommendations on investments, and the large financial interests made judgements on the basis of those reports, not on what they could learn from the Chamber of Commerce or Stanley Wood.

In the late 1860s and 1870s decisions about loans to budding Denver entrepreneurs were often made on the basis of character and financial reports gathered by R.G. Dun and Company, a New York agency that was the nineteenth-century forerunner of Dun and Bradstreet. Beginning in the 1840s, R.G. Dun had confidential investigators (frequently young lawyers) in every state and territory, plus Canada and Europe. A banker or wholesaler, approached for credit by a businessman, could obtain a credit rating on the applicant through R.G. Dun and Company. With this information a creditor could make a reasonably intelligent decision about how large a loan to make or whether he should risk his capital at all.

Almost without exception, the men who entered Denver's power structure were investigated by R.G. Dun. Because they passed the scrutiny of the Dun investigators, they obtained money to build businesses and fortunes. Eventually they controlled the banks, utilities, and major businesses and owned much of the most valuable real estate. Once established, these men not only directed the economic life of the community, they became the respected men who advised eastern and European financiers on where to place their money in Colorado. This enabled the local power elite to direct economic growth along lines in which they held interests, and it empowered them to make or break younger people and newcomers who hoped to get a start in the Queen City of the Rockies.

Only a few men built fortunes and directed Denver's development between 1870 and 1900. Five of them—William N. Byers, Jerome B. Chaffee, Charles Kountze, David H. Moffat, and John Evans—were leaders in the 1860s. The others—James Duff, Walter S. Cheesman, Henry R. Wolcott, James Archer, J.B. Grant, Roger Woodbury, William Gray Evans, Fred Z. Salomon, and Charles Boettcher— entered the power structure one decade later.

All five of the charter members of the power elite were investi-

Charles B. Kountze

gated by R.G. Dun and Company. Despite the fact that John Evans was well established and wealthy before he went to Colorado, he became an early subject for Dun correspondents. According to a December 1874 report, ex-Governor John Evans "Is of exclnt [excellent] char [acter] habs [habits] and bus [iness] ability. Stands high in Col [orado] and is identified with various enterprises here. Was said to have 200M$ [thousand] wor [th] of ppty [property] in Chicago and is e.w. [estimated worth] 3/4 to 1 million dollars." In 1871 William Byers was rated an "excellent man, [with] excellent char [acter]." Three years later the field man noted Byers was of "good char [acter], hab [its] and ability, . . . [with real estate] worth 30-50M [thousands] . . . Credit good." The following year, according to the investigator, "he is regarded . . . good for any he may ask in his line." In the early 1870s Jerome B. Chaffee was judged "emminently safe, reliable and honorable . . . Is wor [th] 600,000 to my own personal knowledge, straightforward, upright bus [iness] man, wor [thy] of unlimted cr [edit]." A similar report was registered on David H. Moffat in 1875. "Young married man of excellent char [acter], habits and capacity [.] Owns 2 fine residences here worth 50M [thousands], and other valuable R.E. . . . in good credit." As early as 1866 the Kountze brothers were described as "rich and well established in business [and] entitled to full confidence." In 1867 their bank was proclaimed to be "one of the most reliable firms in the Union." In 1867 a Dun correspondent reported on Walter S. Cheesman: "In bus [iness] 6 yrs, made money [,] most excellent trade undoubted . . . No better man . . . worthy all confidence." And by 1873, the reporter concluded that Cheesman was in "good credit" and "one of the *staunch.*"

Reports on other civic leaders were similar. In 1871 James Archer was listed as a "man of high character and standing and very enterprising. . . . Probably well known in St. Louis." Two years later he was marked as "one of the substantial men of the city." Charles Boettcher was labeled "a safe man for cr [edit]." The Salomon brothers had good business and character references and "may be credited to any extent that their trade may require," and Roger Woodbury was noted as "a young man of excellent char [acter], habs [habits] is doing a safe and profitable bus [iness] regarded perfectly reliable." One should not conclude from these favorable reports that R.G. Dun and Company refused to say anything about a businessman if they could not say something good. The company, after all, was in business to make money, and if the reports proved unreliable, no one would pay for investigations. Indeed, the mercantile agency

frequently made harshly unfavorable judgements. One Denver lawyer was described as a member of the "D[enver] bar and had brighter
prospects than [a] majority of the lawyers of this Co[unty], he is now
morally [,] socially [,] physically [,] mentally and legally a wreck."
Another attorney was alleged to have "fair legal ability, has accumu-
lated considerable R.E., but it all will be gone if he continues the
course of [sic] life [with] wine and women." One small manufacturing
company was purported to be a "very small affair and not recommended for credit." A bank stockholder was described as "an unscru-
pulous unreliable man."

Those who received high marks from R.G. Dun and Company
found access to investment capital, and most of them used it wisely.
To be sure, there was speculation in mines and some in the fickle
cattle market, but most capital went into transportation, urban real
estate, banking, utilities, and manufacturing—all enterprises that
could do nothing but succeed in a new city that had outdistanced its
rivals and was just beginning to grow.

Many investors took advantage of these colossal opportunities,
but there was a coterie of less than twenty men who inaugurated
services and, through their corporations, dominated the community.
Their strength certainly originated from the vital businesses they
controlled, yet, it was enhanced by group unity. Denver's magnates
never limited themselves to one dimension of the economic empire;
rather, they created an interwoven and interlocked network that
helped them place a vise grip on virtually every significant branch of
the new city's economy.

A key figure in organizing the economy was James Duff. The
Scot was influential because he was an experienced investor who had
more money at his disposal than any person in Denver. He not only
made decisions for the Colorado Mortgage and Investment Company,
he was a confidant and advisor to wealthy British investors, among
them the Member of Parliament from Aberdeen, Scotland—James
Barclay. Duff surrounded himself with successful men who were
intent on building an empire.

These city builders congregated in each other's offices and homes
in the late 1870s and discussed plans for the future. Finally, in 1880,
Duff risked offending his American associates by suggesting that in
the British Isles gentlemen of power had clubs where they socialized
and discussed business. Surely Denver needed such an institution,
Duff's counsel was deemed wise, and in July 1880 the group that was
accomplishing important things in the Queen City incorporated the
Denver Club. The membership of the new club was practically

Seventeenth Street and Glenarm about 1890. The
stone building on the left is the Denver Club.

Henry R. Wolcott about 1880.

synonymous with Denver's power structure and would continue to be so during future decades.

Joining Duff in the Denver Club venture was thirty-four-year-old Henry Roger Wolcott, who became the club's first president. Wolcott was born into a comfortable Massachusetts family in 1846. His father was a notable Congregational minister who gave him a first-rate education in private schools in Providence, Rhode Island and Cleveland, Ohio. While in Providence, young Wolcott met Professor Nathaniel P. Hill of Brown University, a scientist who was preparing to visit Colorado to investigate mining and smelting investment possibilities. Hill liked what he saw and soon organized the Boston and Colorado Smelting Company. Two years after the company was formed in Black Hawk, Wolcott went to the Colorado mining town to join Hill as assistant manager. Soon the clean-shaven, stocky built Wolcott, with dark, wavy hair neatly parted on the left side, was assigned to manage a new branch plant at Alma. Eventually he directed operations of the company's Argo smelter when it was opened in Denver in the late 1870s. Wolcott's knowledge of the smelting business earned him a place on the board of the Colorado Smelting and Mining Company, and he assumed the vice presidency of Colorado Fuel and Iron Company.

The Denver Club's first president had an incredible capacity for work. His mining and smelting responsibilities were only one part of an extremely busy business life. The aggressively ambitious New Englander became well known in east coast financial circles due to his position in Colorado industry. By the mid 1870s he was on the Board of Directors of the Equitable Life Assurance Society, representing that New York corporation in Rocky Mountain investments. Wolcott's growing influence in attracting eastern capital to the West put him in a powerful position in Denver. Between 1875 and 1900 he served on the boards of the First National Bank, the Merchants National Bank, the National Bank of Commerce, and the National Trust Company. Besides his involvement in these financial institutions, Wolcott was a large stockholder in and director of the Denver, Utah and Pacific Railroad. He also became president of the Colorado Telephone Company and was active on the Mining Stock Exchange.

Wolcott did even more. Extremely influential in the East, he was second only to James Duff in acquiring outside capital for Denver and its hinterland. A frequent visitor to Boston and New York, he stayed in the best hotels and dined with financiers. While he lived and worked in Denver, he maintained memberships in several of the most

71

exclusive clubs in Boston and New York and became a personal confidant and advisor to men who had fortunes to invest. The transplanted New Englander became close to Boston financier Henry Lee Higginson, the president of Lee, Higginson and Company, a major Boston investment house. With Wolcott as intermediary and advisor, Higginson put money into such ventures as the Old Hundred Development Company. Managed by Eben Smith, Old Hundred was a prospecting and mining firm which, in the early 1890s, was operating near Leadville. Wolcott made major decisions for the company, especially when it came to buying equipment or seeking more capital for exploration.

Wolcott also worked closely with Henry B. Hyde, president of New York's Equitable Life Assurance Society. Hyde sometimes came to Denver to call on Wolcott, and the Denver entrepreneur made dozens of trips to New York City to consult on matters they both felt were too complex to work out in their voluminous correspondence. Henry R. Wolcott advised Hyde in Colorado coal mining investments and suggested that he join him and Charles Perkins (president of Chicago, Burlington and Quincy) in their exploration into gold mining prospects in Arizona and Nicaragua. Regarding Denver, Wolcott assured Hyde in 1891 that "Denver is holding its own better than any western city, and I am sure our investment here is going to be a profitable one." This apparently impressed the New Yorker. He listened to the Denver leader and took his advice on venturing nearly $1.5 million dollars in the Equitable Building on Seventeenth and Stout, complete with steam heat, electric elevators, imported marble, and a top floor observation walk. Wolcott advised Hyde to purchase all of the $700,000 bond issue that Denver was trying to sell in 1891 for street paving. Although the city was willing to pay 4% to the investor, Wolcott promised he could get 5% for Equitable if they agreed to purchase the total issue.

The insurance company investor had confidence in Wolcott. "You are on the ground," he wrote. You "know everybody and are the most competent to advise me." Assuming Wolcott's reliability, Hyde asked him to investigate the company's attorney in Denver; to let him know "whether our general impression that he is a young man of good capacity and ability is confirmed." Of more consequence, however, was Hyde's desire to enlist Wolcott's aid in deciding on Denver bank investment possibilities. By the early 1890s there were eleven national banks in the young city. Most of these sold sizeable blocks of stock to outside investors. In 1890 Hyde became interested in diversifying his Denver investments even further, and he

The Equitable Life Building.

called on Wolcott for advice. The Equitable president had been approached to purchase stock by directors of the American National Bank, but before making a decision he called on Wolcott for counsel. "Confidentially," Wolcott wrote to Hyde, "there are half a dozen banks in Denver, any of which I would rather favor than the American, and I think the combined insurance carried by the officials of any one of these banks is greater than that carried by the American National." Wolcott recommended the National Bank of Commerce or Moffat's First National Bank; he himself was vice president of the latter bank.

Hyde bought no bank stock in Denver for five years. However, in 1895 he approached Wolcott about Moffat's offer to sell a block at $100,000. Wolcott, who was no longer with the First National, but rather with the National Bank of Commerce, answered that although he had "a high personal regard" for Moffat, and that his relationship was "cordial and pleasant," nevertheless, "I am not willing to advise you to purchase that stock. . . He does not know that I have seen the list of bills and I hope he will not. Moffat is a rich man but he is not always as conservative as a Banker should be. All this is very confidential."

Although Wolcott wanted to attract capital to Denver, he was always candid with men he advised. This protected his reputation as an advisor and helped him keep his contacts open in Boston and New York. Consequently, long after Duff moved back to the British Isles in the late 1880s Wolcott was still a man of power in Denver. He continued to be the major intermediary between the financial leaders in Denver and those in Boston and New York.

Wolcott and Duff were not the only busy men in the Queen City. Several others who joined them at the Denver Club led equally ambitious and active lives. Actually, every man who became a member of Denver's power elite was involved in a variety of enterprises, and they evidently thrived on work schedules that would have killed ordinary people. David Moffat, for example, had time to become actively involved in several major railroad enterprises—any one of which would have taxed the endurance of one entrepreneur. But his activities with the Kansas Pacific, Denver, Utah and Pacific, and Denver and New Orleans railroads took only part of his time. Moffat's name was synonymous with the First National Bank until his death in 1911, and he served on the Mining Stock Exchange and the National Trust Company's board.

The man who went to Denver in the 1860s with little more than his clothing was also a major stockholder in the Denver City Tramway Company, organized in 1885 by John Evans, William Byers, Roger W. Woodbury, William Gray Evans, and several others. Moffat was a close personal friend of William Gray Evans, who became the director of the company. Only one day after the company was incorporated, the mayor and council granted it the right to build railway tracks on any street. No time limit was set for the franchise, and the company's directors soon built a public transportation monopoly.

Tramway chief William Gray Evans did not work his way into Denver's power structure—he inherited his father's seat. Born in 1855, seven years before his father became territorial governor, he never experienced poverty or knew physical hard work. While he was a young boy his parents introduced him to the capitals of Europe, and he was educated in the best preparatory schools in England. He graduated from Northwestern University (his father's creation) in 1877. He then went to Denver to gradually assume his sixty-three-year-old father's responsibilities in local business.

Young Evans' biographer, Allen D. Breck, discovered that as a college student Evans' ambition was to become a cattle rancher. John Evans, however, would not listen to such dreams. He pressured his son into following the family path of urban entrepreneurship. If William disliked the choice made for him he never showed it, for he energetically pursued a variety of businesses which helped him to replace his father as one of the most powerful decision makers in the Colorado emporium. As soon as he arrived in Denver with his Bachelor of Science degree, he began investing in mines and real estate. By 1880 he was a director of the promotional Colorado Industrial Association and four years later he became a Chamber of Commerce activist. All the while, he helped manage the construction company for the Denver and New Orleans railroad, and eventually he became a major stockholder in both the Colorado Savings and Mercantile banks. Besides overseeing the Tramway Company after 1886, he was an officer of the Denver, Texas and Gulf Railroad, and he controlled the Evans Investment Company after his father died in 1897.

W.G. Evans not only inherited the governor's enterprises, he inherited his father's large eyebrows and nose and long, squared chin. Equally important among the things bequeathed to him was his father's knack for choosing useful friends and associates. When he was only a lad of fifteen and off to school beyond the watchful eyes of his parents, William received a letter from his father instructing him to "be careful to select good boys for your playmates . . . avoid such

William Gray Evans

associations as will have a bad influence upon your habits and tend to unfit you for the society of the good and noble in life." By late nineteenth-century Denver standards, "the good and noble in life" was hard work which led to financial security and social standing.

William Gray Evans must have taken his father's advice. Hard work in the field of urban empire building was his life's obsession. He labored untiringly just like his father and the men with whom he associated. His closest friend was David H. Moffat, who was sixteen years Evans' senior. Naturally, Evans became a colleague of the men with whom Moffat fraternized at the Denver Club.

One of the "staunch" men of Denver in its second generation was Walter S. Cheesman. A charter member of the Denver Club with Duff, Moffat, and Wolcott, Cheesman was born on Long Island, New York, in 1838. Unlike Moffat, who was born into a poor New York family one year later, Cheesman had no financial worries. His father was a merchant and saw to it that his son was educated both in the public schools and with private tutors. In the mid-1850s Cheesman left New York for Chicago, where he apparently prospered enough to invest in a Denver drug business in 1860, without leaving the Illinois metropolis. When the Civil War started, the absentee owner of a Denver building and drug business left Chicago and reestablished permanently in Denver.

Denver was good to Walter S. Cheesman. Over the years he grew sleek, fat, and wealthy. He realized considerable profits from the drug business and invested them wisely in real estate. By 1874 the corpulent, sagacious investor recognized that power and substantial fortunes did not exist in the drug business, so he sold out and devoted full time to more lucrative ventures. With Moffat and several others he invested in six railroads, and he became manager of the Denver Union Depot and Railway Company. He joined Moffat and Wolcott on the board of the First National Bank and served with them on the Mining Stock Exchange.

As early as 1870 Cheesman became involved in a major Denver enterprise that ultimately earned him a fortune and did more than anything else to establish him as one of the most powerful men in the community. Influenced by James Archer, Cheesman began to pay attention to the importance of utilities. Archer, who had come to Denver as a promoter of the Kansas Pacific Railroad, was confident that the line would soon reach Denver and make that town the future metropolis of the Rockies. In 1869 he secured permission from the city to organize a gas works and supply the energy for street lighting and private use.

Walter Cheesman

James Archer

Archer was a singular man. He came from St. Louis with important financial connections in Missouri, and he possessed a steellike demeanor that matched his ambitions. He had an unusually long, bushy beard which accentuated his balding head and piercing eyes. His deeply lined face enforced stern features that complemented his attitude toward business. Always one to take a cold, narrow view, James Archer saw that there were money-making opportunities in Denver, Colorado, and that nowhere were those opportunities greater than in utilities. The blunt and candid railroad promoter knew that someone would bring gas and water service to the thousands of people who were destined to settle in the new community in a few years. He prophesied to confidants that nothing could be more profitable than controlling natural monopolies.

The cunning opportunist had just secured the franchise to introduce gas service to Denver—a service that he refused to inaugurate until the Kansas Pacific line reached Denver—when he asked for the water concession from the city as well. Although the town of less than 5,000 souls was amply supplied with well water in 1870, Archer persuaded others that a water delivery system would be necessary in the near future. Walter S. Cheesman joined Archer, David Moffat, Jerome Chaffee, Frederick Salomon, and Governor Edward McCook in incorporating the Denver City Water Company in 1870.

The monopoly ran smoothly from 1872, when they began pumping water to Denver from the South Platte, until James Archer died in 1882. Then trouble began. Archer's widow sold the controlling shares of stock, which she and her husband had owned, to out-of-state investors. By 1889 Moffat and Cheesman, who had little voice left in the company, sold their interest and invested sizeable sums of First National Bank monies into a new company designed to improve water service—and at the same time put their group back in control of the utility. Ultimately, Cheesman and Moffat, with the First National Bank as treasurer, incorporated the Citizens Water Company, located larger and purer sources of water from the South Platte, and set out to destroy the competition. By the early 1890s the bank's water company was delivering free water to Denver until they forced the older company into receivership. A complex series of stock transfers and corporate procedures left the Cheesman-Moffat group in complete control of Denver's water works and pumping stations by 1894. Cheesman became head of the new company, the Denver Union Water Company, and promptly set out to construct a new dam on the South Fork of the South Platte, about forty miles from Denver—at a cost of over $4 million.

Another man closely involved with the Denver Union Water Company monopoly was James B. Grant. Once again, the interlocking of Denver's key enterprises was evident to anyone who cared to look. James B. Grant, who was born on an Alabama plantation in 1848, arrived in Colorado in 1877. He had served briefly in the Confederate Army and then studied agriculture and engineering for three years at an Iowa college. With this background he went to Freiburg, Germany to learn all he could about metallurgy and mining. Upon returning to the United States the young mining engineer went to Leadville, Colorado, where he and an uncle opened the Grant Smelter in 1877. Five years later the German-trained engineer and his uncle moved the smelter to Denver. Soon the thirty-four-year-old ex-Confederate was nominated by the Democratic party to run for governor of Colorado. Elected in 1882, he served until 1885.

Like most of Denver's late nineteenth-century decision makers, Grant maintained a multidimensional career. In 1884, while governor, he helped organize the Denver National Bank with James Duff and several other financiers. Always active in more than banking and politics, he bought stock in the water company and served as vice president in the family business, which became known as the Omaha and Grant Smelting and Refining Company.

By the early twentieth century Denver's power elite had demonstrated remarkable skill and versatility. They had attracted outside capital and had used it to build railroads, utilities, smelters, and banks. Some money was channeled into real estate development, going to make such industrial suburbs as Valverde, Argo, and Globeville or residence communities like Montclair and South Denver. These communities provided sorely needed housing for the growing populace. Once annexed, they helped account for the physical expansion of Denver from six square miles in 1874 to nearly fifty-nine square miles by 1902.

The initiative and manipulative sagacity of these men had been crucial to Denver's growth and development, although natural advantages, especially gold and silver, had been the basis for the emergence of the mountain metropolis. Natural resources aside, however, Denver would never have grown to nearly sixty square miles with over 130,000 people by 1900 without the energy and farsightedness of the entrepreneurs.

The supreme test of their leadership came during the nationwide depression of 1893-97. The "panic of 1893," which crippled the American economy for four years, had many causes. The crisis was precipitated by the collapse of a major British banking house, Baring

James B. Grant

Brothers, in 1890. This event caused thousands of British investors to sell their American securities, which, in turn, put an unprecedented drain on the United States' gold reserve. When the gold reserve fell to the $100 million mark, the stock market collapsed, leaving the economy in serious disarray and draining more from the gold reserve. By 1897 the nation was able to recover because the economic structure was fundamentally sound. Undergirded by railroads and industries that were essential, the economy maintained the capacity to produce once again.

Colorado was not as fortunate as other states in the Union because much of its economy was based on silver production. When President Cleveland lined up the votes to go on the gold standard, an important factor in Colorado's growth and prosperity was undercut. Colorado businessmen and politicians organized in an attempt to get the nation back on a bimetallic standard. But in case that failed (which it did), they made decisions to diversify their own economy. Although the flush times of the 1870s and 1880s were not to return during the lifetime of Denver's late nineteenth-century leaders, the men were able to preserve their community and protect their investments by developing alternative sources for growth. Their efforts insured survival—even modest expansion.

In 1893 the president of the Denver Chamber of Commerce announced that public spirit was at an all-time low in Denver. Little wonder. The price of silver dropped sharply, and mines closed throughout the mountains. Regardless, the business leaders kept faith just as they had done when it was learned that the transcontinental railroad would go through Cheyenne rather than Denver. Their optimism was expressed well by Henry Wolcott. He wrote to Henry Hyde early in the depression that "it will be a short time before things will pick up." Wolcott and his friends pooled their resources and went to work. The Chamber of Commerce mobilized a drive to attract tourists and health seekers. This campaign was started in the 1880s but with renewed vigor during the panic, Colorado was heralded as America's "Switzerland"—a haven for play, rest, and relaxation. Not only did promoters proclaim Colorado to have the most beautiful scenery in the world, they reiterated earlier claims that the region's climate was the most healthful—ideal for people suffering from asthma, tuberculosis, and other pulmonary diseases.

The business leaders did more than renew older promotional techniques; they embarked upon new programs as well. During the depression the Chamber of Commerce encouraged the development of the sugar beet industry. They disbursed seeds through the State

Agricultural College to over 2,000 farmers in thirty-one counties. The chamber also hired agents to teach farmers how to plant and cultivate the crop. The businessmen's organization raised money to pay a fifty-dollar prize to the farmer in each county with the best results, if the county in which the outstanding farmer resided would add $100 to the reward.

Results were more than encouraging. Sugar beet production spread from the Colorado River Valley around Grand Junction to the South Platte Valley in northeastern Colorado, and southeast along the Arkansas Valley. In little more than a decade Colorado was the nation's leading producer of sugar beets, with almost 80,000 acres under cultivation. In 1899 a young German-born banker in Denver, Charles Boettcher, invested in a beet processing factory at Grand Junction. At the same time, he served as president of one of Henry R. Wolcott's ventures—Denver's National Bank of Commerce. Eventually Boettcher encouraged eastern investors to join him in what was to become the Great Western Sugar Company, thus launching the young entrepreneur on a career that would place him in the center of Denver's twentieth-century power structure.

The fruit and orchard industry was encouraged during the depression of the 1890s, ultimately helping to make agriculture more important to Denver's economy than the cattle business had been before its crash in the late 1880s. In October 1893 the city sponsored a fruit and orchard fair designed to exhibit produce, stimulate sales, and encourage production of apples, pears, peaches, plums, quinces, grapes, and ground cherries. Produce was exhibited, samples were given to prospective buyers, and conferences were held to promulgate the latest scientific growing techniques.

In 1895 civic leaders, united by William N. Byers, organized the first of several annual Festivals of Mountain and Plain. People all over the nation were encouraged to attend the gala affair. The festival, unlike anything done anywhere except the Mardi Gras in New Orleans, lasted for three days. The first day was devoted to exhibits of Colorado's agriculture, industrial, pastoral, mining, and mercantile enterprises. The second and third days were dominated by parades complete with floats, marching bands, and military reviews. The climax of the three-day event was a ball with the crowning of the festival queen. The purpose was two-fold. The extravaganza was favorably played up by such respected magazines as *Harper's Weekly*; so it attracted tourists. Besides bringing in money from tourism, the festival promoted agriculture and business enterprises.

During these lean years, the Chamber of Commerce actively

sought manufacturers to locate in Denver. Officers of the organization specifically recruited textile mills, stocking and shoe factories, potteries, and glue manufacturers. They argued that they would offer no subsidies because Denver was an ideal city. There was "intelligent and inexpensive labor," cheap fuel, an excellent climate, raw materials, and "no competition for 600 miles." These arguments were obviously persuasive. Thanks to investment capital raised in New England by Henry Wolcott, a cotton mill and a knitting factory relocated from Massachusetts to Denver. Indeed, manufacturing establishments grew, the value of their products increased, and overall industrial employment expanded. The three major smelting companies, Boston and Colorado, Omaha and Grant, and Globe, increased their productivity every year except 1893 and 1894. This was due, in part at least, to the renewed search for gold during the depression. The campaign yielded at least fifty new camps in a score of communities by 1900.

The Chamber of Commerce vigorously pursued its program to attract conventions to the mountain city. By offering free meeting and exhibiting facilities, they persuaded the Odd Fellows, the American Society of Civil Engineers, the Horticulture Society, and National Educational Association to hold their meetings in Denver in the late 1880s. During the 1890s boosters encouraged the National Educational Association to return, in addition to attracting new conventioneers, among them the General Federation of Women's Clubs.

These efforts allowed Denver to survive the depression. The result was that by the twentieth century the Queen City's prospects were less lofty than they had been ten years earlier, but they were based on sounder, less speculative economic foundations.

Almost as if to celebrate the survival of the depression, as much as to boost future prospects, three books appeared between 1899 and 1901. Unabashed, self-congratulatory volumes, each was conceived and prepared by Denver civic boosters to venerate the power elite in their own city and other parts of Colorado. A *Portrait and Biographical Record of the State of Colorado* appeared in 1899, featuring prominent men of affairs which the compiler had found mostly in finance, industry, mining, utilities, and politics. Two years later the aging president of the Chamber of Commerce, William N. Byers, wrote a massive leather-bound tome which weighed nearly nine pounds. *The Encyclopedia of Biography of Colorado* appeared in 1901, and it was divided into two parts. The first section outlined the chronology of important events in Denver and Colorado history; the second part featured biographies and steel plate engravings of the men who, in the words of the tireless promoter, were the "noble, courageous and progressive men who braved the perils and hardships of frontier life, withstood the privations of the Territorial time, and have been the chief builders, not of the corner stone alone, but of the grand superstructure of the commonwealth."

That same year another Denverite, Jerome C. Smiley, published for the *Denver Times* a booster *History of Denver* which outdid Byers' book in length if not in weight. Smiley even surpassed the old promoter in celebrating the past and predicting a greater future. Chronicling Denver's development in copious detail, Smiley filled his prodigious undertaking with the most glowing biographical sketches of Denver's men of power. Like Byers, Smiley had no room for women or minorities because in his estimation only the empire builders were worthy of adoration. His biography of Walter S. Cheesman was typical of the hero worship that pervades the *History of Denver:*

> Mr. Cheesman, as our readers will have learned in this Story of Denver, was a conspicuous member of that remarkable group of men, comparatively few in numbers but of indomitable faith and courage, that undertook in defiance of what to most men seemed insurmountable obstacles, the building of the pioneer railways in the Denver region; and followed with other great undertakings that were also potent in making this city what it is in the opening year of the Twentieth Century.

The concluding chapter of Smiley's booster record began with a vision unrivaled by even the most sanguine members of the Chamber of Commerce. "Remarkable as developments and progress have been in the past," he wrote, "it would seem that they are to be overshadowed in relative magnitude by those that are yet to come."

Turn-of-the-century civic spokesmen were understandably delighted that Denver had grown from less than 5,000 to over 133,000, that railroads had come providing jobs and access to the outside world, and that the mountain metropolis now had all the modern utilities that made urban life comfortable. Building a great city, after all, was no ordinary accomplishment. It is only natural that those who reaped the benefits of this triumph should celebrate and venerate the men who were most responsible for such a success story.

If building Denver was in and of itself a positive act, an unequivocal good, then its history would be written only around the accomplishments of such leaders as Duff, Moffat, Byers, Archer, Wolcott, the father and son Evans, the brothers Kountze, Cheesman,

Grant, Woodbury, Salomon, and a few others. These were the energetic decision makers who built the city, nurtured it through difficult times, and placed it permanently into America's network of regional metropolises. Nevertheless, for all of their energy, ability, and foresight, they were often calloused, myopic, and greedy. Their monument was remarkable but riddled with flaws. Those people who never aspired to the ranks of the elite, or who tried to get there and failed, recognized only too well the human price that was paid when material achievement was the highest priority of urban life.

Chapter 4

The power elite was responsible for more than the physical expansion and business development of Denver during the generation after 1870. The quality of life in the mountain and plain metropolis was largely a result of their decisions as well. To superficial observers such as eastern journalists, the Colorado community was a "Magic City" not only because it mushroomed as if by magic, but also because in a few years the leaders had built a city of highest quality. This observation was partly accurate. Denver's leaders had built quality into their community, but it was primarily for themselves and the city's image.

Writers for magazines usually wrote what their readers wanted to read, and that is one reason why men who wrote for the middle and upper class readers of *Harper's* and *The New England Magazine* praised the power elite and dwelled upon the most attractive aspects of Denver life. It is also true that when writers for major eastern magazines went to Denver, they were squired about by civic boosters, housed in the Windsor, Brown Palace, or Metropole hotels, and entertained at the Denver Club and Tabor Opera House.

Not surprisingly, when these men returned East to their writing desks, they wrote as Julian Ralph did for *Harper's* in 1893 that "Denver is a beautiful city — a parlor city with cabinet finish — and it is so new that it looks as if it had been made to order, and was ready for delivery." A writer with *The New England Magazine* one year earlier said that "the chief pride of Denver is in its homes, which rank with those of the leading eastern cities, and in point of elegance and comfort are unsurpassed by those of any city of its size in America." Even in the 1880s, a *Harper's* author proclaimed Denver to be a "metropolis, a center of refinement, a place rich in itself, influential, and the admiration of all beholders." In continued praise he wrote that "rarely is the sky obscured," and "socially Denver may be called a charming place."

These writers acclaimed Henry R. Wolcott, Roger W. Woodbury, and David Moffat for their contributions to Denver, publishing photographs of them as well as pictures of homes, churches, colleges, and business buildings which they and others had erected for the community. These claims, of course, contained veracity. Wolcott secured eastern money for a monumental construction program in downtown Denver. He raised over $600,000 plus the cost of the site for the Boston Building at Seventeenth and Champa, and he secured over $1.4 million for the Equitable Building at Seventeenth and Stout. Wolcott and Duff raised the funds to put the Denver Club into its elegant stone quarters at Seventeenth and Glenarm in 1888 and Duff was behind the investors who built the 400-room Windsor Hotel, as well as the Barclay Building at Eighteenth and Larimer and several state buildings downtown. Local banks and outside investors helped build the massive Union Depot plus several other functional and attractive sandstone and granite buildings.

These investors gave Denver a look of modernity and elegance. Older store buildings and homes were torn down on land owned by Evans, Byers, and Cheesman. On those sites the most modern offices were constructed. Usually ranging from five to nine stories in height, these business structures from Fifteenth to Eighteenth between Larimer and Stout became the skyscrapers of nineteenth-century Denver.

The men of the power elite not only were turning older business and residential districts into profitable high-rise investment property, they were also building villas and mansions for themselves in previously undeveloped parts of town. Whereas Fourteenth Street had once been the neighborhood of the elite, now the high land near the capitol became fashionable and exclusive "Capitol Hill," where Grant, Cheesman, Kountze, Moffat, and a number of silver and cattle barons built homes with an eye to permanence and extravagance. Colonial, southern Norman, and Roman styles influenced the architects, and no money was spared on the cupolas, towers, and mansard roofs. Most of these high-ceiling, two- and three-story homes were complete with carriage houses and servants' quarters, along with landscaped gardens, lawns and trees, and ornate wrought or iron fences.

Denver's power brokers possessed more than expensive offices and homes: they built ostentatious socializing clubs which were as replete with imported furniture and interior-design materials as their houses. Their life-styles were not allowed to suffer on Sundays either, for they generously contributed to the construction of grandiose churches and cathedrals. The Episcopalians laid the cornerstone of St. John's Cathedral in 1880, and with that began the race to build bigger and more expensive edifices. With a competitive fervor reminiscent of cathedral construction in medieval Europe, each denomination seemed determined to keep up with or surpass the others. After St. John's was started in 1880, the First Congregational Church was built in 1881 on Glenarm near the future home of the Denver Club. The wealthiest Baptists followed in 1883 with the First Baptist Church on Stout between Seventeenth and Eighteenth. It contained an auditorium with a 1,200-seat capacity. In 1888 Trinity Methodist outdid most of the competition with a massive structure, complete with a $35,000 organ. Four years later the upper economic class Presbyterians unveiled their new Central Presbyterian Church at Seventeenth and Sherman, also resplendent with a new organ. The wealthiest Jews were not surpassed by the Christians. In 1898 the doors of massive Temple Emanuel at Sixteenth and Pearl were opened.

Jerome Smiley explained that church members felt a need to move to larger churches in "a more desirable location" and that the church construction was only one part of Denver's "great forward movement." Another part of the forward movement, of course, was the private school building program in which the power elite figured prominently. Civic boosters pointed with pride to the work of their leaders in private education, as did the magazine writers who helped foster the image of Denver as a cultured, up-to-date city. Henry Wolcott helped found Colorado College in Colorado Springs. He also underwrote his sister's exclusive college preparatory school for girls (boys could attend only the elementary grades)—The Miss Wolcott School. John Evans continued his interest in private higher education even after the Colorado Seminary was forced to close in 1867. Twelve years later the seminary idea was revived, culminating in the founding of a Methodist seminary and the University of Denver, with financial backing from Evans, J.B. Grant, Mrs. Elizabeth Iliff Warren, and several other prominent people. Even after John Evans died, his family, as well as the Grant, Iliff, and Warren families, continued to back the university and seminary in the difficult years ahead.

Denver's leaders, then, were building the good life for themselves and their associates. To live among them and move in their circles was a fortunate experience which inevitably would color one's view of the city. For example, a visitor who lived among the upper walks on Capitol Hill for a time in 1880 viewed the new city in a most favorable light. "Denver is the most substantial [*sic*] built city," Rezin H. Constant wrote in his diary. Visiting friends who lived on Welton between Thirteenth and Fourteenth, Constant could view the homes of Governor Routt and James Archer from his host's veranda. In July 1880 he noted "There are the most exquisitely beautiful lawns in Denver I ever saw; great varieties of Roses . . . in full bloom; Fuchias, in short, every desirable flower. . . . " Constant was impressed by Governor Routt's carriage and spirited horses, which, he estimated, cost $3,000. Routt, however, was not alone when it came to sporting fancy rigs and horses. "The number of fine carriages," Constant wrote, "fine rigs of every description, excels anything of the kind I ever saw in any City." Constant noted that the sidewalks were "diamond-shaped marble." Although the streets were not paved, the city maintained eighteen sprinkling tanks which were used daily to keep down the dust.

Denver's leaders had paved sidewalks to fringe their homes, and they had fancy carriages for predusk parades on watered-down streets. The rich had modern offices to make their work days comfortable, and they maintained exclusive clubs and churches where they could socialize and worship. They made the "grand tour" in Europe, they built private schools which only their children could afford, and they built elegant hotels that fit the budgets of only wealthy tourists or out-of-town business associates. As one visitor phrased it in 1880, Denver was a "most aristocratic city;" and it most certainly was for the elite.

Denver's people of wealth gradually withdrew into their own little world for many reasons. Partly, insularity and formality were fashionable. Life was lived that way in older cities like Boston and New York (to which Denver liked to compare itself), and as wealthy Denverites travelled about Europe they could not help but observe that the social classes kept their distance from each other in that venerated part of the world. Equally important in pushing the leading citizens into their isolated world, though, was the fact that the city they had built was unpleasant. Like the legendary Dr. Frankenstein, they were creating a monster that threatened their own quality of life.

Glowing images of Denver promulgated by eastern journalists and local boosters aside, many parts of the city were dirty, noisy, and ugly. Dust and grit continually filled the air of the city as winds blew the top layer of the graded streets in every direction. Despite attempts to keep the thoroughfares sprinkled, relief came only when rain or snow fell. But then mud, sometimes ankle deep, replaced the choking, eye-irritating dust as a city-wide nuisance. To be sure, the business

Looking up Seventeenth Street from the train depot

district was equipped with wooden planks for sidewalks. Nevertheless, the rains were often bad enough to lift the boards from their intended locations next to buildings and wash them out into the muddy and horse manure-laden streets.

When dust or mud did not plague the urban dwellers, other sources of irritation kept tempers short. People who lived and worked near the three smelters in northern Denver always coped with black smoke and coal dust. Worse, though, were the thermal inversions which blanketed the entire community in a grey haze of pollution, obscuring all views of the mountains. Soot collected on window sills. The coal residue darkened windowpanes, and it hastened wash day as collars and cuffs grew discolored in a few hours.

Soot-blackened objects were not the only eyesores in Denver. Old photographs reveal litter on major business streets, and tidy citizens angrily protested the trash filling the gutters and alleys. Protests were also raised against fruit and vegetable peddlers who dumped their unsold, rotting produce in vacant lots or back alleys, yet, it was difficult to distinguish the sellers' refuse from the garbage pitched by residents into all sorts of out-of-the-way crannies.

Frontier Denver had not been a quiet place. During the 1860s people frequently complained of noises from the saloons or from the Indian camps along the South Platte. Still, if the winds were not blowing, one could hear the water wash through the rocks in the river while strolling near its course and listen to calls of crickets and birds. By the late nineteenth century old noises were gone. The Indians had been driven away, and the calls of magpies and insects were drowned by the clatter of railroad cars, the groans of locomotives, and the rattles of ubiquitous horse-drawn trucks. The new hum of the city was loud enough to mute even saloon revelry unless a passerby was almost to the door.

Eyes and ears were not the only parts of the body offended by the boom city. All the senses had to adjust to Denver's success. A stench almost always plagued working class neighborhoods near the smelters, around the railroad yards, and along the river. If the winds were still, nauseous miasmas gradually diffused throughout most of the downtown business district. Industrial and stockyard odors were bad enough, but the noxious smell from raw sewage was most repulsive. Human waste disposal was a serious problem for a city that grew as rapidly as Denver. As late as 1880 no sewers existed, although a system was under construction. Most residences had cesspools or watertight privy vaults, and the city did remove vault wastes periodically in horse-drawn, closed tanks. Untreated sewage was drained into the South Platte from the business district throughout the 1870s, leaving that river thoroughly contaminated. By the late 1870s the stench from the Platte and open cesspools was so loathsome that the city undertook a sewage construction project. By the time it was finished in the mid 1880s, the metropolis had grown so large in physical size and population that the newly built sewer lines were sorely inadequate. By the early twentieth century, over 250 miles of underground sewer pipes had been constructed, but the entire system, inadequately treated, flowed into the river. At times the polluted river could be smelled all over northern and central Denver, but the people who lived along the course of the South Platte were continually enveloped by malodorous air.

Other repulsive sights and smells bothered Denverites. Dead animals were a constant annoyance. A man retained by the city to cart away carcasses hauled off an average of 1,000 animals per year during the 1870s, with the number of remains declining only slightly during the next two decades. Household pets made up a mere fraction of his freightage because the most talked-about nuisances were dead horses, mules, and swine.

Live animals apparently detracted from the pleasantness of urban life as much as deceased ones. Runaway horses and recklessly driven ones sent walkers and bicycles scurrying constantly. Well into the 1890s, people accustomed to urban life griped incessantly about neighbors raising chickens and milk cows. But these grievances aside, dogs pestered Denverites more than anything. Although the police

Denver in 1876

were frequently ordered to corral strayed mules and swine, until the early twentieth century the stray dog problem was the most troublesome of all save drunkenness. In the mid-1870s the council passed an ordinance requiring unleashed dogs to be muzzled and licensed. Nevertheless, scores of unlicensed and unmuzzled canines roamed the streets of Denver, singly and in packs. In 1876 the city offered a twenty-five-cent bounty to any citizen who brought a dog to the city compound, dead or alive. Although dozens of boys engaged in this lucrative enterprise for a year to two, the problem was so far out of hand by 1878 that the police rented an express wagon and patrolled the streets shooting every stray within range of their shotguns. The first week the police boasted a kill of 103, and they hauled the unlucky animals to a local tannery. Despite their anger over the number of strays, citizens were outraged by the new method of control. The sight of wounded dogs, dragging partially shot-off legs and dangling intestines down major thoroughfares, was too much. The public outcry forced a halt to the shootings until 1883. At that time, several children were attacked by dog packs, and the shotgun patrol went back on the streets to wrestle with the canine problem until it was brought under control around the turn of the century.

Juveniles, too, ran in packs and harassed city dwellers during the boom era. Several bands of boys loitered near the saloon around Wazee and Blake, pestering passersby verbally if not physically. Gangs of boys were frequently charged with assault and theft. Two groups distinguished themselves in the 1890s by stealing from freight trains, stoning the street railway cars, and hijacking them for free rides. The "Klondike Kids," a group of white youths, became notorious by 1897, as did a band of young blacks who dubbed themselves the "Ragged Lovan." In the early twentieth century the "Riverfront Gang" became even more notorious than its two predecessors.

Juvenile crime, however, was insignificant compared to adult lawbreaking. Burglaries were daily occurrences throughout the nine-

93

teenth century, as were crimes of violence. Some citizens blamed this on the large numbers of men who rode the rails into Denver and preyed on the growing city. Such men were viewed as degenerates who were too lazy to work. Regardless of what inspired criminals, one thing was certain—only a few criminals were ever arrested because the police force was inadequate. Denver's lawmen were underpaid by national standards. Consequently, they were always consuming free drinks in saloons rather than walking their beats. Furthermore, Denver had too few law enforcement agents because the city refused to spend the money. In 1878, for example, the *Rocky Mountain News* urged more money for the police. Denver had only one patrolman for each 4,116 citizens. New York and New Orleans, on the other hand, had one policeman for each 400 citizens, and St. Louis and Cincinnati each had one per thousand.

Part of Denver's high crime rate was the inevitable result of hard-core poverty. Civic leaders denied that poverty was a problem in Denver. If there were a few poor people, their plight was self-inflicted; they were lazy or they spent too much money on liquor. Promulgating the image of a prosperous Denver, The Chamber of Commerce announced in 1890 that "Truly it may be said that Denver is a city of homes." The following year the image was reinforced, when the chamber boasted that no "cheap and unsightly shanties" can be found in the Queen City. Such rhetoric was simply untrue. No one who lived in Denver and ventured beyond Capitol Hill and the renovated business district could miss the ubiquitous signs of human misery and poverty. All along the right bank of the South Platte, beginning as far north as the Omaha and Grant smelter and extending south as far as Colfax, was a strip of factories, warehouses, and railroad yards, interspersed with dwellings of Denver's poorest citizens. Stephen Leonard, in his dissertation on "Denver's Foreign-Born Immigrants," described one section of this strip. "The half square mile between Colfax Avenue, Speer Boulevard and the Platte River. . . . In 1890 . . . nearly 8,000 persons, more than 2,000 of them foreign-born, crowded that neighborhood's boardinghouses, small homes and hotels, raising the population density there to at least 15,000 per square mile. . . ." Farther north and east of this densely populated working class neighborhood were even more abject living conditions. Around the Omaha and Grant smelter and near the river and railroad yards were hundreds of families living in tar paper shacks, dwellings built of discarded crates, and tents.

From the late 1870s until the early twentieth century, destitute people were found living along the river in tents and hastily made shanties with little or no heat, suffering continually from malnutrition, scarlet fever, typhoid, cholera, and pneumonia. Rachel Wild Peterson, a survivor of a tent dwelling in 1880 who devoted over twenty years of her life to aid the poor, found hundreds of sick men, women, and children, infants and mothers dying in childbirth, and several destitute people frozen to death. Some of these unfortunates drank too much, some found escape in morphine. Often people from this miserable environment were arrested for stealing food or poaching coal from the railroad yards. The children who were trapped in these surroundings were frequently left homeless. They moved in gangs, roamed the streets begging, and got into trouble with the law. These people contributed to Denver's growing crime problems, but the cause of their antisocial behavior was less their own fault than the fault of those who encouraged them to come in the first place.

The men who built Denver and its enterprises were always urging people to come to the magnificent mountain metropolis. They promised jobs, profits, and restored health. At the same time, they kept wages as low as possible, callously used human resources, discriminated against people they assumed to be inferior, and did little to help those who fell into unfortunate circumstances. Their task, as they saw it, was to build a city, acquire fortunes, make life as comfortable for themselves as possible, and do little about equality of opportunity.

No Denver builder deliberately set out to exploit people. Nevertheless, in the myopic quest to develop a hinterland, to attract settlers, factories, railroads, and investors, virtually no attention was paid to the human costs of urbanization. Unskilled laborers were always exploited. Indeed, one of the Chamber of Commerce's promotional arguments was that Denver's labor force was "intelligent and inexpensive." Keeping wages low was viewed as good for business and the community's image, regardless of resultant hardships for workers. As late as 1899 smelter workers labored hard, twelve-hour days, frequently contracted lead poisoning, and were paid only $1.50 a day. Later that year a movement was begun to raise those wages to $2.00. A writer for a local magazine, *The Mecca*, which always supported the interests of James B. Grant and Henry Roger Wolcott, quipped: "If smelter work is hard and injurious at a dollar and a half a day, is the injury less at two dollars?"

Smelter owners' exploitation of workers had effects far beyond injury to workers. Judge Ben B. Lindsey found that a boy who was brought before the county court in 1901, charged with stealing coal from the railroad tracks, and convicted, was a victim of circumstances

A puddler in the Argo smelter

leading directly to a smelter. The father of this Italian family was bedridden from lead poisoning which he had contracted at the smelter. The company provided no compensation for job-related disabilities. The family, according to Lindsey, was "living in two rooms in a filthy shack, with the father sick in bed, and the whole family struggling against starvation." Lindsey talked with the boy "and found him not a criminal, and a bad boy, but merely a boy. He had seen his father and mother and the baby suffering from the cold, and he had brought home fuel from the railroad tracks to keep them warm." Such conditions notwithstanding, the railroad companies kept detectives posted to prevent coal thefts and insisted on prosecution of all men and boys (and their number was legion) caught stealing.

These were not the only abuses. Railroads recruited Italians to build and repair track. When there were no more jobs, the corporate leaders displayed no qualms about discharging hundreds of workers in a society that offered no unemployment compensation. Stephen Leonard found that in 1884, three years after the railroads had recruited laborers in Italy, 700 Italians were laid off in Denver and left to starve and suffer in their hovels along the banks of the South Platte.

In other areas of the economy, still more stories of exploitation and misery abound. Rachel Wild Peterson took a young woman into her house as a boarder, trying to assist the poor lady while she attempted to make ends meet on the meager wage she earned in a laundry. When the laundry worker got her hand caught in a wringer at work, she was sent home. Although Mrs. Peterson arranged for her to be attended by a doctor, the mangled hand gradually swelled to three times its normal size. In a few days the hand had to be amputated—and it was done in the Peterson house, of course, because proper surgical facilities in a hospital were beyond the budget of such unfortunates.

The "one-lunged army," as the thousands of pulmonary disease sufferers were called, did not find much balm in Gilead either. A writer for *Harper's* in 1893 reported that approximately 30,000 members of that "army" lived in Denver, but that they came with money and education and were recovering and contributing much to the cultural and business development of the city. Lawrence C. Phipps, the wealthy Republican party leader, J. Jay Joslin, the merchant who founded the Haydn and Handel Society, and E.B. Field, who distinguished himself with the Colorado Telephone Company, come to mind in the vein described by *Harper's.* On the other hand, there were many more victims of lung disease who went to Denver and were too poor to get the rest and good food required for recovery.

As early as 1868 Denver's Board of Trade advertised the city as having a climate "exceedingly favorable to consumptives." In Denver they were sure to find "instantaneous relief and rapid and permanent cure." Such claims, which were designed to attract settlers, brought thousands to the mountain city in quest of a panacea. Not all tuberculosis, asthma, and bronchitis sufferers were as well established as Phipps and Joslin. On the contrary, scores of destitute people spent their last dollars just to reach the cure-all climate of Colorado. So many weak, dependent people had found Denver by the 1880s that the Chamber of Commerce announced that their city wanted "manufactuers and capitalists," not folks in need of "easy positions."

Despite these discouraging warnings, the healthful image was already imbedded in the popular imagination. Furthermore, occasionally in the 1890s the boosters even forgot the stipulations and bragged to the world, in 1895, for example, "old age carries off a few each year, but the balmy climate, the pure air, the excellent sanitary conditions, endow Denverites with nearly perpetual youth." So the impoverished ill continued to make the trek to Denver. Some regained their health and lived normal lives in the Queen City, yet many who went there were neglected and hungry, and died even sooner than if they had remained at home with friends and relatives. Rachel Wild Peterson took a few into her small central Denver house, but

Rachel Wild Peterson

her book underlines the fact that many were allowed to lie down on pauper's beds, suffer malnutrition, and gradually slip into death unmourned and unnoticed.

Children were allowed to suffer all over urban-industrial America in the late nineteenth century and early twentieth centuries, and Denver was no exception. Bernard Rosen discovered that throughout the 1870s and 1880s many abondoned boys and girls walked the streets of Denver. To cope with this problem, the state and local authorities made it easy for adults to adopt children. However, the commonest way the waifs were handled was to bind them out—literally indenture them—to people who were able to secure employment for them as recompense. This system was abusive at best, for the law did little to protect children who worked. It was only a misdemeanor as late as 1887 for factories, mills, and smelters to employ children under fourteen; and the law was usually winked at when violated. Not surprisingly, many overworked children ran away from the families and jobs to which they were "bound out," and soon they took to stealing and joining gangs. Once apprehended by the police, tried, and convicted, children were thrown into Denver's filthy jails where they were not segregated from adult criminals of their own sex.

Children, like many unfortunate adults in Denver, suffered not so much from maliciousness on the part of business leaders and the general citizenry, rather, they were overlooked in the wake of the obsessive quest for growth and profits. They were not injured from design, but from the narrowness of vision that comes from measuring success in terms of status and material wealth, from the callousness that inevitably evolves when property rights are placed before human rights. Certain ethnic groups, though, had treatment meted out to them which was far more severe than neglect and economic exploitation. They were deliberately mistreated for being who they were.

Lynchings and public hangings, which were not unheard of in frontier Denver, were shunned between 1870 and the early twentieth century. Still, one legal public hanging and two lynchings occurred in Denver after 1870. It is significant that the victims were black, Italian, and Chinese. These three ethnic groups were not only exploited, they were unconscionably harassed by the majority population. The Italians in Denver, according to the federal census, numbered 608 in 1890 and 999 in 1900. These figures, however, are low estimates. Hundreds of transient laborers came in and out who were never counted. Most of Colorado's Italians came after 1881 when the Denver and Rio Grande management sent agents to Italy to recruit employees and paid the workers' transportation to the Rockies. Employed by the railroads all over the region, this predominantly male group tended to congregate in Denver during the winter or whenever they were laid off by the railroad companies. Hundreds of other Italians, in Denver on a temporary basis, undoubtedly escaped the attention of the census takers.

Italians were disliked by the general population because few of them spoke English and because they were practicing Roman Catholics in a predominantly non-Catholic society. In addition, most of them were young, unmarried men, who came without families. They were viewed as potential threats to the womanhood of Colorado. Because of these prejudices, Italians were given the most menial jobs on railroads or in factories, and they were denied access to better opportunities when any workers other than blacks or Chinese were available. Barely able to earn sustenance under the best of circumstances, these immigrants were subject to layoffs by the railroads and were forced to live in abject poverty on both sides of the Platte near the railroad yards.

Occasionally, sensitive Denverites called attention to the plight of the Italians and urged the community to offer them a helping hand. The editors of the *Rocky Mountain News* and the Denver *Republican* called attention to the crowded and unsanitary living quarters to which Italians were restricted in the Bottoms north of Seventeenth Street. But nothing was done to alleviate the situation. When thoughtful citizens raised money for a group of laid off, stranded Italian railroad workers in southern Colorado, some civic leaders in Denver deplored the actions as unwise charity that would lead the immigrants to expect such help all of the time.

Stephen Leonard's dissertation contains evidence that Italians were frequently harassed. Doing everything they could to survive, immigrant children sometimes picked watercress along the banks of the South Platte and took the fresh greens uptown to sell. After selling the produce, they scavenged cigar butts and sold them for pennies among the poor workers back in the Bottoms. When sympathetic voices were raised over the hardships such people were forced to endure, a Denver philanthropist countered by saying, "The majority of the children belong to the dagoes, who would probably follow the same thing if they had thousands of dollars." The writings of Judge Ben Lindsey and Leonard's research show that Italians were forced to gather driftwood from the river for winter fuel, and when that ran out, they had no choice but to steal coal. While Lindsey understood their plight and tended to go easy on such offenders, Judge Platt Rogers meted out stiff jail sentences, especially if an interfering watchman was harmed.

Public bigotry toward the Italian population grew worse during economic recessions. If the labor market was glutted, the public blamed the southern European workers. In 1893, for example, a lynching occurred. An Italian bartender named Dan Arata allegedly killed a customer. After he was arrested, a mob assembled outside the city jail, hurling shouts of "Hang the Dago" to nervous police guards. Then, in the presence of an estimated 10,000 onlookers, the nucleus of the mob assaulted the jail, dragged Arata from his cell, hung him on the nearest cottonwood tree, and filled the body with bullets. The next day an enterprising ghoul cut down the blood-stained branches and sold sections for ten to fifty cents a piece to morbid souvenir collectors. As the editor for the *Colorado Catholic* analyzed it in retrospect, the murder probably would not have occurred had the alleged criminal not been Italian.

Being Italian was certainly a factor in Arata's murder. It is likely, however, that if the man had been Chinese or black a similar end would have befallen him. Thirteen years earlier a Chinese citizen of Denver was lynched by a mob at Nineteenth and Lawrence. He was strung up on a lamp post after being brutally beaten by a mob of whites during the bloody "Chinese Riot" of October 1880.

The riot was the culmination of the anti-Chinese sentiment that had been rising since 1869, when the transcontinental line was completed in Utah. Hundreds of Chinese roadbed workers who had been recruited from abroad were dismissed. Some made their way to Colorado seeking employment with the railroads that were just starting construction in the territory. But the Chinese were not welcome. Both native Americans and immigrants from Europe hated them. Not only did they have yellow skin that was assumed to be inferior, but few of them spoke English, the majority were males, and they were usually followers of Buddhism, Taoism, or Confucianism and were therefore considered heathens. Their eating habits and style of dress appeared as unique as their religions. As a consequence, they found railroad work increasingly difficult to get, and they were run out of the mining towns where they tried to find employment as cooks, laundrymen, and common laborers.

Ultimately, most of the Chinese who remained in Colorado found their way to Denver. Nearly 250 had arrived by 1880, and almost 1,000 resided there ten years later. Denver became the center of Colorado's Chinese population because there were more opportunities to make a living in the bustling city than anywhere else in the state. Viewed as inferior-minded, subhuman beings by most Coloradans, the Chinese were forced to do work that others found unattractive. The majority did other people's laundry, worked in restaurants, or served as janitors and servants. Some had opium dens where people of any color could go, smoke a pipe, and briefly escape from the boredom or pain in life.

Denverites who held no qualms about drinking alcohol to escape reality were prejudiced against opium. Despite the fact that no federal or state law forbade its use until 1914, the city fathers passed a local ordinance which they enforced from time to time. The local statute was actually used to harass the Chinese den keepers, because white patrons were seldom arrested. On the contrary, they were viewed as victims of an evil Chinese practice.

Local laws regarding prostitution were also used to discriminate against the Chinese. Although Denver was a wide-open town throughout the nineteenth century, historian Gerald Rudolph found that while police winked at the law most of the time, they frequently arrested and fined Chinese prostitutes despite the fact that they represented a small minority of the street women.

Most of Denver's Chinese lived in Hop Alley, which was along Wazee Street between Fifteenth and Seventeenth. Chinatown remained there, according to Rudolph, until a faction of the community established another neighborhood in the mid-eighties on the West Side around Blake and Thirteenth. Eventually, a third neighborhood was settled in 1889 on Holladay Street between Twentieth and Twenty-first. It was in the first Chinese quarter where the infamous riot started on Sunday, October 31, 1880. Several days before the fracas, local newspapers had been editorializing against the Chinese. On October 23 the *Rocky Mountain News* printed an inflammatory statement: "John Chinaman—The Pest of the Pacific Coast—The Heathen Who Have Ruined California and Are Now Slowly Invading Colorado—Workmen Starving and Women Following Prostitution Through Competition of the Wily Heathen." Other news commentators attacked the Chinese for selling opium, especially when it was learned that an eighteen-year-old white man had died from a perforated intestine which a doctor said *could* have been caused by using opium.

The immediate cause of the dispute seems to have been a poolroom fight between a Chinese and a white. When the altercation attracted attention, anti-Chinese bigots joined in the Hop Alley fracas. Before long, wide-scale fighting erupted. Looting and burning of Chinese living quarters and businesses ensued. The violence quickly grew uncontrollable, and police and sheriff's deputies tried to quell it. Even the fire department was called to spray the belligerents. The battle which began about noon lasted until nearly midnight. Only after David Cook and his Rocky Mountain Detectives intervened was order restored.

Scores of Chinese were beaten by rioters, and one was killed at Nineteenth and Lawrence. Only the flight of the Chinese—many went into hiding once the fighting and looting began—prevented more injuries and deaths. Several heroic white families did their part in saving lives, as some of them took victims into their houses and hid them from the angry mob. Mayor Richard Sopris, who did all he could to allay the uprising by using policemen and firemen, finally called on Cook to intervene. During the melee the Sopris family hid several Chinese in their own home.

The city did reimburse the Chinese for nearly $54,000 in property damage. Nevertheless, the anti-Chinese sentiment failed to dwindle during ensuing years. Owners of buildings where the Chinese lived charged high rents but refused to keep the quarters in decent repair. Furthermore, local entrepreneurs discriminated against these immigrants and made it extremely difficult for them to find work. Despite the fact that the Chinese remained segregated in laundries, small shops, and restaurants, the Bureau of Labor statistics of Colorado reported in 1890 that over 1,000 Denverites could be employed if the Chinese were not in the laundry business. Official attacks on the immigrants were effective. Many moved to the West Coast or returned to China, and the Chinese Exclusion Act passed by Congress in 1882 ended the recruitment of more laborers from the large Asian nation. Although nearly 1,000 Chinese resided in Denver by 1890, their numbers dropped to 306 by 1900 and continued to decline during the twentieth century.

The black population of Denver was treated less harshly. Blacks, who numbered only 237 in 1870 but grew to nearly 4,000 by 1900, certainly were denied equality. In Colorado, as in all of the United States, they were viewed as inferior to native and foreign-born whites in intelligence and propensity to achieve. At best, they were considered superior to other nonwhites, particularly Chinese and native American Indians. Not recruited by the railroads, after 1870 blacks went to Colorado on their own because they hoped the West might offer more opportunities than older sections of the country.

Their story is complex. Until the early twentieth century blacks fared much better than the Chinese. A white editor for the *Colorado Graphic* wrote an article in May 1890 which typified, in a patronizing way, how some whites ranked blacks above the Chinese: "Less labor for the Chinamen and more for the white and colored men of Denver would reduce the numbers of the former. The *Graphic* has often wondered why the Negro citizens of Denver do not pay more attention to the laundering art and supercede the Mongolian. . . . We believe there is a profitable field open for our colored citizens in the laundry business. . . ." Not willing to accept such condescension from a white journalist, E.H. Hackley, editor of the black newspaper *The Statesman*, replied that "the colored man is not confined to any single channel of trade, he is an all around man and success from a boot black to a banker, from a newspaper courier to a financier, when he is given an honest chance. He has washed the Caucasian's dirty duds many a year, but you will never see him washee, washee, allee somee Chinaman."

To Hackley's view, if blacks sought laundry work dominated by the Chinese, they would be taking a step backward. Laundry work was thought to be a demeaning occupation which the Chinese almost monopolized because few Denverites were willing to do it. Blacks, on the other hand, were making strides in the Colorado city. Although many were janitors and common laborers, or did domestic work including washing and ironing in the homes of wealthy whites, increasing numbers were finding their way into "respectable" occupations. In 1880, for example, a group of blacks petitioned the mayor to appoint one of their people to the police force. Mayor Sopris responded by assigning Isaac Brown a full-time position with a beat on Larimer Street. A year later John Bell was also given a full-time patrolman's position. Blacks found good jobs with the railroad companies as well. Whereas Chinese and Italian workers were relegated to the ranks of common labor with the railroads, blacks were not so restricted. Some blacks did work as gandy dancers and roadbed builders, but an increasing number found employment as porters. This was an important step forward because porters were well paid relative to laborers, and they could dress well and remain warm and clean in a job that required no back-breaking physical exertion.

Blacks discovered other opportunities to prosper and gain status within their own ethnic community. Unlike the Chinese and Italians, they had a relatively large and stable population. The majority of Denver's blacks were *not* predominantly male and transient. Indeed, by 1900 women outnumbered men 2,042 to 1,881, and families were the rule rather than the exception. The bulk of Denver's blacks by the late nineteenth century lived segregated north of the central business district along Larimer and Blake, although the more prosperous began moving toward Five Points along Welton in the early years of the new century.

The existence of a relatively large, stable, segregated, family-oriented community created economic opportunities. If they could not find opportunities in business and the professions in the white world, they could at least do so among their own people. A prosperous, if small, black middle class was emerging by the 1890s. There were three black churches with full-time ministers. Several newspapers competed with Hackley's *Statesman*, including *The Star, Argus, Negro World,* and *African Advocate.* Blacks had their own physicians, including one woman, Dr. T.G. Steward, as well as their own saloons, restaurants, drugstores, millinery shops, insurance agents, funeral homes, and various other businesses.

Other breakthroughs pointed to a better life for some blacks. In 1892 Beatrice Thompson secured a job with the state government. L.D. Rivers was made a guard at the city jail in 1898, and four years later a black was elected to the state legislature. In the late 1880s Barney Ford built a house on Capitol Hill, and in 1898 his wife was included in the *Social Year Book.* Furthermore, the *Denver Republican* in March 1890 reported that more blacks per capita owned property in Denver than most cities. This symbol of success came when a few black and white entrepreneurs provided low down payment loans in the 1880s to families who were having difficulty finding rental property.

Despite these token achievements in Denver's white-dominated world and the upward mobility within the black community, Denver blacks were not treated equally. Disillusionment and frustration clearly existed, and with good reason. The editor of the *African Advocate* no doubt expressed the feelings of many blacks when he wrote in November 1890 that "No recognition of political preferment can ever establish the Negro's claim to equality. No law, written or unwritten can ever force the American people to concede to the Negro all rights and privileges enjoyed by the dominant race." As the title of the paper indicates, editor J.N. Walker saw expatriation to Africa as the only answer to his people's problems.

Although the majority of blacks were not willing to emigrate, there were constant reminders of their second-class citizenship which must have made them appreciate Walker's stand. The only legal public hanging after the 1860s took place in 1886, and the condemned man was Andrew Green, a black, convicted of murdering a streetcar driver. Eugene Frank Rider, in his dissertation "The Denver Police Department," shows that blacks were continually harassed by police. In 1877 Fannie Gray was arrested simply because she was walking along the streets saying that her name was Susan Snowdrop. By 1898 angry black citizens were still claiming that people of their race were regularly hassled by police and arrested with no charges ever filed. Local news items corroborate their complaints. Black gamblers and prostitutes, like the Chinese, were arrested while white vice went unnoticed, and interracial married couples complained about abuse.

Further evidence of discrimination can be found in social statistics. Blacks were segregated into the poorest schools, and many families had such low incomes that their children were forced to work. Consequently, by 1900, when only 0.1% of the native white population was illiterate, and only 4.1% of the foreign-born, 11.2% of Denver's blacks could neither read nor write. Death rates also indicated lack of equality. Whereas 17.6 native whites per thousand died each year, 21.9 blacks died, only slightly better than 22.1 for foreign-born whites. The reason for the high mortality rate was that blacks were denied access to most hospitals and sanitariums. While some facilities would admit them if they could afford a private room, such expensive medical care was out of reach of Denver's ordinary black.

Blacks were denied access to more than hospitals. Although a state law was passed in 1895 prohibiting discrimination in public facilities, blacks were in fact denied admission to most restaurants, hotels, theaters, and bathhouses. Even the International Sunday School Convention segregated blacks in separate rows of seats when it met in Denver in 1902, thus encouraging black clergymen to urge their race to boycott the meeting.

White leaders openly underlined their biases on several occasions. In 1895 a state law was passed legalizing segregated schools. Several years earlier, in 1879, this white determination to keep the races apart was made clear at a public meeting. Black leaders had called a conference to raise funds for helping southern blacks caught in Kansas without jobs or money to move to Colorado. William Byers, Thomas Patterson, and John Evans, counseled against such action, suggesting that blacks would experience just as much prejudice in Colorado as in the South. Most whites who attended the conference felt that southern blacks were best fitted for agricultural work, and thus, few opportunities would be available in Denver. Mayor Sopris said that perhaps one hundred families could be accommodated inasmuch as blacks were good construction laborers and domestics. To encourage the thousands in Kansas to come, however, would be an unwise move because they could never be absorbed into the economy.

Even though Denver was in the midst of a campaign to attract settlers, it was clear that blacks were not welcome. Henry O. Wagoner said that if emigration to Colorado was good for whites, he could not understand why it would not be good for blacks. A white politician cut off the discussion by saying that "Colorado would not be an inviting field to the blacks."

Horace Greeley of the *New York Tribune* popularized the slogan "Go West, young man," arguing that the frontier offered the greatest opportunities for men seeking a start in life. "Go West, *white* young man" seems more accurate in retrospect. Actually, only about four thousand blacks were in Denver in the late nineteenth century. The *Denver Republican*, March 17, 1890, estimated six thousand, which might be more accurate if one counts transients such as cowboys and railroad workers who would not get counted by census takers. Regardless, these figures suggest that few blacks believed that the West held any special opportunity for them. Indeed, in 1860 approximately 86% of America's blacks lived in the slave states, and by 1910, 83% still resided there.

If women, especially white women, paid attention to Greeley, they must have assumed the "young man" embraced mankind rather than just the male sex of the species. Thousands, many of them unattached to husbands or parents, went to Colorado in search of opportunity. In 1860 there were more than six men to each woman. By 1870 men still outnumbered women by a ratio of seven to five. The gap closed rapidly after 1870, until in 1900 women slightly outnumbered men by about 1,000 out of a total population of 134,000 in Denver.

Women who sought employment in Colorado's major metropolis met either challenging opportunities or exploitation and discrimination, depending upon their qualifications and the field they chose to pursue. According to a study by James A. Atkins, by 1905 women earned much less than men (sometimes only half the wage of men) for doing identical work. Whether they worked as cooks, bakers, or clothing salespersons, women's wages were significantly lower than those of men. The only area that did offer equality of economic opportunity was small business. The records of R.G. Dun and Company show that many women went to Colorado in the 1870s to establish retail businesses, especially millinery shops. If they were deemed honest, hard-working, and efficient shopkeepers, Dun correspondents usually regarded them as good credit risks, even if they had no assets to use as collateral. Dun investigators seemed to admire and urge credit for women who had the ambition to start a business of their own, especially if they had to put up with an unemployed, lazy, or drunken husband.

Another area of the ecomomy that offered excellent opportunites to women was writing and publishing. Atkins' book shows that only in newspapers and publications did women earn on par with men, and salaries in that field were high compared to other areas open to women. Those who could work in publishing were few in number. Indeed, they represented a small educated elite. Only eighteen women were employed in the field in 1905, although the numbers were probably larger in the 1880s and 1890s. Minnie Hall Krauser remembered that there were only four newspaper women in Denver in 1898, when she and Minnie J. Reynolds organized the Denver Women's Press Club. Still, many others worked as free-lance writers or served on the staffs of Denver's numerous magazine companies.

Venturesome publishers tried to make Denver a national publication center. At least two dozen periodicals were originated, edited, and published in the city. However, only a few magazines experienced long and prosperous lives in the Rocky Mountains. Most either went out of business or moved their headquarters to Chicago, Kansas City, or the East Coast. The depression of the 1890s hurt some of these ventures, but distribution costs to the populous, magazine-buying eastern states and the competition for advertising contacts hurt those who attempted to make Denver a mecca for writers and editors. *Outdoor Life* and *Sports Afield* were two successful periodicals published in the Queen City, along with a host of more obscure and less successful journals like *The Mecca, Why?, The Western Architect, Stamp, The Great Divide, Swastika, Denver Inter-Ocean, The Modern World,* and *Business Women's Magazine.* Some of these were business, booster, and trade journals; others were more literary. Within this community of publishers were scores of women. They held positions as publishers, editors, and copyreaders, and the magazines provided a market for their free-lance verse and stories.

Women like short story writer, novelist, and *Denver Republican* editorialist Patience Tucker Stapleton or Louise Lee Hardin, editor of *Business Women's Magazine,* were no more typical of Denver's women than was gynecologist Dr. M.C. Farnham. The typical woman who came to Denver and attempted to make it on her own had neither the benefit of an eastern education nor a small amount of savings to start a millinery shop. Some found husbands in the new city, but many were forced into laundry, restaurant, or domestic service where the hours were long, the work was hard, and the pay was incredibly poor.

Hundreds of young women who expected to find work or husbands in the Queen City found neither. Because they were uneducated, broke, and without prospects, they were forced into prostitution. The least fortunate were the young women who went to work for a "solid man," as pimps were called in nineteenth-century Denver. He procured customers and a room and took at least half of the earnings. Rachel Wild Peterson remembered one young woman who came to her for help in getting out of the "business." Her "solid man" went into Rachel's house with a gun, insisting that she return to work for him. The man failed to enslave this young woman, but no doubt he was more successful with others.

The typical house of ill fame in Denver was not one of the handsome parlour houses decorated and operated by the famous madames Mattie Silks and Jennie Rogers on Holladay Street (formerly McGaa Street and by the late 1880s, Walnut, and then Market Street), where the "soiled ones" were well fed and elegantly dressed. On the contrary, the typical house was a small, dirty, dark "crib house" where a madame oversaw four or five girls and collected half of the money they earned in the tiny room or crib containing a chair, a bed, and a washstand. Women in these dens were given little rest, and they were poorly fed and cared for. Once they became pregnant or sick, they were turned out on the streets to fend for themselves.

Life was more luxurious and comfortable in the elegant parlour houses but was far from the excitement and romance of the popular imagination. Only the most beautiful young women could work for Madames Silks and Rogers. The madames made certain that the women were well fed and insisted on good grooming and elegant dress. The prostitutes, however, had to purchase their own wigs and dresses. Because the madames kept such a large percentage of each employee's income, little was left over to buy new wardrobes. An R.G. Dun investigator discovered that one enterprising Denver woman known locally as Madame Croze, made her living selling wigs and lending money at usurious rates to the parlour girls who needed cash for clothing. According to the Dun correspondent, Madame Croze in the mid-1870s "is loaning money . . . to 'soiled ones' at 365% per annum . . . is undoubtedly worth considerable money, holds chattel mortg [ages] on ½ the furniture in the Holladay St. 'Places of Pleasure' and wardrobes etc. of the occupants." Apparently women as well as men exploited prostitutes in nineteenth-century Denver.

Rachel Peterson discovered that young women in larger, expensive houses were not thrown on the street when they became ill. They were carried off to filthy and crowded tenements where they got the most casual medical care. When a woman died, the madames made one final gesture of thanks to the ones who had so lucratively served them. The funeral was paid for by the madame, and sometimes

109

Rachel Peterson was asked to officiate the religious dimension of the service.

Most citizens were never touched by the social extremes in the booming city. They lived comfortably in the middle class, and seldom if ever did they walk among the eminently successful on Capitol Hill or the poverty stricken in the bottoms near the South Platte. The middle class was one more isolated segment of an increasingly fragmented society—a society with a decreasing amount of human interaction. The poor, the Chinese, the Italians, the blacks, and the very wealthy each huddled in their own neighborhoods and remained ignorant of each other's way of life. As a result, it became increasingly difficult to unite the community in solving social and physical problems.

To be sure, some attempts at change were made, but they were often selfish, callous, or shortsighted efforts which alienated people rather than united them. By 1900, for example, Denver had over 800 miles of streets. Of this total, only twenty-four miles were paved, and these were all on Capitol Hill and in the business district. In the view of many citizens, Denver's power elite took care of themselves and neglected other parts of the city. The charge was true regarding street improvements, but that was only part of the story. Civic leaders saw that streets important to themselves were paved first, but by the standards of most cities, they were generous with money for recreational areas. By the turn of the century Denver had amassed over 400 acres of land for a dozen parks, equally distributed throughout the city. This movement was inaugurated during the administration of Mayor Richard Sopris (1878-1881) with the purchase of land from the state for City Park. Acquisition of land continued over the next two decades, especially when Sopris was commissioner of public parks during a ten-year period after he left the mayor's office.

These efforts notwithstanding, many people believed that civic leaders paid too little attention to the city beautiful. In 1895 Martha A.B. Conine and Mrs. Jasper D. Ward organized the Women's Club of Denver. By 1898, according to a report Conine published in *Municipal Affairs*, their club had 1,000 members and was making significant progress toward cleaning up Denver. To discourage littering they pressured city hall into placing rubbish cans around the city, and they encouraged merchants along Sixteenth Street between Arapahoe and Curtis to hire a man to clean that filthy thoroughfare which the city refused to maintain.

The Woman's Club did much more. Offended by the ubiquitous, weed-covered vacant lots in the poorer sections of town, they started the "Pingree Gardens" project. Owners of lots were persuaded to allow cultivation of the land, and several fallow plots were converted into vegetable gardens by lower economic class residents. While the efforts of the Woman's Club were worthy in one way, they served to alienate the poor families who reaped vegetables from the garden space. In a most condescending and patronizing manner, Martha Conine argued that the "Pingree Gardens" project was significant because it put "a dependent and indolent class" to work and at the same time provided them with food and cleaned up the city.

When middle and upper class Denverites tried to improve social conditions, it was too frequently done in this smug, holier-than-thou way. The original impetus was often self-serving, as in the case of the Woman's Club aversion to weeds. Then, the motive was twisted to seem beneficial to those who supposedly would not help themselves. The fight against poverty was similarly rationalized.

There was no war on poverty in Denver—skirmish describes it more precisely. As Bernard Rosen discovered, state and local services for the sick and poor were inadequate. Little money was spent caring for the unfortunates. The public viewed the poverty program as a tool to drive the problem elsewhere. Rather than trying to understand *why* there were so many destitute children and unemployed adults and then working to correct the cause, the commonly expressed solution was to rid the community of indigents. State law required each county to stop ignoring lunatics, but the charge was to give each one ten dollars, a suit of clothes, and a railroad ticket out of town. Destitute children were treated in much the same way. Arapahoe County officials started industrial schools for children in the 1880s and in 1895 a home for dependent children was established. The county did search for adoptive parents for orphans because the county facilities were overcrowded. If adoption was impossible, they indentured the waifs to families who could find them employment.

Rachel Wild Peterson learned that if she found young men in jail who she deemed to be genuinely decent but in trouble because of hardships or mistakes, she could arrange to have them released as long as she procured railroad tickets for them and personally saw that they boarded the next train to their hometown.

Most upper economic class Denverites turned their backs on the poverty class, although the lower echelon had become a permanent dimension of society. Stephan Leonard claims that with the exception of H.B. Chamberlain, none of the foreign investors who lived in Denver and made fortunes off the state's resources and labor gave anything to charity. Ancestor worshipers and booster historians like

Street urchins

to point with pride to the generosity of Denver's elite, but few wealthy residents gave much of their fortunes to help the downtrodden. Millions of dollars were put into massive churches, private dwellings, social clubs, office buildings, private schools, foreign travel, and political campaigns. Precious little in comparison went to help others. W.S. Cheesman did donate some books and rent a building for a public library; and after his death his wife agreed to build a park pavilion if she could glorify her husband's name by labelling the area Cheesman Park. David Moffat was never noted for philanthropy in

Denver, but he did return some of his money to his hometown of Washingtonville, New York. Imitating Andrew Carnegie, Moffat erected the Moffat Library and Hall to serve the people and immortalize himself.

Only the wives of Denver's power elite seemed sensitive to the poor. Elizabeth Byers continued her dedicated work in the Ladies Union Aid Society which she had organized in the 1860s, and was instrumental in reorganizing it into the Ladies Relief Society in 1874. Margaret Gray Evans, the territorial governor's wife, was active in local charities and became president of the privately supported Denver Orphan's Home. Between 1874 and 1890 the Ladies Relief Society raised as much money as they could from private sources. They dispersed food and clothing and ultimately established a kindergarten, a day nursery, a free clinic, a home for destitute women and children, and a home for the aged.

These were worthy and well-meaning endeavors. Still, only a small percentage of the needy found help. Philanthropists had difficulty raising enough money to meet ever-growing needs, which became especially acute during the depression of the 1890s; but their own narrow views of who deserved help ruled out many of the poor. The Ladies Relief Society refused to aid people who they did not find "worthy." Indeed, they carefully screened those who sought help. They were determined to help only those who conformed to, or were willing to conform to, middle class standards of hard work, moral purity, and sobriety. Even after the Charity Organization Society—an umbrella organization that brought several private charities under one directorate to make fund raising and distribution more efficient—was formed in 1887, the same biased measuring stick was used to arrive at the "worthiness" of prospective welfare recipients.

Bernard Rosen says that Denver's philanthropists who worked for the Charity Organization Society were less committed to finding causes of poverty and actually aiding the poor than they were in instilling "self-respect, self-reliance and self-help" qualities in those seeking relief. The welfare workers throughout the late nineteenth and early twentieth centuries tenaciously adhered to the belief that if the poor were perfected, poverty would not exist.

This myopic brothers' keepers view of the lower economic classes was manifested in all sorts of ways. Rachel Peterson's autobiography reveals that some local officials assumed that if a person was converted to Christianity he or she was worthy of being released from jail and given a new start; her experiences further show that if a woman on relief became pregnant out of wedlock, the Charity Or-

Thomas A. "Parson Tom" Uzzell

ganization Society would take her off the welfare rolls immediately because she was no longer one of the "worthy."

Other biases were inherent in Denver's largest private charity federation. The black community supported Ada McGoway's Colored Home and Orphange Association for three years after it was founded in 1899. When the community was unable to finance the facility in 1901, the home closed with not one dollar from white citizens or philanthropists going to its rescue.

114

The Gospel Wagon

The most effective and least judgmental charity was disbursed by those who lived among the poor. Rachel Peterson and her friends at the People's Tabernacle came from the lower economic class themselves. They understood the problems of the needy. The People's Tabernacle was a nondenominational Protestant church. Located at Nineteenth and Blake throughout the 1880s and 1890s, it moved to larger quarters at Twentieth and Larimer in 1900. "Parson Tom" Uzzell oversaw the religious and philanthropic activities of the tabernacle and coordinated the charitable labors of his volunteer workers. "Parson Tom's" corps of volunteers generously gave of their time and meager earnings. Without fanfare they visited hospitals and jails, took the sick and unemployed into their simple homes, and personally ministered to the infirm and dying who lived in tents along the river and in tenements of the overcrowded slums. Rachel Peterson was one of Uzzell's volunteers. She rescued young women from houses of prostitution, and she bought a tent dwelling for an unwed mother thrown off the Charity Organization Society's relief rolls. Tom Uzzell used his own modest resources to open a "Friendly Shelter" in the heart of Denver's slums. There he fed, sheltered, and clothed as many as 400 men at one time who were disease-ridden, drunk, or down on their luck. He preached a little gospel to the indigents, but he never made conversion to Christianity, temperance, or middle-class morality a measure of worthiness or a requirement for help.

Rather than conducting fund-raising drives for magnificent edifices, Uzzell, Peterson, and an army of co-worshippers both black and white solicited money to buy tents for the homeless and furniture and clothing for the needy. They worshipped in the austere tabernacle, served free breakfasts of coffee and pork and beans from its kitchen, and spread their gospel from the seats of bicycles and a crude, horse-drawn vehicle dubbed the "Gospel Wagon." The distance between Uzzell's volunteers and the fashionable Ladies Relief Society was farther than the city blocks separating the bottoms and Capitol Hill. Rachel Peterson saw and felt the enormous gulf between them when she was asked to go to Trinity Methodist Episcopal Church to advise the women members how they might establish a home for fallen women. She wrote at the time that "Trinity Church is one of the leading churches of our city, and the leading society ladies of the city attend it." The ladies she addressed that afternoon in the late 1890s included the first ladies of the Byers, Kountze, Routt, Rogers, and Vaile families. Although they were cordial and tried to make her feel welcome, she was uncomfortable with her chapped, red hands, being the only one among the 150 women without kid gloves and a fashionable satin dress.

The extent to which Denver had become a fragmented city, where various groups never interacted or understood one another, was symbolized at that Trinity Church meeting. The women of Trinity had no notion of the kind of women they wanted to help, how those women got where they were, or what could be done to free them from their peculiar bondage. Nevertheless, they were reaching out—they were trying, and they had the good sense to seek out a Rachel Peterson to help them bridge the light years that separated the isolated worlds existing in the new Denver.

Despite the barriers, some of the wives of Denver's power elite helped relieve symptomatic pains of the sufferers. They channelled some of the money earned by their empire-building husbands into local reform. Elizabeth Byers built a home for destitute boys, Margaret Evans donated a lot to Rachel Peterson so that she could erect a tent and carry on her work, and Mrs. James B. Grant, Mrs. J.A. Thatcher, Mrs. N.P. Hill, and Mrs. Charles Kountze furnished some of the eighty-five rooms in the YWCA Young Women's Home built at Eighteenth and Sherman in 1899.

Ethnic and religious pride probably played as important a role as alienation in the efforts made by Denver's minorities to care for their own. The Catholic Church opened several facilities for the aged, infirm, and orphaned. St. Vincent's, St. Clara's, and the Good Shepherd homes were started in the 1880s, followed by a facility for Italians, the Queen of Heaven Orphanage, a few years later. German Franciscans at St. Elizabeth's Church helped destitute German immigrants, and Swedish Lutherans built the National Swedish Sanitarium in Denver in the early twentieth century. The Jews maintained a burial society dating back to the 1860s, and they built the National Jewish Hospital in the early part of the new century. The Jewish Relief Society was organized in 1900. Particularly aimed at helping the East European Jewish immigrants, it incorporated other Jewish relief societies. Frances Weisbart Jacobs and Rabbi William S. Friedman both did yeoman work in these societies, and they worked for the nondenominational Charity Organization Society.

All these efforts notwithstanding, poverty was a major and largely unconquered problem by the early twentieth century. Added to poverty were scores of economic, political, and physical problems which grew worse each year and demanded immediate attention. A stumbling block to finding solutions was the widespread social disorganization. Rather than working together, combining human and fiscal resources, Denver's multitude of interest groups were at best not communicating, or worse, they were fighting. What the Queen City desperately needed was a leader who knew his city intimately, understood the needs and desires of the diverse groups that stood isolated or at loggerheads, and was skillful enough to find areas of agreement among them. Only then could Denver unite to solve the myriad problems which were endemic in a new city that had been so successful in attracting railroads, factories, and thousands of people.

Part III
The City Beautiful,
1904-1923

Chapter 5

The man who saved Denver from chaos in the early twentieth century, pulling a wide diversity of groups together so that problem-solving decisions could be made once again, was Robert Walter Speer. Born in Cassville, Pennsylvania, in December 1855, young Speer spent his early years there and in nearby Mount Union. One of four children in a moderately prosperous family, Robert Speer's education at the Dickenson Academy in Williamsport, Pennsylvania, was paid for by his father, who was a Union officer during the Civil War. After receiving secondary education, the academy graduate took a ticket agent job in Shirleysburg and ultimately found office employment with the Pennsylvania Railroad. However, his career with the railroad was cut short. In 1877 his sister was diagnosed to be in an advanced stage of tuberculosis, and brother Robert decided to take her to Colorado. Margaret Speer was unhappy with the place they found in Pueblo, and in less than one year her brother took her back to Pennsylvania, where she died within a few months.

By early 1878 Robert Speer began hemorrhaging from the disease. Not wishing to meet his sister's fate, he returned to Colorado, where fresh air and ranch life helped restore his health. By 1880 the twenty-five-year-old Pennsylvanian was in Denver, working first as a carpet salesman and then as a real estate agent. Approximately five feet, ten inches tall, the thin newcomer to Denver gradually gained weight as he won his battle with tuberculosis. When he made a quick trip back to Pennsylvania in 1882 to marry Kate Thrush, his childhood sweetheart, he was strong and robust, even slightly rotund.

The young couple returned to Denver immediately after the wedding, and the bridegroom resumed his work as a real estate agent. Not content to devote his entire time to business, Speer became active in the local Democratic party. In 1884 the party placed him on the ballot for the city clerkship, and in a close election, he won. The following year the local Democracy persuaded President Grover Cleveland to appoint Speer postmaster, a position he held until the Republicans turned him out four years later. In 1891 Governor John L. Routt, a Republican, named two Republicans and one Democrat to the newly created fire and police board. Considered by regulars of both parties to be "sensible and safe," Speer was the Democrat that Routt named to the board.

From the beginning of his tenure on the police and fire board, Speer was a sagacious politician. Working equitably and effectively with the two Republicans, he gradually secured places for many Democrats in the fire and police departments. In 1897 Governor Alva Adams selected Speer as police commissioner, and two years later Governor Charles S. Thomas placed him on the board as fire commissioner. In 1901 Thomas put Speer in charge of the patronage-laden Board of Public Works, where he controlled a sizeable budget (about 50% of the city's expenditures) to build and maintain everything from sewers to parks. By the early twentieth century, Speer had scores of workers in the police, fire, and public works departments indebted to him for their jobs. Furthermore, he had a large voice in saloon licensing, and it was common knowledge that he could enforce or wink at laws regulating gambling, saloon closing, and prostitution. In short, Robert W. Speer, not yet fifty years old, had a political organization that could raise money and turn out a large bloc of votes. He also had a large personal following among the lower economic class of Denver. He used his influence with the police to ease the heavy hand of the law when boys were caught stealing coal or when destitute men had stolen food for their families. Speer also understood, rather than attacked, men who got drunk to escape their problems. In a word, Speer had friends. Blacks, Italians, Jews, Germans, and native whites downtown and in the Bottoms know Robert Speer—and they liked and trusted him.

The Denver which Speer was destined to direct for nearly two decades, until his death in 1918, was socially and economically complex and beset by problems. With a population of 134,000 in 1900, Denver increased nearly 60% in the next ten years, growing to over 213,000. By the end of the next decade the city boasted a population of over 256,000, a 20% increase over 1910. Despite the population explosion during the first twenty years of the new century, Denver's boundaries remained unchanged. Annexations in 1902 brought Denver to nearly fifty-nine square miles, where it remained until World War II.

Robert W. Speer at the time of his first-term election

The new arrivals were far from homogenous in ethnic makeup. Twenty-five thousand foreign-born residents inhabited the Queen City in 1900, and nearly thirteen thousand more joined them by 1920. The black populace grew from just under 4,000 to over 6,000 during those years. Approximately 4,000 Jews (mostly German) resided in Denver at the turn of the century, but a large influx of Russians and other East Europeans brought the total population of professed Jews to 11,000 in 1920. Nearly 35,000 Catholics resided in predominantly native Protestant Denver by 1920, and nearly 2,000 of those represented a new ethnic minority from Mexico.

Ethnic diversity created tensions. When housing, sewers, water service, public transportation, police and fire protection, and street construction failed to meet increasing demands, the majority population tended to blame newcomers, in particular the foreign-born, for the problems. When new residents were not judged culpable, many citizens charged politicians with inefficiency or raged against the public service corporations, accusing them of ignoring public needs in the blind quest for profits. What no one apparently recognized—or at least no one spoke out on the issue—was that rapid growth inevitably created urban problems. Actually, Denverites were proud of their growing city. They applauded the booster efforts of the Chamber of Commerce, newspapers, and the State Board of Immigration, whose staffs worked untiringly to attract settlers, investors, and businesses.

Boosters were phenomenally successful in enticing people (mostly native whites) to Denver and its hinterland. Such efforts were viewed as a positive good inasmuch as property values appreciated, the tax base increased, and Denver could boast that it was one of the twenty-five largest cities in the United States. This typically American assumption that success should be equated with more industry, an expanding population, and an ever-growing urbanization was so pervasive that it prevented all but the most eccentric from suggesting that perhaps "success" itself was the cause of urban problems. Instead of asking penetrating questions about growth, Denver's citizens, at the least, quietly acquiesced as the boosters tried everything imaginable to attract people and capital. If problems existed, causes would be sought elsewhere.

The state spent more money to boost Colorado during the early twentieth century than it had in the previous years. With a larger budget than ever before, the Board of Immigration published its goals for the next few years: "To collect reliable information and statistics regarding agriculture, stock-growing and feeding, horticulture, mining,manufacturing, climate and health in Colorado, and to publish the same with a view to attracting health-seekers, tourists, investors and prospective settlers to the state; . . ." Booklets, pamphlets, and brochures were disseminated throughout the country, pointing to Colorado's present advantages and future prospects. Complementing efforts of the Board of Immigration were activities of numerous state agencies. Hundreds of thousands of dollars were spent to encourage farming. Not only were earlier efforts to stimulate sugar beet and fruit-growing production continued, but the state fostered newer agricultural pursuits in such areas as scientifically controlled beekeeping. Colorado was also proclaimed as one of the most progressive states in farm-to-market road construction, having built over 40,000 miles of highways by 1916.

Denver's Chamber of Commerce was committed to the city's hinterland just as much as were state agencies. Indeed, in 1913 the organization's slogan was "Build Colorado First." But even earlier, the chamber made hinterland development a top priority. In 1906 it persuaded the United States government to spend $60,000 on dry land farming experiments. Their findings stimulated irrigation and dry land farming in eastern Colorado in particular, and consequently bolstered the service dimension of Denver's economy. In 1909 the Chamber of Commerce sponsored an apple exposition to place Colorado on the map as an apple-producing state, and the next year it organized boys' and girls' agricultural clubs to create interest in farming all over the state. During 1913, the chamber's year to "Build Colorado First," they sponsored a "Plowing Carnival" in Denver and introduced a flax-growing campaign. That year the Denver promotional organization launched the first Annual Stock Show, aimed at encouraging stock raising and agriculture and making Denver the center of agricultural business in the West.

The Chamber of Commerce did more than promote agriculture. The booster organization hired full-time staff members to relieve businessmen of doing more than advisory work. Throughout the early twentieth century, the Chamber of Commerce (which changed its name in 1916 to the Denver Civic and Commercial Association) published maps of Colorado and folders on Denver. The association distributed photographs labeled "Denver on a Sunday Morning" to newspapers all over the nation as they expanded efforts to attract visitors. To encourage tourism the chamber led the way in persuading the federal government to make the Mesa Verde cliff dwellers' region a national park in 1906, and the promotional organization spent thousands of dollars lobbying to get a tourist playground near Estes

Park (Rocky Mountain National Park), set aside by Washington in 1915. Throughout the second decade of the century, the association devoted itself to attracting 200,000 tourists a year, even going so far as opening a branch office in Los Angeles for a time after World War I.

Tourism and conventions were closely related, and the promotional agency spent large sums of money encouraging both. Trying to create an image of Denver as the "Convention City," the Chamber of Commerce put herculean energy and time into constructing facilities, advertising available hotels and restaurants, and doing whatever was necessary to bring organizations to Denver. The chamber aided the city in building the half-million-dollar Denver Auditorium at Fourteenth and Champa, which was the largest assembly hall in the United States when it was finished in 1908, with the exception of New York's Madison Square Garden. Boasting a seating capacity of 11,500 for the auditorium, the promoters claimed that Denver's hotels could accommodate nearly 100,000 people. They did provide for 75,000 visitors of the Benevolent Protective Order for Elks when that organization held its national gathering in Denver in 1906, and the city made room for an even larger gathering of Elks in 1911. The Grand Army of the Republic was attracted to Denver as were the Christian Endeavor Societies. The big coup, though, was getting the National Democratic Convention in 1908. In order to win the honor, Denver raised $100,000 for a delegates' entertainment fund, and this helped convince the national committee that Denver was the ideal place for their presidential nominating business. The widespread publicity that Denver received from the Democratic National Convention drew more large meetings during ensuing years, among them the National Good Roads Convention in 1910 and the Public Lands Convention in 1911.

Occasionally the Chamber of Commerce found itself facing dilemmas—indeed, almost working at cross purposes. On the one hand, they wanted to preserve the state's natural beauty for attracting tourists and conventioneers. This aim was manifested in lobbying for national parks and in one successful drive to get billboard advertising taken out of mountain wildernesses. On the other hand, chamber leaders hoped to entice industry and develop the hinterland, which meant that preservation of natural resources would have to be sacrificed. The chamber joined representatives from several western states in 1907 and held a Lands Convention in Denver to protest President Theodore Roosevelt's conservation programs. Sheepmen and cattlemen from all over the Rocky Mountain region were there to protest the grazing restrictions on public lands. Coal producers were furious over a new law which prohibited mining in major portions of the public domain. Small and medium-sized lumber industries were angered by the Roosevelt-inspired legislation restricting open timber cutting. The smaller lumbermen argued that only the big corporations would get access to federal timber because large organizations could out bid everyone else on the selected areas that were to be opened to the highest bidder. Prudent use of public land was consistent with Denver's promotion of tourism but inconsistent with attracting and helping industries. Ultimately, the Chamber of Commerce joined the anti-conservationists in the convention of 1907, and again in 1911. With modest success they fought to keep the public domain open to private exploitation. In short, local boosters argued that states east of the Mississippi had been free to utilize resources in the past, and it was unfair to prevent newer states from having the same opportunities. In conjunction with this attitude, the chamber not only opposed environmentally healthy goals, it established committees to prepare inventories on coal and lumber resources. These statistics were published as part of a larger program to lure extractive industries to Colorado.

Denver's Chamber of Commerce joined local businessmen and bankers in other activities to promote growth. After 1910 they recognized the importance of the federal government to urban development. When rumors that Ft. Logan might be closed in 1911 began, promoters lobbied to block the move with attractive incentives to the United States Army. During World War I civic leaders hoped to capitalize on the extraordinary federal spending. Millions of dollars were being pumped into lucky communities around the nation. By 1918, through a fund-raising drive headed by the Civic and Commercial Association (formerly the Chamber of Commerce), businessmen and banks contributed enough money to purchase the site for Fitzsimons Hospital. By leasing the land to the government for ninety-nine years at one dollar a year, they encouraged the government to build its military personnel recuperation center in Denver. In 1920 local activists persuaded Congress to appropriate money for a large expansion of Fitzsimons Hospital. When the government agreed to enlarge the facility to accommodate 800 more patients, the Denver Civic and Commercial Association took credit for the project and argued that over $4 million per year of federal money, considering payrolls and purchases, would be injected into the local economy.

Although the Commercial and Civic Association spearheaded most promotional schemes in the twentieth century, private corporations continued to allocate funds for boosterism. Despite the fact that businesses underwrote the chamber and expected it to take over public relations which corporations largely had handled in the nineteenth century, local entrepreneurs still spent sums over and above their annual contributions to the chamber. Businesses, for example, raised most of the money for the Democratic National Convention and for such projects as buying the land for Fitzsimons Hospital. Corporations sometimes promoted Denver when they furthered themselves. In 1915 the Denver Union Water Company published a booklet on its own history. Designed to give the company a public servant image, it also was intended to be a piece of advertising for Denver. Page one proclaimed "Sunshine, Pure Air and Pure Water Make Denver an Ideal Place in Which to Live," and the Chamber of Commerce photograph of "Denver on a Sunday Morning" covered one entire page.

Sometimes Denver got free publicity in other cities as a result of financial transactions. In 1914 Harris Trust and Savings Bank in Chicago offered for sale over one quarter of a million dollars worth of Denver municipal bonds. The city had sold the bonds for viaduct construction. The Chicago investors were selling the bonds at 4¼%. As a means of announcing their sale, they circulated a form letter which celebrated Denver in a most glowing manner:

> Denver, the capital of Colorado, is the largest city between the Missouri River and the Pacific Coast. In addition to the products which it handles from the tributary agricultural section, the City is in close proximity to a great mining region and does a large business in machinery and manufactured goods. Its mercantile interests are diversified and extensive and the City is noted for its many fine public buildings and improvements. There are twenty-nine banks, having an aggregate capital of $5,127,550 and total deposits of over $50,000,000.
>
> Denver is an attractive railroad center, having eight different lines of steam railroads, including the "Santa Fe," "Burlington," "Rock Island," and the "Union Pacific."

Publicity for the mountain metropolis also came out of Kansas City. Denver was eloquently described by the editors of *The Great Southwest Magazine*. Founded in Denver in the early twentieth century, this travel and regional promotional magazine moved its headquarters to Missouri in 1909. After relocating in Kansas City, *The Great Southwest Magazine* continued to publish articles and photographs of Colorado, dwelling upon the beauty, opportunities, and advantages of the Queen City and its environs.

These booster efforts were obviously successful. Not only did Denver boom in the early years of the twentieth century, but the outlying portions of the state, which were served by the burgeoning service metropolis, expanded as well. The state's population increased from a little over one-half million in 1900 to almost 940,000 by 1920. Inextricably tied to population expansion were striking developments in agriculture and industry. Farm population and productivity increased during the first two decades of the twentieth century, adding to the prosperity of the state and its bustling service city. As agricultural enterprises expanded, so did railroad traffic and miles of track. By 1914, 5,739 miles of track were in operation, an increase of over 1,500 miles since 1890.

Railroads voraciously consumed coal, and there was an ever increasing demand for the black fuel in houses, office buildings, and factories all over the mountain state. Millions of dollars in eastern money flowed into Colorado's rich bituminous coal regions of Los Animas and Huerfano counties south of Denver and into the smaller northern area around Boulder, Louisville, and Lafayette. Although the rich quality of Colorado's coal had been recognized early in the state's history, the demand was not great until years later. Only about 437,000 tons were mined in 1880. By 1890, however, smelter and railroad consumption brought production to 3,000,000 tons. As fuel use for homes and industry mounted, production increased each year, with over 12,500,000 tons produced in 1920.

By promotional design, Denver became a regional metropolis because of the campaigns to attract capital, develop agriculture, promote industry, and tempt newcomers. Given the prodigious problems concomitant with reaching regional metropolitan status, it is appropriate to recall Dr. Samuel Johnson's observation of the dog walking on his hind legs. The act was not performed gracefully, he noted, but one "is surprised to find it done at all." Using Johnson's perspective, the remarkable thing about Denver during the first twenty years of the new century is not that it suffered from graft and corruption, or that every problem was not solved or solved equitably, but that the city survived—and rather well at that.

Without Robert W. Speer, Denver would not have come through one of its most difficult periods of growing pains with so many accomplishments and so few scars. The city was disorganized and nearly chaotic when Speer became mayor in 1904. Businessmen had lost control of the town partly because their own enterprises demanded so much time; also because the diverse populace had come to believe that corporate interests were antithetical to their own. Interest groups consisting of minorities, the poor, small and large business, organized vice and crime, and moralistic reformers each had their own interests to protect and goals to attain. No leader existed who found areas of agreement among these motley concerns. No businessman or politician was able to serve a variety of persons, win their confidence, and thereby embark upon a substantive urban problem-solving program.

Robert Speer was a master broker who possessed that rare talent of understanding mankind from all levels of society. He knew his city and its people better than most of his contemporaries. He was blessed with the political acumen which enabled him to bridge the gulfs between conflicting groups by winning their confidence and then persuading each that they must compromise with others if any were to prosper and survive.

Speer demonstrated his political agility in 1903 and 1904 when battles raged over Denver's new charter. In 1902 the Twentieth Article to the state constitution was adopted granting Denver home rule, thereby giving the city the authority to draw up its own charter and control its internal affairs. Scores of individuals and groups had their own panaceas to solve Denver's problems, and they wanted these incorporated in the new charter. Moral reform was fashionable throughout urban America in the early twentieth century, and Denver had its share of people who hoped to legislate morality. Civil service was also viewed as a cure-all for urban ills, as was municipal ownership of public service corporations. The result was that a loosely united coterie of journalists, lawyers, politicians, men's and women's civic associations, the Anti-Saloon League, and Women's Christian Temperance Union managed to draw up a charter and present it to the voters in fall 1903. The proposed charter called for strict regulation of public utilities and ultimate municipal ownership, as well as municipal civil service extended to the police and fire departments. The charter proposal was also designed to close "disreputable" saloons by raising license fees from $600 to $1,000 a year, and it contained a prescription to abolish gambling and policy making in the Queen City. Incredible, but true, the activists believed that the spoils system, abusive corporations, and immorality could be banished from Denver with the new charter.

The only problem with the proposed charter was that its provisions offended too many people. Leading bankers and businessmen owned stock in the utilities corporations, and they were not about to see their interests destroyed without a fight. Promoters from the ranks of business and finance who had worked hard to make Denver a popular convention center knew that the wide-open nature of the city was an important attraction. Likewise, the thousands of Denverites involved directly or indirectly with brewing, wholesale liquor, gambling, saloon (and its handmaiden—prostitution) enterprises viewed moral reform as similar to a smallpox epidemic. To Robert W. Speer and other professional politicians who worked diligently to create a political organization based on patronage, and to those who held the spoils of that system, civil service was as welcome as another fire and flood. Not to be overlooked were Denver's immigrants and indigents. Since 1891 Robert Speer had been using his power on the police, fire, and public works boards to find jobs for the needy and to ease the impact of the law. Speer even inaugurated a food and lodging coupon program in 1900. Each policeman was instructed to locate the destitute and distribute the coupons, which could be redeemed for cash from the city. The recipients of Speer's welfare program were no more inclined to see his base of power erased by a new charter than were the gamblers and prostitutes whom he protected. But others in the city disagreed.

Clyde Lyndon King, an idealistic young political science Ph.D. from the University of Pennsylvania, was dedicated to political reform in Denver. He described the proposed charter as one "drawn in the interests of many." Judge Ben Lindsey, a self-styled reformer who fought for the charter's passage, saw it in the same vein—as a document designed to protect "the rights of the people." The wealthy, politically ambitious editor of the *Rocky Mountain News*, Thomas Patterson, envisioned the charter as a document that would "centralize responsibility for city government . . . [in] the people." The question though, was which "people" would benefit from the new charter?

Robert W. Speer had himself to protect, but he also sincerely believed that most Denverites would prefer a new charter that did not run a bulldozer over Denver's polity and economy. Thus, the balding, greying, bowtie-sporting president of public works began putting together a coalition that effectively and efficiently directed the city except for one four-year interruption from 1904 until May 1918. Speer's coalition brought together a wide range of disparate, even potentially antagonistic, groups. The poor and working-class people, of course, had supported their longtime friend for his employment and welfare programs. During his years of service on the police board, Speer accepted the inevitability of prostitution and befriended

Edward Chase

the saloon and gambling element. He was espcially close to its czar, Ed Chase, the handsome, mustached, and urbanely dressed man who had gone to Denver in the early 1860s. He opened a small tavern and gradually built a gaming and entertainment empire. Chase earned enough money during more than three decades of entrepreneurship to pay cash for a home on Capitol Hill, yet, despite the fact that he had as much money, if not more, than the elite, he never socialized with most of them.

The stigma attached to Chase's career prevented him and his successor, Vaso L. Chucovich, from joining the Denver Club, but Robert Speer genuinely liked and befriended both men. Chucovich was born in Yugoslavia in 1858, and he emigrated to America when he was nineteen. Spending the next eighteen years in California, Nevada, and Omaha, Nebraska, Chucovich arrived in Denver in 1895. By that time he was thirty-seven years old, wealthy, fluent in English, and well schooled in games of chance. The astute discoverer of the American rags-to-riches dream immediately associated with Chase and Speer. Never one to drink or gamble himself, he invested in Denver real estate, became active in local politics, and ultimately bought Chase's finest gambling, drinking, and eating establishment, the Arcade, at 1611-13 Larimer Street.

From Chase and Chucovich, Speer got money to help the needy. In return, the Speer-controlled police force closed its eyes to violations of liquor and gambling ordinances. Speer developed a similar working arrangement with Denver's madames. They provided money for the party and welfare coffers, and Speer reciprocated by allowing them to do business as long as they remained cloistered around Market Street and avoided abusing the customers.

Speer's supporters in the downtown wards provided the basis of a potent political organization. Indeed, Speer had the largest bloc of votes at his beck and call of any person in Denver. Nevertheless, he was no "boss" as his enemies sometimes charged. He could count on the support of these interests only so long as he gave them something in return, and he could offer them nothing if he lost his influence in local government under the new charter. Furthermore, these core city supporters notwithstanding, Speer could not "boss" the city or swing an election without backing from the outlying wards.

No one recognized the fragile nature of his position more than Speer himself. Consequently, he went to the city's corporate and financial elite and suggested an alliance that would be beneficial to all. Among the men confronted by Speer were Walter S. Cheesman, who presided over the Water Company, Tramway king William Gray

133

Evans, and Charles J. Hughes, who served as attorney for the Water and Tramway companies, as well as for the First National Bank, the Union Pacific Railroad, and Coors Brewing Company. Through these men Speer made contacts with attorneys and executives affiliated with the Gas and Electric Company, the Telephone Company, and those involved in sugar refining, smelting, cement, and the stockyards.

Heretofore, these business magnates had directed Denver's decision-making process on their own, and with little competition. From the early days of railroad promotion through the depression of the 1890s, Denver's power elite had been synonymous with the business leadership. They had directed the building of the city and had secured through docile—almost puppetlike—mayors and councilmen whatever they desired. Their influence had won them sewers and paved streets in their neighborhoods before anyone else had such improvements, and they gained scandalously favorable franchises for their utilities corporations. Public Service franchises had been granted in perpetuity until the legislature placed a twenty-year time limit on such transactions in 1889. But even with the two-decade restriction, the franchises of the street railway and utilities companies were described by Clyde L. King in this manner: "none secured pecuniary return to the city and none gave adequate protection to public needs." King oversimplified the history of public service corporations only slightly. Incredibly small fees were paid to the city—at least small in comparison to what was required of similar corporations in other cities. The companies not only used city property and paid little in compensation, but they had a free hand in deciding consumer fees and rates. And because the public service corporations were monopolies by 1900, the citizens had no choice but to pay the charges.

By 1903, however, Denver was too large and diverse for the business elite to control. Many citizens were tired of being exploited, and now a proposed charter was before the public which would strictly regulate and eventually socialize the natural monopolies. The previously all-powerful decision makers were in trouble. The city had prospered as they hoped it would, but it had grown unruly in the process.

Robert Speer personally owned no utility corporation stock, and his own interests were not threatened by municipal ownership. On the other hand, the predicament faced by those who did stand to lose fortunes suddenly coincided with his own. The proposed charter could destroy Speer's little empire as well as the businessmen's larger one. Both groups recognized this and agreed it was time for an alliance. Denver lore tells us that Speer was bought by the corporations in 1903; that in return for his organization's votes, the corporations would put up money for Speer and his henchmen and steal the election if necessary. Ultimately, so the popular history continues, Speer would be elected mayor, and he would give the corporations preferential treatment as long as they could keep him in power and pay the price.

A deal was indeed made in 1903, but the facts are significantly different. Speer suggested to business leaders that if they would pay workers to get out the downtown vote, and if they also encouraged their employees and friends to vote against the charter, it could be defeated. The business elite, after all, had public service, railroad, and smelter workers they might influence, which would present a considerable addition to Speer's own faithful followers. The next step would be to draw up a new charter proposal ignoring civil service, leaving saloon and gambling houses untouched, and making municipal ownership of public service corporations so difficult that it would be almost impossible to achieve. Speer, however, had a condition tied to the agreement. The corporations would have to become more sensitive to the needs of the community; they would have to be less abusive and pay a fair revenue to the city for public improvements. In effect, Speer did not say, "I can be bought." On the contrary, he said, "I'll help you survive if you help me survive." For this scheme to work effectively, though, Speer made it clear that the corporations would have to accept regulation in the same way that the gamblers, saloon keepers, and prostitutes had agreed to be overseen.

Ultimately, the alliance was consummated. Compromise for survival transcended party politics and socio-economic class differences. Due to Speer's broker politics, gamblers, tavern keepers, prostitutes, indigents, and laborers were doing battle alongside bankers, corporation lawyers, and directors of the city's utilities. Not only were capitalists and proletarians uniting, but Republicans and Democrats were ignoring party regularity in Denver's Armageddon. Speer was a Democrat, as was Charles J. Hughes, the influential lawyer. Yet, some of Hughes' closest friends, business associates, and clients, William Gray Evans and Lawrence Phipps for example, were powers in the Colorado G.O.P.

The hastily created organization went into action immediately. There was little time to mobilize for the September charter fight. But as Speer predicted, they were successful in defeating it, and they did so by a 7,200 vote margin. Correspondence between Judge Ben

135

Charles J. Hughes, Jr.

Lindsey and Walter S. Cheesman three years later contains evidence that corroborates charges made in the local press. The corporations funneled thousands of dollars to Speer, who subsequently used the money for paying workers to get people to the polls; and officials were bribed to pad the voting lists with fraudulent names. A later investigation revealed over one thousand names of deceased or unidentifiable residents on the lists in 1903.

Such corrupt practices were certainly unnecessary. Without the illegal votes, the charter was defeated by over 6,000 votes. And when the new charter favorable to Speer and the corporations went to the citizens in March 1904, it passed without the "ghost" and "repeater" vote. Irregularities were discovered the following May when Speer was elected first mayor of "home rule" Denver. But once again, the army of partisans that carried Speer to victory was large enough to win without vote fraud, suggesting that a plurality of Denverites believed Speer would best serve their interests. Precinct and ward workers apparently were not confident of enough honest support; perhaps Speer himself was not confident. Their faith must have been restored by the outcome of the mayoralty race, for it was the last time substantiated charges indicated that Denver's new leader had resorted to vote fraud to insure his victories. To be sure, the public corporations and the liquor and gambling interests put money into subsequent campaigns, but it was used to pay the ward heelers and precinct captains to get out the legitimate voters, not to resurrect the dead.

If voting irregularities tarnished Speer's ascension to the mayor's office, his tenure there was a positive good for Denver and the majority of its citizens. What he was able to accomplish between 1904 and 1912, and again from 1916 until his death in May 1918, was by any standard substantial and remarkable. Indeed, his achievements were monumental and humane. Where his business elite predecessors managed the city with an eye to attracting railroads and capital and building the edifices to house the economic vitality such enterprise brought to Denver, Speer did much more. With utmost efficiency he launched a city beautiful movement, expanded public services, and declared war on poverty. He also regulated the public service corporations without destroying them or giving Denver a reputation as a city unsafe for capital investments; and he made the city's wealthiest citizens aware of ways in which they could contribute to the community and the needy. Thus, he reduced class tensions and conflicts.

Rather than a "boss," as his opponents charged, Speer became an able manager and coordinator. He served as a mediator to promote communication; he identified problems and brought together a variety of groups who possessed resources for solutions. Perhaps most importantly, he *listened* to citizens rather than dominating or shoving them, and he sincerely tried to meet their demands or requests. He frequently took his plans to the public. A popular speaker—some said he was charismatic—Speer rallied support from the podium as well as from intimate meetings around his office desk.

In January 1907 Speer delivered a speech at the Brown Palace which summarized his political philosophy. Mirroring what he had already done, and forecasting what he would do in the future, the mayor declared, "I believe city government should be progressive along conservative lines—push needed improvements and add the ornamental at the lowest possible cost. Refuse to be puritanical or used in spasms of reform, yet earnestly strive for betterment year by year along all moral lines."

Speer's philosophy of making government "progressive along conservative lines" was manifested in the way in which he worked with Denver's business community. He assumed that big businesses, even natural monopolies, were good as long as they were not abusive and paid their fair share to the city which, in turn, gave them valuable franchises. Under the Twentieth (Home Rule) Article to the state constitution, the city council could no longer grant or extend franchises. The public had the right to vote on each franchise. In 1906 Mayor Speer urged Denverites to vote new charters to the Tramway Company and the Gas and Electric Company, arguing that the stockholders of each had inaugurated necessary services to Denver by risking their money. Now they had a right to continue to earn profits as long as they provided good services at low rates and compensated the city for use of its property.

Compensating the city was not something the public service corporations had contended with before. Speer, however, refused to advocate new franchises unless Evans agreed that the Tramway would pay the city $60,000 annually for park and boulevard maintenance, and unless Gas and Electric Company president Henry L. Doherty agreed to $50,000 a year for the same purpose. Recognizing they had little choice—without Speer's backing the franchises would surely be voted down—the executives acquiesced. Speer then went to voters and urged their support, put his organization to work, and the franchises were extended for twenty years.

Speer did more for the business community than sustain the franchises. He cut red tape for investors seeking building permits in the central city, and when he unveiled a program of ornamental street lighting, the business district was the first to benefit. When complaints of high insurance rates due to minimal fire protection reached his ears, Speer responded with additional fire hydrants and a new station in the central business district. When the Chamber of Commerce and local boosters bemoaned the lack of facilities necessary for making Denver a convention center, Mayor Speer responded with a successful bond issue drive to build the City Auditorium. To beautify the downtown business district, Speer appropriated city funds to bury unsightly telephone and electric lines; and of the $10 million he approved for storm and sanitary sewers and street and alley paving, the first sections of the city to benefit were Capitol Hill and the commercial sections of downtown.

Unlike most of his predecessors, Speer demanded reciprocity from business. The mayor, who early gained a reputation for pounding his fist on his desk when angry with uncompromising businessmen, forced the Union Pacific, Chicago, Burlington and Quincy, Colorado and Southern, and the Denver, Northwestern and Pacific Railways to pay almost 90% of the cost of a viaduct over the railroad crossings on Twentieth Street. This dangerous thoroughfare had been the scene of several accidents as street traffic tried to dodge the passing of freight and passenger trains. After months of discussion, and the railroad executives still refusing to pay most of the expenses for a viaduct, Speer pushed an ordinance through the council calling for watchmen to stop every train at Nineteenth and Twenty-first streets until street traffic had cleared. This threat of tying up the railroad's movement finally brought the companies into line. The viaduct was opened in 1911, with the city paying under $67,000 of $614,000 total costs.

In much the same way, Speer pressured the railroads and the Tramway Company to pay two-thirds of the cost of the West Alameda Avenue subway. Thanks to the construction project, railway tracks crossed the South Platte and the old water canal bridges, and the tramway and passenger traffic went underneath in a 1,300-foot subway. Once again, the purpose was to avoid collisions. Tragedies frequently occurred at this spot before the subway was built.

Speer used bargaining power for other purposes. Beyond the $50,000, he insisted that the Gas and Electric Company pay annually for park and boulevard maintenance, in addition to other concessions. The mayor developed a close working relationship with Henry L. Doherty, the brilliant young man who became president of the Denver Gas and Electric Company when he was only thirty years old.

139

Henry Doherty

Doherty was born in Columbus, Ohio, in 1870. Like a character from a Horatio Alger story, at age twelve he went to work for the Columbus Gas Company, where he toiled as an office boy, eventually working his way into maintenance work. Always fascinated by machinery, he studied the company's equipment and kept it in good order. While still a teenager he invented devices to modernize and increase the efficiency of gas and lighting appliances. So impressive were his technological innovations that the Columbus company promoted him to chief engineer and assistant manager. Doherty, who was thin and fastidious and wore a closely cropped beard, was soon recognized as an unusually gifted technical expert. Before Doherty was thirty, the New York-based financiers, who owned the controlling shares in the Columbus utility company, placed him in an engineering consulting and managerial position with over a dozen other companies in which they held stock. By the time Doherty went to Denver in the 1890s, he was serving companies in nine states including Colorado.

Doherty was in Denver much of the time, although he maintained a residence in Wisconsin (several of his companies were there) and an office in New York City. The youthful prodigy was a member of the Denver Club and close to William Gray Evans, Walter S. Cheesman, Henry Roger Wolcott, and Charles J. Hughes. Despite Doherty's elegant life-style, the man became friendly with Robert Speer. The corporation executive liked the politician's candor and learned to appreciate his compromise approach to city politics.

This meeting of the minds resulted in the Gas and Electric Company's survival, as well as in benefits for Denver. Speer, for example, had received evidence from anti-public service corporation spokesmen which convinced him that when the company converted to the new arc lamp for street lighting, it actually cost them less to burn than the older models. Company officials had increased rates, arguing that the new, brighter lights cost them more to operate. Armed with his evidence, Speer confronted Doherty. The result was that rates were reduced by one-third. In 1912 Doherty responded to another call from Speer. After the city voted a $2,685,000 bond issue to acquire land for a civic center, Doherty, who by then controlled a utilities holding company in New York, purchased the entire bond issue.

Another natural monopoly, the Telephone Company, had been using city streets for its lines since the 1870s. Never required to obtain a franchise, the company earned profits every year and never paid anything to the city. Once again Mayor Speer put his "progressive government along conservative lines" into action. Assuming that the company, which had been started and managed by F. O. Vaille, had every right to remain private and profitable, Speer nevertheless demanded compensation for Denver. Vaille had retired in 1884, and his successor, Edward B. Field, was the man with whom Speer negotiated. Field was a slight man in his mid-fifties when the mayor took office. Never physically strong—indeed, Field had gone to Denver in 1879 for his health—he looked more like a meek and retiring Sunday school teacher than the powerful head of a major corporation. Balding, round-shouldered, and emaciated, Massachusetts-born Edward Field appeared boyish next to the husky mayor. Field's demeanor, however, did not match his personality. A hard-nosed businessman, he had worked strenuously to build a profitable corporation. He was proud of his achievement, had earned a fortune, and was not about to be pushed around by reformers who had threatened to hamstring his company with strong regulations. Anti-corporation leaders such as Edward P. Costigan and Ben Lindsey viewed Field with a jaundiced eye and charged that he invested large sums of company money in politicians who would benignly neglect his company's abuses. Mayor Speer was not intimidated by Mr. Field. On numerous occasions Speer told Field that the company must pay for using city property or the people would take matters into their own hands. Ultimately, Field compromised, and in 1912 the directors of the Colorado Telephone Company began returning 2% of their firm's gross income to the city.

Speer's role as a mediator was not always played between the corporations and the anti-corporation citizens. By the early twentieth century business community leaders often fought among themselves, having shed the unity they displayed during those embattled years of the 1860s and 1870s, when survival was everyone's major concern. Once Denver's position as a regional metropolis was secured, members of the business community increasingly disagreed about directions the city should take.

Denver's skyline emerged as an issue in 1908, and Mayor Speer finally put the contestants to rest with a compromise. That year a realty company from the West Coast came into Denver with plans to build a fourteen-story skyscraper. J. Paul Mitchell, in his study "Progressivism in Denver," found that both major newspapers, the *Post* and the *News*, applauded the proposed building because it would update Denver by converting it to a vertical city such as New York. The problem, according to Mitchell, was that an old city ordinance prohibited the construction of buildings over nine floors high. David Moffat, who had already agreed to rent the first floor of the new building, joined the newspapers in the cry for modernization. Opposition came from the Bennett and Myers Realty Company. It owned many downtown buildings and earned high rents (some said exorbitant rents) because of the scarcity of downtown office space. City Art Commissioner Henry Read took the realtors side, not because he cared about rent rates, but because he wanted Denver to keep its horizontal posture for preserving the view of the mountains. E. B. Field opposed the fourteen-story structure for similar reasons. The city council was as divided over the building code as was the business community. Finally Speer brought the opponents together and got all to agree to a twelve-story compromise. This new limit governed Denver for the next half-century. The only exception was the D. and F. tower, which was already under construction.

Speer worked untiringly to make businessmen more sensitive to community needs and to the wishes of each other. Beyond these efforts, though, he used his influence to persuade Denver's wealthiest citizens—the people who had made fortunes in the Queen City—to give some of their riches back to the community that had been so good to them. In his January 1907 address, Speer called for "generous citizens" to become "benefactors." Denver needed a beautification program and it was only right, he argued, for the elite to help pay for the face-lifting. The mayor said that monuments should be raised to outstanding leaders; observation pavilions, fountains, parks, and drives were needed to bring sophistication to the city. He called for philanthropists to build a museum, an art gallery, a horticulture building, and a gateway to the city park. For the next eleven years Speer made the same plea, rephrasing his thoughts in 1909 by saying: "We want the good opinion of our fellowmen while here, and to be kindly remembered after we have passed on. I know of no better way than to cultivate and unfold some blossoms along life's path, add rest stations, play stations and beauty spots along the way. The time will come when men will be judged more by their disbursements than by their accumulations. Denver has been kind to most of us by giving to some health, to some wealth, to some happiness, and to some a combination of all. We can pay a part of this debt by making our city more attractive." Such was Speer's plan for "adding the ornamental at the lowest possible cost."

Most wealthy citizens applauded the concept but did little to bring it to fruition. At first only a few responded with more than promises. Subscriptions from individuals and corporations helped build the Pioneer Monument at Colfax and Broadway, and an outsider, steel king Andrew Carnegie, gave $200,000 toward the Denver Public Library at Colfax and Bannock, plus an additional $80,000 for four branch libraries. Walter S. Cheesman's widow and daughter contributed $100,000 for the observation pavilion in the Congress park which now bears the water baron's name.

In December 1916 the mayor delivered a speech entitled "Give While You Live." This time the idea generated more enthusiasm, perhaps because the mayor could now point to tangible results of this crusade. By the time of his death in 1918, a little over $500,000 was given to the city for beautification purposes, but it was still a modest response considering the money that existed in Denver. An early Speer biographer, Edgar C. McMechen, catalogued the donations in detail. The Stockyards Association built an outdoor swimming pool at Elyria Playgrounds, Joseph A. Thatcher contributed money for a fountain, and John Clarke Mitchell underwrote the Dennis Sullivan gateway to City Park. S.H.P. Voorhies paid for a gate at the Civic Center, as did Joshua Monti. The Junius F. Brown family donated an art collection, and Mrs. Joseph Standly added an annex to the Museum of Natural History. Finlay L. MacFarland contributed the cost of two gateways to the Mountain Parks, and J.K. Mullen and Stephen Knight ordered bronze statues for the Civic Center. Several other benefactors who preferred to remain anonymous gave donations to Speer's beautification program as well.

If the elite's response to Speer's call for sharing the wealth was less than overwhelming, it probably made some of the city's poorer citizens less antagonistic toward "malefactors of great wealth," as they were dubbed by cynical pundits. What impressed the lower economic class most, however, were the specific measures Speer took to prove that his administration was as concerned with the poor as with the rich. He employed uneducated and jobless Mexicans, Russian Jews, and Italians and raised the wages of city laborers to $2.25 a day. A bathhouse and showers were installed in lower downtown so that slum dwellers without such facilities could wash somewhere other than in the river. Speer oversaw the construction of a city bakery during the World War, with the dual purpose of providing low cost bread for the poor and simultaneously putting to work a number of "human wrecks," as McMechan described them. During this time the mayor used city labor to plow vacant lots into victory gardens, and he persuaded the Water Company to provide free irrigation. This was as much a humanitarian program as it was a patriotic endeavor, for it furnished fresh vegetables to many of Denver's poorest families.

Mayor Speer and his wife Kate never had any children of their own, but both of them devoted time and energy to Denver's youth, especially the poor. Speer often maintained that his wife was his ablest political advisor, and her interest in children was reflected in many of the mayor's activities. At his behest, more city money was spent on playgrounds and playground equipment than at any other time in Denver's history, with much of it going into lower economic class neighborhoods. It was Speer who asked the Stockyards Association to build a swimming pool in the immigrant-dominated, working class neighborhood of Elyria; and when the bathhouse and shower installations were being planned, the mayor said he hoped those facilities would become havens for newsboys.

Speer also worked closely with Thomas Uzzell, James Goodheart, and a number of other ministers of the social gospel. Uzzell's "Friendly Shelters" often received a helping hand from the city, as well as personal contributions from Robert and Kate Speer. Jim Goodheart founded the Sunshine Rescue Mission for men, women, and children derelicts, and, like Uzzell, Goodheart found the Speers eager to help the cause. Goodheart always had access to the mayor's office, and he frequently sought the mayor's assistance in pardoning a convicted criminal whom he felt deserved another chance, especially if the malefactor was a young person or a man whose wife and children were destitute because the head of the family was in jail. Speer's commitment to Goodheart and his confidence in the social worker's judgement and success came to fruition in early 1918. Speer created a new office of city chaplin, and he named Goodheart to the post. Goodheart's charge was to make the rounds of the jails, hospitals, and institutions and give spiritual comfort and advice to all who wished such help. If Goodheart found persons in need of welfare, or if he discovered prisoners worthy of pardon, he was to take his recommendations to the mayor. This is precisely what he had been doing since 1904 anyway, but in 1918 Speer wanted the program formalized so that his leniency toward convicted criminals would be less criticized.

Clearly Speer worked as well with the poor as he did with the business elite, yet he never ignored the middle class. Most Denverites fell between the socioeconomic extremes. They had no need of clothing, food, and fuel handouts, and at the same time they controlled no major businesses that could be affected one way or the other by local politics. To this class of people Speer made most of his grandstand plays. Understanding that they wanted services at the lowest possible cost, he continually emphasized the achievements of

Entrance to Jim Goodhart's Sunshine Rescue Mission.
Courtesy Western History Department, Denver Public Library

An interior view of the Sunshine Rescue Mission.
Courtesy Western History Department, Denver Public Library

his administration and boasted how little they cost taxpayers. His public addresses always focused on such issues. During his first term, for example, he pointed with pride to his innovative garbage removal program. Whereas most cities of Denver's size allocated between $20,000 and $50,000 annually for garbage removal, Denver was paying a mere $1,500 because Speer had arranged for the Hog Grower's Association to haul away the trash for only the price of an inspection fee.

In 1909 Speer's administration began publishing and distributing free a small weekly magazine entitled *Municipal Facts*. Although it cost approximately $20,000 a year to print, the mayor justified it as an important vehicle of communication between the government and the taxpayer. Through the pages of *Municipal Facts* the administration gave the people a detailed accounting of where their tax dollars were going, complete with before and after photographs to illustrate his beautification programs. The magazine complemented Speer's many speeches, as it was designed to convince citizens that never before were so many extensions of services and new programs provided for so little money. The magazine advertised several "clean-up" and "paint-up" campaigns in which home owners were encouraged to dress up their houses and yards to make the city more attractive. The government, too, was doing its part in making Denver sparkle. City streets received a scrubbing daily, and sidewalks were washed three times a week. The mayor even presided over a parade in which all the street cleaning equipment and crews were put on review.

With unabashed pride, the city leader celebrated each physical improvement made by his administration. Every street and alley that was paved and each mile of storm and sanitary sewer that was opened was reported and mapped like the progress of a victorious army. The greatest hoopla was reserved for monumental construction projects such as the public library, the Museum of Natural History in City Park, the second lake in Washington Park, the Welcome Arch in front of the railroad station, and the ambitious park and boulevard system.

With much fanfare, Speer brought urban planner George E. Kessler to Denver as a consultant. Kessler had brought international attention to Kansas City, Missouri, for the park and boulevard system he unveiled there. This German-born expert on the city beautiful helped Speer's administration bring order and function to Denver's beautification program. Under Speer four park districts were created, and the system of parks was increased to embrace over 1,183 acres. Consisting of only 572.6 acres when he took office. Speer more than doubled Denver's park acreage and spent over $1.5 million on improvements. With Kessler's help a boulevard and parkway system was designed. Speer Boulevard was constructed along Cherry Creek, complete with concrete walls for beautification and flood control. Marian Street Parkway was built, too, and that project involved buttressing, terracing, and reinforcing the City Ditch. Ultimately, two beautifully landscaped parks (Cheesman and Washington) were connected by a functional and beautiful green roadway, and the city had a boulevard and parkway system of eighteen miles for Sunday strolling, bicycling, and touring.

Not all of Speer's ideas for beautifying Denver came from George E. Kessler. In 1911 Speer toured several European cities as a guest of the Boston Chamber of Commerce. Among the many mayors who made the trip to study European cities, Speer, according to nationally known reformer Lincoln Steffens, studied more and learned the most. It was in the urban showplaces of Europe that Denver's mayor found inspiration for many of his planning ideas, and he did his utmost to apply them to Colorado's Queen City.

148

In Speer's quest to find ways to serve all of Denver's interest groups—to prove that he was neither owned nor controlled by any interest or faction—he continually offered the olive branch to his opponents. Making peace with Denver's so called "reform element," however, was no easy task. A difficulty inherent in dealing with Denver's early twentieth-century, self-styled reformers, led by Judge Ben Lindsey, lawyer Edward P. Costigan, journalist George Creel, city attorney and later mayor Henry Arnold, social worker Josephine Roche, and *Rocky Mountain News* owner Thomas Patterson, stemmed from their lack of unity and purpose. A letter to Costigan in 1910, cited in Roland De Lorme's dissertation, summed up the problem: "We are a queer set. The man that is willing to fight the Water Company . . . will strenuously object to enforcing the same rule against the Gas Company, the Telephone Company, or the Electric Company. Some peculiar ties hold the most of us from being more than one-fourth sincere in our pretension. . . ."

This motley group had one aim in common after 1904, according to George Creel, and that "was to kick out Mayor Bob Speer." From there, however, the similarities ended. One of the central figures who hoped to oust Speer was southern-born and Harvard-educated Edward P. Costigan. A flamboyant young man who had practiced law in Utah before going to Denver in 1899, Costigan was an eloquent speaker, a dapper dresser, and a possessor of charm and wit. One of the most selfless and sincere of all the anti-Speer forces, he viewed Denver as only one battleground in a larger war. From his first days in Denver he became convinced that large corporations controlled not only Denver but all of Colorado, and they did so at the expense of the majority of citizens. Hoping to wrest the political control away from the mine and smelter owners, the utilities corporations, railroads, and banks, he wanted to see the interests of farmers and laborers represented in government.

To Costigan's view, the masses in Colorado were represented in neither the state nor national governments. He believed that the economic elite controlled the state assembly, protected their own interests there, and used that body to send partisans of the rich and well-placed to the United States Senate. Certainly there was ample evidence to support the Costigan viewpoint. With the exception of Thomas Patterson, who served in the United States Senate from 1901 to 1907, Colorado's legislature during the late nineteenth and early twentieth centuries had secured places in the Senate for a number of friends of big business. Edward O. Wolcott, for example, was a singularly undistinguished lawyer whose only claim to the office

149

Edward P. Costigan.
Courtesy Western History Department, Denver Public Library

seemed to come from being Henry Roger Wolcott's brother. Never distinguishing himself in Washington, Senator Wolcott attracted the most attention for being a big plunger at gambling casinos. Symbolically, he died at Monte Carlo.

The legislature's selection of Simon Guggenheim in 1906 was more evidence of the greedy "Beast," as Lindsey dubbed the capitalists, at work. Only forty years old when he was elected to the Senate, Guggenheim symbolized the advantages of great wealth. Born into the fabulously rich, smelting and refining Pennsylvania Guggenheim family, the strikingly handsome, dark-haired and dark-eyed young man was well-schooled and well-travelled before the family placed him in charge of its Colorado enterprises. Young Guggenheim went to Colorado in 1889, and local newspaper reporters followed his social life as much as his business endeavors. When he married Olga Hirsh of New York City in 1898, a combination of jealous and admiring eyes devoured the news of the wedding, officiated by Denver's Rabbi William S. Friedman, and the reception in New York's Waldorf-Astoria Hotel.

While Guggenheim was serving Coloradans in Washington, the state assembly did the unforgivable, by the standards of Costigan's followers, when it elevated Charles J. Hughes, Jr. to the Senate. Recognized by virtually everyone in Colorado as the state's most brilliant attorney, Hughes was nevertheless inextricably identified with the corporations. He had represented David Moffat and the First National Bank since 1894. Furthermore, his clients numbered among Colorado's most influential business organizations, among them the Tramway Company, the Denver Union Water Company, Coors, several sugar beet refineries, and the Union Pacific. Beyond this, Hughes had successfully defended the Tramway Company in numerous personal injury cases, and he had found tax loopholes (legal, but unpopular) for the utilities companies.

Such were the interests Costigan fought, and he never wavered from his position. Indeed, when he had an excellent chance to be elected governor in 1914, "he lost it deliberately," said George Creel, "by his defense of the striking coal miners" in the Trinidad-Ludlow region. Typically, the Bull Moose Republican supported Woodrow Wilson in 1916 rather than cast his lot with his own party's darling of the corporations, Charles Evans Hughes. Largely because of his consistent refusal to compromise with the business interests in his party, Costigan's ambitions for public office were not realized until he was elected to the Senate in 1930.

Motivated differently was Ben Lindsey. Deferred to by most Denver reform-crusaders as their leader (because of his international reputation), Lindsey was a puzzle of contradictions. During his years as Judge of the County Court (1900-1907), and then Judge of the Juvenile and Family Court (1907-1927), he devoted incredible energy to working with juveniles. In 1899 he wrote the legislation creating a juvenile court. A model of its kind, it attracted attention throughout the United States and in other parts of the world, as hundreds of social workers hoped to adopt his innovation of treating juvenile offenders as juveniles—not as adults. Thanks to Lindsey's efforts, separate courts were established for children. When they were incarcerated for crimes, they were confined in institutions separate from adults, and the emphasis was on rehabilitation rather than mere punishment.

Lindsey's own correspondence shows that when juvenile reform was his highest priority, he found working with Mayor Speer a decided advantage. Speer was eager to help facilitate Lindsey's plans. The mayor listened to the judge's appeals and then followed up with money for swimming pools, playgrounds, and recreation centers. Speer instructed the police department to cooperate with Lindsey on matters involving the young offenders. When Lindsey organized the Juvenile Improvement Association in 1903—an organization designed to get youngsters involved in wholesome activities and find them decent employment—he found Mayor Speer a frequent and generous contributor. The broker-politician not only put his own money into the association, he used his influence to get Ed Chase and Vaso Chucovich to make sizeable donations as well.

Judge Lindsey did not shy away from taking money from Chase and Chucovich, and he never hesitated to call upon the mayor for help in expediting juvenile programs. Lindsey solicited and received large contributions from Lawrence Phipps, Walter S. Cheesman, and the Denver Union Water Company. At the same time, he used a contact inside the Gas Company to find jobs with that corporation for some of his waifs; and the judge accepted free passes for several years from the Denver and Rio Grande and Colorado and Southern railways so that he could cut traveling expenses while making speeches all over the country. As late as 1906 he was complimenting Speer, and in 1907 he was still recommending Charles J. Hughes, Jr. to people who wrote to him asking for the name of a good lawyer.

Surely the "Kids' Judge" found as much support for his programs for minors from Denver's political and business elite as he

George Creel.
Courtesy Western History Department, Denver Public Library

could have wanted. Little wonder then that these one-time supporters reeled in anger and dismay when he launched a major writing campaign against them in 1908. That year, through the aid of Lincoln Steffens, Lindsey published a series of attacks in *Everybody's Magazine* against Denver and its political and business leaders. Two years later the essays were published in book form and titled *The Beast*. Precisely what prompted the little man—he was five feet five inches tall and weighed 100 pounds—to tackle the entire power structure he had worked with so well before is uncertain. His ablest biographer, Frances Anne Huber, argues that he finally recognized that the alliance between big corporations and politicians was responsible for the juvenile problem; that his reform efforts for children were meaningless as long as "the Beast" remained in control. In short, he awakened to Costigan's position about a decade after the liberal Republican had seen the light.

More critical and cynical observers believed that Lindsey never recovered from a nervous breakdown which he suffered in winter 1905. Other pseudo-psychologists insist that he had a Napolean-like complex stemming from his deprived childhood and small physique. Subconsciously he had to take on new challenges once his juvenile court and improvement association ideas were institutionalized. It is true that he insisted on running for governor in 1906 despite the fact that his party (Democratic) refused him the nomination. His Independent ticket failed miserably, and then he began spending more and more time at his typewriter attacking those who were more successful in politics.

Whatever caused Lindsey's metamorphosis, it was sufficient to place him permanently into the anti-corporation and anti-Speer camp. There he became a colleague of Costigan and several others who were determined to destroy "the Big Mitt," which was George Creel's name for Lindsey's "Beast." Creel went to Denver just in time to further his career and reputation as a "voice of the people" in cities ridden with tainted politicians. Born and raised in Missouri, he began a journalism career in Kansas City. Working for the avidly Republican *Kansas City Star*, he devoted much of his time to disparaging the growing Democratic organization led by James Pendergast. From there he went to declare war on Cincinnati's George Cox. Although he admitted that "Cox made Jim Pendergast and the Denver gang look like baby-faced amateurs," he joined Senator Thomas Patterson's *News* and used it as a vehicle to barrage Speer and his supporters as if they were worse than Cox and Pendergast combined.

Josephine Roche

Close to Lindsey, Costigan, and Creel was Josephine Roche. The daughter of the wealthy owner of Rocky Mountain Fuel Company, she graduated from Vassar in 1908 and earned a master's degree at Columbia University in 1910. A repentant noblewoman, she went to Denver after doing social work in New York. She threw her lot with Lindsey and Costigan by organizing women voters against Speer and worked to root out prostitution in her spare time.

Rather quickly, the leaders of the anti-Speer movement pulled together a sizeable following. Eventually a loosely knit coterie of dissatisfied persons—each with their own little crusade in mind—grew convinced that if Speer could be removed, God would be in His heaven and all would be right in the world, or at least in Denver.

People who wanted municipally owned utilities climbed on the bandwagon, as did those who frowned upon saloons and houses of ill fame, which Speer segregated and protected. The Women's Christian Temperance Union and the Anti-Saloon League entered the parade, alongside a host of fundamentalist Protestant ministers who were tired of seeing compromises with Satan. Pastors of Denver's larger churches, especially those patronized by the social elite, refused to support the union; and the movement found little encouragement from local Catholics or Jews. "Only Father O'Ryan and Rabbi Kauvar," said Creel, "gave us pulpit support." A local taxpayers' association became convinced that their taxes would be reduced if Speer quit spreading so much money on his "propaganda" magazine and sundry beautification programs; and the women's Civic Federation was certain that Denver could be run more efficiently if "professional politicians" were removed from public office.

Robert Speer's removal—the panacea for Denver's ills—came more quickly and easily than most members of this strange coalition expected. When Speer's city attorney, Henry Arnold, went over to these forces, Speer saw no alternative but to refuse to seek re-election in 1912. Henry Arnold charged that the public service corporations were paying far too little in taxes, while small home owners were being over taxed. Unilaterally, he reassessed the properties of the utilities corporations and reduced from the budget $650,000 in home owners' taxes which he said had been added "secretly" by Speer. The mayor denied the charges and fired Arnold. In doing so, however, he allowed Creel and other journalists to martyr the city attorney. Speer's impetuosity raised serious questions about his integrity, and left him no sensible alternative but to retire. Elated by this unexpected event, the victorious reformers rallied behind Henry Arnold and elected him mayor in 1912.

What ensued for Denver was four years of chaos. Lofty idealism turned into abject failure. Mayor Arnold was inundated with demands for the 2,100 city jobs at his disposal. Each of the groups which backed him argued that they had first priority, and after the appointments were made, few supporters were happy. In quest of greater economy, Arnold stopped publication of *Municipal Facts* and took the axe to city-funded programs. Judge Lindsey, who had demanded more efficiency at city hall, was one of the first to scream when some of his pet projects were redlined by the new champion of efficient government.

The anti-Speer victors learned that they disagreed over many other issues besides the city funds and job allocations. One faction

156

demanded the closing of all saloons, while cooler heads counseled strict enforcement of the Sunday closing law. Some of the same moralists who hoped to turn Denver into a dry city also wanted every prostitute rounded up and jailed, while others urged gradual shutdowns in the red-light district accompanied by medical examinations, hospitalization where necessary, as well as some kind of rehabilitation program for the "soiled ones."

One social worker was appalled by the war on the red-light, or "crib" district. "I am greatly distressed about the order against the cribs on Market St. . . . Where can they go?" George Creel and Josephine Roche had the answer. They herded the women off to jail, forcing them to submit to medical examinations and treatment when prescribed. Then they organized a committee to send the tainted ladies back to their homes if they had relatives or friends outside of Denver, or place them in family custody if their homes were in Denver. The women who either had no family or refused to admit it were then turned over to another group of moral legislators who assumed the responsibility of finding "manual" occupations for the fallen unfortunates.

Denver's new leadership had still other divisive issues with which to contend. They grew embittered toward each other over the national election in 1912. Some backed Theodore Roosevelt and others rallied behind Woodrow Wilson. When one faction mobilized to "*re*-form" Denver's government, there was no agreement on whether that was a good idea, let alone who the new commissioners should be. In the meantime, Mayor Arnold fell out with George Creel over saloon regulations, and he fired Josephine Roche from the police department. She had been assigned there to help solve the prostitution problem, and she and Arnold disagreed over policy. This power struggle culminated with Arnold and his followers opposing the new commission-government charter, and with Lindsey, Creel, and Roche leading the backers of a second panacea for the Queen City.

Despite the fact that the *Post*, the *Times*, and the *Republican* fought the charter movement, it carried the city by a three-to-one majority in February 1913. One reason for its overwhelming success at the polls was the disclosure that Mayor Arnold's budget saved Denver only $13,000 even after he cut welfare programs and abolished the $20,000 a year for *Municipal Facts*. Thus, in June 1913 a five-man commission replaced the reform mayor and his court. They had lasted only one year.

The charter victory and subsequent election of a commission

government was the last gasp of a reform movement that was hopelessly divided before it took over city hall. With Speer out of office, the only unifying issue was gone. Political infighting consumed valuable time and energy that should have been spent on city services. The final blow came when the leadership disappeared. In 1913 George Creel packed his bags and moved to New York, and crusading Thomas Patterson sold the *News*. Ed Costigan turned his attention to the gubernatorial election in 1914, and when the war broke out in Europe, Josephine Roche was called to Washington, D.C. to organize a foreign language service bureau. Only Lindsey and Arnold remained, and they were not even speaking to each other.

Without leaders and without Speer for a whipping boy, commission government carried Denver aimlessly along until 1916. By that time many one-time idealists had their fill of "reform" government which saved very little money, left the city more embattled and disorganized than it had been in 1904, and did not even keep streets and sidewalks clean in the summer or the snow cleared in the winter. Not surprisingly, many of Robert Speer's opponents joined his loyal supporters in 1916. They repealed the commission form of government and reinstated the able manager to his old office.

Mayor Speer had only two more years to pursue his broker-style politics. During that time he planted thousands of trees, advanced his Civic Center project, and opened the path to an imaginative mountain park system. On the afternoon of May 13, 1918 he left his office feeling ill. He died of pneumonia the following day.

Thousands of mourners filled the Civic Auditorium and lined the streets outside on the day of his funeral. Not since the Democratic National Convention a decade before had so many people congregated there. In retrospect, most of Denver's citizens seemed to agree that the remarkable thing about Robert Speer was not that he failed to transform Denver into a utopia, but that he enabled the city to survive and made it a more attractive community in the process.

The era of Robert Speer did not really end in 1918. A strong leader leaves momentum in his wake which cannot be throttled with last rites. His two successors, W.F.R. Mills and Dewey C. Bailey, were unimaginative mayors, and they allowed the city to function on the fading energy created by the Speer administrative bureaucracy. The year 1923 more accurately symbolizes the end of Speer's Denver. That year the Civic Center he inspired was constructed, and a new leader with an energetic and enthusiastic view toward the future, Benjamin F. Stapleton, was sworn in as mayor.

Chapter 6

The Denver that Robert Speer dominated for two decades offered a quality of life superior to anything up to that time in the city's history. To be sure some old problems lingered. Smog, for example, continued to plague Denver during the early twentieth century. Although the automobile was not yet a major factor in air pollution, extended use of coal for home heating and industrial energy left the Queen City blanketed in a gray haze each time the weather bureau announced a thermal inversion. Persistent efforts by the Chamber of Commerce to encourage energy conservation as a way to abate smoke proved ineffective, as did a weak smoke abatement ordinance passed by the city council in 1911. Indeed, by 1921 the Chamber of Commerce was still pointing to the irritating smoke with horror, but little beyond discussion of the problem came from the campaign. As long as most citizens agreed with Speer and the business community that population and industrial expansion were desirable, no relief was in sight.

Along other fronts Denver adjusted well, even progressed, in the struggle to improve quality of life amidst prodigious growth. The city bought the water company in 1918, and other natural monopolies were forced to be more sensitive to the people they served. The Tramway Company, railroads, and private citizens made financial contributions to Speer's city beautiful and functional movement. These resources, combined with tax dollars, helped make Denver one of the showplaces of urban America. Denver had received applause from national circulation magazines in the late nineteenth century, but these articles always focused on the offices and homes of the elite. Unattractive and decadent sides of the urban center were ignored or glossed over, leaving readers with a distorted image of the city.

159

Denver's smog problem about 1920

During the Speer era, nationally circulated magazines directed toward city planners, engineers, and architects noticed Denver for the first time. Journals such as *Architectural Record* and *The American City* published numerous pieces on Colorado's largest city, describing with praise and detail the park and boulevard system, the Auditorium and Civic Center, street paving innovations, fountains, and the civic benefactor approach to beautification.

Speer's physical innovations did more than attract the attention of urban planners. Truly the city beautiful program was an aesthetic achievement rivaled by few American cities, but it went much farther. To Speer's mind the city beautiful was not simply another art gallery where people gazed upon but never touched the treasures. While such emotional and psychological stimulation was important, people needed places to find physical involvement as well. While Speer's predecessors did spend money to improve parks by planting grass, shrubbery, and trees, they told people to remain spectators by placing "Keep Off The Grass" signs on every tempting lawn. Speer doubled the park acreage, covered them with recreational equipment, removed the no-trespassing signs, and circled the Washington Park lakes with sand for beaches. Denverites were encouraged to use their recreational areas—not merely look at them.

Denver's citizens had other free entertainment besides playground and outdoor bathing facilities. The Tramway Company paid for the City Band and several touring bands to play in Denver's parks on weekends. The company polished its image while underwriting these outdoor concerts, but it also increased company revenues by filling its railway cars with passengers going to and from the festivals. For the price of a tramway ticket, budget watchers could take in free concerts and low-cost entertainment at Elitch Gardens. Located in northwestern Denver in what had been the township of Highland, the Gardens comprised about seventeen acres of flowers, trees, and orchards, complete with a zoo, theater, miniature railroad, and steam-powered carousel. John and Mary Elitch established the outdoor park in 1890. The following year John Elitch died, leaving his widow to manage the entertainment center alone. For nearly a decade she maintained the Gardens with the aid of her assistant, Thomas Long. She and Long married in 1900, but he died soon after, leaving her alone again to manage the programs. Until World War I the cultured, creative, and dedicated Mary Elitch Long offered her programs to Denver's citizens at the lowest possible cost, with many concerts and children's programs open free to the public. She was more concerned with providing quality entertainment than she was

Mary Elitch

with making a profit. Sadly, she was forced to sell the Gardens in 1916 to meet outstanding debts.

Mary Elitch Long's contribution to Denver was outstanding. Not only did she provide entertainment for the masses, she played a significant role in keeping classical music and light opera alive in Denver during the early twentieth century. Grand and light opera was routine fare for Denverites in the 1890s. Horace Tabor's Opera House and The Broadway at Eighteenth and Broadway regularly featured outstanding productions during those years. These houses attracted the foremost traveling companies from the eastern theater syndicates. The depression, however, worked havoc with the arts in the same way it destroyed banks and businesses. Horace Tabor lost the opera house in 1896, and The Broadway went bankrupt as well. According to Sanford Linscome, the eastern syndicates bypassed ailing Denver, leaving grand opera nothing but a memory in the new century. Only the determination of Mary Elitch Long kept light opera in Denver. She employed Italian-born Raffaelo Cavallo to conduct classical concerts and light opera. Mrs. Long helped keep the tradition alive because, added to the troubles at the Tabor and The Broadway, Denver's tastes were turning to light musicals.

Without such persons as Mary Elitch Long and a number of immigrant groups, Denver would have been deprived of an important cultural dimension. Between 1900 and the years immediately following the war, Mary Long, Henry Housley, and several dedicated German, Italian, and Swedish music lovers enriched the entertainment fare of musicals, marching bands, and ragtime. Henry Housley promoted a symphony orchestra in 1900, but the effort failed. Then, in 1903 a trio of Germans, Fritz Thies, Frederick Schweikler and Cordelia Smissort formed the Symphony Orchestra Association. Raffaelo Cavallo conducted the symphony for a time and was followed by Horace Tureman, and later by Henry Housley. The German and Italian communities patronized the new association, but in 1908, when it fell into financial difficulty and the leadership appealed to the public for subscriptions to establish a permanent orchestra fund, only thirty-five men contributed. Sanford Linscome found that only one man save the promoters "gave a dollar without being urged, solicited and sought again and again." *The Denver Post* in 1906 was correct when it editorialized that ". . . we in Denver are in the musical elementary stage."

Linscome's significant study, "A History of Musical Development in Denver, Colorado, 1858-1908," shows that sophisticated music almost ceased to be available in the early twentieth century.

162

Except for performances at Elitch Gardens, the productions of the Swedish Orpheus Society, and the chamber music quartets which played in the private homes of German immigrants on a regular basis between 1884 and 1921, there would have been few people to keep the classical musical tradition alive, especially after the symphony fund drive failed in 1908.

Classical music may have been in trouble, but other signs indicated that Denver was adjusting well to growth pains. Educating the youth had been high on the priority list from Denver's founding days, and public schools were provided even before Auraria and Denver consolidated. The power elite took more than a casual interest in public education during the early boom years. In the 1870s key members of the decision-making community, David Moffat and Roger Woodbury, served on the school board. Henry R. Wolcott, who was active in promoting private educational institutions, also took an interest in public schools. He established a prize for the outstanding public reader among female high school students, and Roger Woodbury established a public speaking prize that was open to both boys and girls.

By 1900 Denver had twelve school districts which derived most of their income from property taxes assessed by district. Already in 1900 historian Jerome C. Smiley alerted local citizens to the dangers of the property tax system. "The worst feature of the system," he wrote in his *History of Denver*, "is that it prevents an equitable per capita distribution of the city's school taxes." District Number One, which embraced half of Denver's taxable property, was located in the center of the city. Property holders in the area were assessed about one-sixth as much as those in outlying districts. Residents in sparsely populated sections of the city carried a much heavier tax burden to keep their districts up to par with Number One, and, as Smiley concluded, "it is difficult to discern sound reasons for perpetuating a system so inequitable, and which appears to be the one conspicuous defect in our most admirable educational structure."

Growth over the next twenty years broadened the tax base in outlying districts. Still, inequities remained. The problem was particularly acute in areas that needed new facilities. In 1918 the Chamber of Commerce entered what had become a city-wide debate on school funding. Chamber leaders proposed special city-wide bond issues for school construction, with the school board distributing the money in whichever districts displayed the greatest needs. In 1919 a $2 million school construction bond issue was endorsed by Denver voters, and for a time, at least, the construction problem was solved equitably.

Denver was not only providing adequate schooling for its youth, but classes in elementary and secondary education were offered at night for adults. The Longfellow Elementary School and Manual Training High School were accommodating over 1,200 diploma-seeking adults by 1915. Besides these adult education facilities, a few churches were offering classes in English and American government to help the foreign-born qualify for naturalization. Such classes notwithstanding, a Denver public school teacher was convinced that educational opportunities for the poor were entirely too limited.

Emily Griffith, a petite woman with large, melancholy eyes, pursed lips, and titanic idealism and energy, set out in 1915 to revolutionize traditional attitudes toward public education. Born in Ohio in 1880, Emily Griffith never married and spent most of her life in education. She taught in a rural Nebraska school when she was only fourteen and moved to Denver in 1895. For twenty years she taught elementary grades in the Queen City's public schools, until she assumed the office of principal at the Opportunity School in 1915.

Emily Griffith

Opportunity School was her own idea. It was not only unique in Denver, it was a pioneer effort without precedent anywhere in the United States. Sometime before 1915 Miss Griffith came to believe that vocational and academic offerings should be available to people of all ages during both day and night. Adults and working children, she felt, should have access to programs whenever they had time free from home or work. If only given the opportunity to improve themselves—to prepare for occupations or life in general without the pressures of fees, restricted hours, or grades—more citizens could find success, security, and fulfillment.

Miss Griffith's proposal did not come to fruition without opposition. Some school officials argued that adult education should be offered only at night and that those who wanted vocational training could find it in local barber colleges and automobile mechanic shops. Other opponents believed that the public school system should only be in the diploma granting business, that helping citizens learn a single trade was not its function. But Emily Griffith disagreed. With the enthusiastic support of newspaper reporters and journalists, especially those with *The Post*, her program was endorsed by the school board in 1915.

The old Longfellow school was renovated for the purpose, and in 1916 the Opportunity School opened its doors. During the first year, nearly 2,400 students enrolled. They were served by thirty-eight faculty members. Blacks and whites, men and women, native and foreign born, of all ages, went to Opportunity School. There they pursued, free of charge, the classes that would meet their needs and schedules. There were beginning level classes in English and arithmetic, as well as typing, bookkeeping, sewing, and drawing. Courses in carpentry, auto mechanics, sheet metal work, radio operation and repair, as well as nursing and fashion design provided a wide variety of choices for those seeking career alternatives. Foreign-born students enrolled in English and civics classes, and everyone had access to a free bowl of soup prepared by Miss Griffith and her aides. Over the years, hundreds of former Opportunity School pupils gave testimony to the help they received from the program. Some found jobs for the first time thanks to knowledge gained there; others earned promotions or started enjoyable careers because of skills acquired at the Griffith school.

During World War I, Opportunity School took on new importance. Young men were trained in short courses to do specialized tasks in the army, and women destined for Europe learned to drive and maintain ambulances. Women who remained on the home front acquired skills in vocations such as auto mechanics and electronics, which had always been the privileged domain of men. After the war, returning veterans flocked to Opportunity School to learn new trades as they took their places in the peacetime economy, and wounded veterans prepared for occupations that they could handle with permanent disabilities.

In 1933 Emily Griffith retired, and the school was renamed in her honor. By the date of her retirement, the newly christened Emily Griffith Opportunity School was in larger quarters. It had served over 100,000 students and distinguished itself as a successful, innovative facility where children and adults, both retarded and normal, were taught in one institution.

Emily Griffith did not labor alone to make Opportunity School successful. The late Elinor Bluemel, who wrote a history of the school, said that the Tramway Company gave the school free advertising on its cars, local businesses cooperated by hiring students, and persons with useful skills donated their time as instructors. Scores of unnamed citizens contributed time and money to the school, and one generous woman saw that a piece of meat was delivered to the school kitchen daily so that the free soup kettle would contain a more nourishing fare.

That Denver's unfortunates found the city more hospitable in the early twentieth century was apparent in still other ways. Judge Ben Lindsey not only inspired legislation for a juvenile court and oversaw the development of a more humane system of corrections for minors, he made Denver a better place for working youth. During those years few people questioned the need for some children to work. Many poor families, especially among the first-generation immigrants, wanted their offspring to share in the task of providing for those in the family who were too young, too old, or too ill to work. And then there were the homeless children. Some were cared for in orphanages, but the directors of those institutions assumed that anyone over twelve or thirteen years old should share the responsibility of paying for his or her sustenance. Sensitive social workers hoped to find safe employment for adolescents and at the same time provide them with decent living quarters. With the support of politicians, Lindsey improved the child labor law in Colorado. Although child labor was not abolished—few assumed that it should be—working conditions were improved.

Lindsey and his supporters were particularly concerned about the problems connected with work in the mines, smelters, and mills. In the late nineteenth century a weak bill was enacted which made it a

Judge Benjamin B. Lindsey on the far left with several boys
in the Juvenile Court.

A group of children at a day nursery

misdemeanor for someone to employ anyone under fourteen years old in mines and mills. The maximum penalty was only fifty dollars. With this ridiculous law, factory and mine owners continued to employ youngsters, working them long hours for wages considerably less than they would have to pay adults. In 1903 a new bill, drawn up by Lindsey and several social workers, became law. The new legislation made the president of an offending company responsible for hiring children under fourteen. Conviction carried a penalty of ninety days in jail. Three years after the bill's passage, Lindsey was so pleased with the results that he wrote to Lincoln Steffens, "I think today we have as satisfactory conditions with reference to child labor in Denver as in any city in the Union."

Lindsey's efforts did more than get children out of dangerous jobs. His new court system was more effective in rehabilitation than the old system, and the Juvenile Improvement Association did much to steer Denver's youth away from crime. The Improvement Association received support from Speer, the police, real estate companies, and the school board. Concerted efforts were made to give indigent youth wholesome food and lodging, places to play, and safe employment. In 1917 Lindsey wrote a letter to Speer summarizing the effects of Denver's juvenile programs:

> Through the co-operative work with the police department, real estate agents and others we are able to save thousands of dollars annually which would otherwise be lost by depredations on property by young boys and gangs which in every city are furnishing one of its biggest problems.
>
> We are also in touch with every school in Denver and have to deal directly or indirectly with Denver's fifty thousand children . . . offenses have been decreased several hundred per cent during recent years through this co-operation. . . . It means a savings of several thousand dollars in property to our citizens, to say nothing of the great help to the boys and girls which cannot be estimated in money.

While significant progress was made in child welfare, the larger problem of aiding the poor was far from solved. For many years the growing numbers of needy had haunted sensitive citizens. County and local government appropriations helped, but even their efforts, combined with tax dollars, left many deserving poor unaided. In the past, well-meaning citizens and social workers tried to solve the problem by purchasing one-way train tickets for indigents. Pushing the problem off on another town seemed to be the most practical solution. Sending paupers back to their home communities, of course, solved only a small part of the problem. Hundreds of indigents had no place to return to, scores were too ill to travel, and many children were too young to turn out on their own. Furthermore, throngs of newcomers arrived daily in response to pleas of booster propaganda. Some newcomers had money to tide them over for awhile, some had skills which enabled them to get into the job market without difficulty. Others, though, brought nothing but faith in the promise of American life or hope that Colorado's highly touted, salubrious climate would work miracles on their health.

Religious leaders took the lead in raising private funds for charity in the late nineteenth century. In 1887 the Reverend Myron W. Reed and Frances Wisebart Jacobs joined two clergymen from London, Father William J. O'Ryan and Dean H. Martyn Hart, in trying a centralized charity organization which had been tested in Liverpool years earlier. The plan was to have one central body collect a single donation from businesses and individuals and then distribute the receipts to all independent charity organizations. This program was designed to make disbursements more efficient and make it more convenient for donors who were usually solicited by over a dozen separate organizations.

During the first year, the Charity Organization Society raised $21,700. The next few years were equally good. The depression, however, left the society almost moribund. Despite efforts to revive it during the next few years—the name was even changed in 1913 to the Denver Federation for Charity and Philanthropy in hopes of creating new community interest—support was disappointing. Between 1913 and 1917 federation spokesmen claimed that funds were only half of what was needed. Community interest was at an all-time low.

Had it not been for the $10,000 annual appropriation from the city council, and for the food and lodging coupon program instituted by Robert Speer, social workers would have been helpless. Finally, the year that the United States entered the World War, federation leaders went outside of Denver for help in revitalizing their program. In Erie, Pennsylvania, they found Gary T. Justis. He had innovated the "campaign" approach to charity fund raising. Mr. Justis went to Denver in 1917 and turned the Denver Federation for Charity and Philanthropy into a dynamic, successful organization. Prior to Justis' arrival, the federation had only three full-time, paid staff members. The other workers were volunteers. The task of the old staff, as they envisioned it, was simply to go out into the city, raise as much money as possible, and allocate resources on an equitable basis. Justis argued that he needed a much larger professional staff. Their charge would be to make a survey for defining specific needs and estimating costs as precisely as possible. The federation then would run an annual campaign to raise the money to meet those estimated costs.

With the freedom to handle the federation as he saw fit, the experienced social worker and fund raiser put his plan (which had worked well in Erie) into motion. New staff members were hired, surveys were taken, and a major fund-raising drive was held. Justis published and circulated pamphlets that outlined welfare programs and listed all contributors by name, including the amount of their contribution. Justis' tactics were eminently successful. In 1922 the organization was renamed the Community Chest. Although no previous organization had collected and disbursed so much money, some of the welfare recipients and social workers felt that the personal touch was disappearing from welfare—that the impersonality of the large umbrella system was obliterating what little human interaction had existed between the classes.

Margaret Evans Davis (the daughter of William Gray Evans) remembered that although her mother's generation actively worked to abolish poverty, once the Charity Organization Society was formed personal involvement by the upper economic class ended. Whereas it had been "the thing to do" for socially prominent women to collect clothing and raise funds for the poor, organized charity took over the function, leaving wealthy women in philanthropy nothing to do but write checks. Consequently, young women of position studied languages and music in Paris or Dresden or went on the grand tour in Europe. There was no way to follow in the benevolent footsteps of their mothers.

The Justis program might have contributed to impersonality in welfare, but the trend was well under way several years before he went to Denver. In any case, the benefits from his approach to altruism offset most liabilities. An outstanding achievement of Justis' program was that blacks were included. The early years of the new century brought no outpouring of concern for minorities. The Charity Organization Society allowed black philanthropic institutions to collapse. For the most part, blacks were left to care for their own, with a few white churches occasionally coming to their aid. In 1910, for example, the Church of Brethren organized an Industrial and Mission Training School for blacks in Denver. Once in awhile, whites would support the enterprise with donations for tents and equipment.

When Gary Justis took over the charity federation, black charities were welcomed for the first time. This brought relief to one community that was never affluent enough to properly care for its own welfare needs. In the years prior to Justis' arrival in Colorado, blacks found no substantive support from any white group except Robert Speer's political organization. They received food and lodging coupons from the white politician, and he saw to it that blacks were given a fair share of city jobs. Indeed, the black's Republican weekly, *The Statesman,* editorialized that "Speer had made it possible for Denver negroes to show the largest number of employees in the Fire and Police Departments yet in the history of the city . . . we take increasing delight in commending [Speer's administration as it continues] . . . to show . . . fairness toward us."

Blacks usually voted for the party of Lincoln and Reconstruction, but when Speer ran for office, they crossed party lines and supported the local Democrat. Their loyalty to him is understandable in light of his determination to disburse welfare and the spoils of victory and of his refusal to join in the chorus of other civic leaders who continually urged blacks to leave the city. The *Denver Post* frequently counseled them to leave Denver and form their own ethnic colonies in eastern Colorado. Occasionally the *Rocky Mountain News* offered similar gratuitous advice, as did Simon Guggenheim, John Shafroth, Julius Gunter, Elias Ammons, and William E. Sweet.

The white press and party leaders were not alone in seeing black farming communities as a solution to the black search for economic opportunity. Many blacks themselves, especially those who were inspired by Booker T. Washington, saw colonization as a chance to become self-sufficient and prove their worth to whites. In the late nineeenth century black communities were founded in Kansas and Mississippi as survivors of slavery and black codes moved from the Deep South to make a new life outside white-controlled environments. Historian Margaret Picher has done pioneer research on this subject. Her findings show that as early as 1905 the Colorado Negro Business League was raising money and making plans for an agricultural colony in the mountain state. Leading white Republicans, among them Guggenheim and General William Palmer, supported this businessmen's movement, hoping, no doubt, to keep these men loyal to the G.O.P. and at the same time encourage them to segregate themselves and thereby avoid embarrassing squabbles over integration.

171

Ultimately, according to Picher, blatant Republican endorsement of the project led to dissension within the Negro Business League. The 1905 plan failed, and a black Democrat, Oliver T. Jackson, ventured out on his own to found the Dearfield community in Weld County. For almost a decade and a half after 1910, Jackson attracted settlers to Dearfield from states east of Colorado, and he persuaded some families from inside the state to join him. Denver blacks, however, viewed the experiment in segregated, rural self-sufficiency with something less than enthusiasm.

The various attitudes of Denver's blacks toward Oliver Jackson's agrarian dream reveal much about the people's aspirations and about social and economic conditions in black Denver. Only a few moved to Dearfield. That most people held this view is not surprising given the quality of life in the city. Blacks were not finding openings equal to those available to non-blacks, but there were just enough signs of success to make Denver a city of hope. Between 1904 and World War I, more blacks found employment in state and local governments than ever before. Furthermore, an increasing number started small businesses which earned them profits and status.

Beginning about 1904-1905, the center of Denver's black population began shifting from the downtown neighborhood along Arapahoe, Curtis, and Lawrence, between Fifteenth and Twentieth, northeast to Five Points. A few families moved northwest near Elitch Gardens. Five Points became the most stylish black community by the end of the war, embracing over 30% of Denver's blacks. The neighborhood encompassed about two square miles of residential and business real estate, emanating from the five-point intersection of Welton, Twenty-Seventh Street, East Twenty-Sixth Avenue, and Washington. James Atkins wrote that Joseph D. D. Rivers, the editor of *The Colorado Statesman*, was a Virginia-born graduate of Hampton Institute and personal friend of Booker T. Washington. Rivers applauded the drift of blacks into Five Points, and he used the editorial pages of his newspaper to encourage them to invest in real estate, establish their own businesses, and make their community as clean and as attractive as possible.

With over two thousand blacks in Five Points by 1915, and more moving there each year, new economic opportunities offered lines for advancement within the black community. Cafes, a pool hall, saloons, a funeral home, cleaning and tailoring businesses, and real estate agencies were opened by enterprising men. Several women ran millinery and wig shops. Much to the chagrin of J.D.D. Rivers, a couple of gambling rooms were in operation as early as 1905, and these continued unmolested under the friendly eye of Mayor Speer. Besides businesses, advancement occurred in the professions. James Atkins wrote that "clustered around the intersection [Five Points] there were eight churches . . . three physicians, two dentists and one lawyer." A small branch of the American Woodmen fraternal insurance organization headquartered there too.

Some of these business and professional people invested money in Oliver Jackson's Dearfield experiment. They purchased town lots on a speculative basis but had no intention of moving to a high plains farming community themselves. Quite simply, they were doing too well in Denver to find anything attractive about the colony besides investment possibilities. Evidently most of the less successful blacks—those who were working as laborers, janitors, and domestics—preferred to trust their future to Denver rather than Dearfield. Just enough people were making it in "Five Points" to give them hope. Moving to a new community where success was problematical at best seemed unwise.

Other blacks shunned the Dearfield scheme because they saw it as a dead end for their people. An increasingly vocal group of young men found the exhortations of Booker T. Washington to be futile amidst changing realities. Washington had urged his people to be courteous to whites, to stay to themselves, work hard, become prosperous and independent. Eventually, he predicted, whites would be impressed by what they saw black people do for themselves, and gradually the dominant race would extend opportunities. An increasing number of thoughtful blacks recognized that this was no way to gain their rightful place in society. Whites met the "Uncle Toms" with continued discrimination, and worse. In the South, lynchings had reached epidemic proportions by the time of World War I. Those who demanded freedom rejected on principle the self-imposed program of segregation preached by Oliver T. Jackson. Go to a semiarid farm and try to survive with the purpose of proving their worthiness to whites? Never. Instead, they rallied around Clarence Holmes, a Howard University dental student who went to Denver in summer 1914 to organize a branch of the National Association for the Advancement of Colored People in his home city.

The NAACP approach to equal rights proved little more effective by the early 1920s than Jackson's colonization effort. NAACP leadership increased its following but effected few changes in white-dominated Denver. Jackson's experiment flourished briefly until farm commodity prices dropped sharply in the 1920s. An exodus from Dearfield began during those hard times for all American farmers. The little community is deserted today.

The Speer era provided some opportunities for blacks in state and local government, and the United States Post Office opened a few positions. Overall, however, when blacks were able to achieve significant economic gains and social recognition, they did so within their own community. Greater Denver was no land of fortune for people with black or brown skin.

Italians found Denver more hospitable than when they first arrived. Several factors account for the change. During the first twenty years of this century, the resident Italian population climbed from just under 1,000 to almost 3,000. Prior to 1900, hundreds of transient Italian workers inflated their population well beyond 1,000, but by 1920 most of Denver's Italo-Americans were permanent residents, and therefore not so unattractive to the majority of the city's inhabitants. Not only was the transient element gone, more Italian women had migrated to the Colorado metropolis. Families were typical rather than unusual among these southern European immigrants by 1920, making them more attractive to the family-oriented society. Furthermore, the Catholic church was playing an increasing role in Italian community life—educating the young in parochial schools, building churches, a college, and establishing recreation and welfare facilities. These were taken as signs that Italians were proving themselves stable and willing to care for their own people.

The nineteenth-century Italian neighborhood was served by two Jesuits, Fathers G.B. Guida and F.X. Gubitosi, who oversaw the construction of Sacred Heart Church at Twenty-Eighth and Larimer in 1879. The following year they established a school on Lawrence between Twenty-Eighth and Twenty-Ninth. Almost a decade later another Jesuit, Father D. Pantanella, went to Denver. He was instrumental in founding the College of the Sacred Heart (now Regis College) north of Berkeley Lake near Federal and West Fiftieth Avenue. The opening of the college, and Father Mariano Lepore's Mount Carmel Church at Navajo and West Thirty-Sixth Avenue in the 1890s, were followed by the Missionary Sisters of the Sacred Heart's school on Navajo and West Thirty-Fourth Avenue in 1902 and the Reverend Mother Frances E. Cabrini's Queen of Heaven Orphanage in 1905. These institutions symbolized the Catholic church's efforts in encouraging Italians to move northwest across the South Platte and away from the increasingly noisy, crowded, dirty, and run-down older neighborhood.

Denver's Italians needed little prodding. Starting in the early years of the new century, they vacated their tents along the river.

Some of these poorer immigrants moved to Lawrence and Larimer, renting the tenements vacated by more successful families who were relocating around Kalamath, Lipan, Navajo, Osage, and Pecos between West Thirty-Second and Forty-First Avenues. The most impoverished, who remained in the older Italian colony, were usually employed as laborers and domestics, the work typically done by Italians in the late nineteenth century. In the later period, though, they worked their way into more lucrative livelihoods. Eventually they purchased or rented small, single family houses on the north side of the Platte. Italians were employed at all levels of Mayor Speer's government, all the way from street crews to the police force and the assessor's office.

Like the blacks, Italians discovered advancement through businesses which served their own tightly knit community. Barbershops, restaurants, and imported food stores prospered in the heart of the North Side, and so did three Italian newspapers, *Il Roma, La Capitale,* and *Il Risveglio.* But unlike the blacks, scores of Italians were able to open businesses which served the larger metropolitan area. Francesco Mazza and N. Borelli started macaroni factories and sold their pasta to stores and restaurants all over the city. The Vagino brothers built the American Beauty Macaroni Factory and turned it into a profitable interstate corporation. Several liquor, wine, cigar, and imported food wholesale houses were established which served retailers in greater Denver.

Other Italians gravitated to the produce business. By the early 1920s, they dominated that segment of Denver's economy. Enterprising immigrants, many of them former laborers from coal mines and railroad gangs, rented or purchase land to grow fresh fruit and vegetables. Between Louisville and Denver, several families started truck gardens. They grew fresh produce on the marginal farmland, then hauled it into Denver by horse-drawn trucks and sold it to peddlers (almost always Italians) who retailed the food door-to-door or from street corners. Between 1900 and 1920, Italian immigrants acquired what had been considered worthless land along the Platte and Clear Creek. Land that was covered with river rock and scrub oak was cleared, fertilized, and cultivated north from the Twenty-Third Street Viaduct to West Thirty-Sixth Avenue. A strip for several miles along Clear Creek above the Platte was similarly transformed. In 1922 Giovanni Perilli wrote that a "spot that was changed from a 'Prairie Dog' waste to a pleasant view lies on the southwest line of Denver City and is reached by the City Tramway cars. Here are located a number of young Italian-Americans in the cultivation of plants for the table. These youngsters," Perilli continued, "have been there but a few years, each owning from a three to a ten acre plot." By 1920, Italian-Americans dominated the local truck gardens, and they represented the majority of the fresh produce wholesalers and retail peddlers who crowded the City Market each morning before sunrise.

Already by the late 1920s, most Italians had graduated from the more menial tasks of unskilled labor. They found their way into Italian-dominated places of employment, and some of the children of these families were making their way into the professions and the white-collar class. Per capita, they secured many more "status" positions than blacks. Each passing year they secured more jobs in law offices, on the staffs of the district attorney and the county sheriff. Children of immigrants hung out their shingles as lawyers and physicians, and the Italian community took great pride in Joseph E. Bona's appointment as vice president and general manager of the Olinger Mortuary Association, one of the prestige funeral businesses in Denver.

Equality of opportunity was becoming a reality rather than a dream for most of Denver's Italian-Americans. Their determination to learn English, their hard work and thrift, their strong attachment to family and church, and their generous care for their own orphans and destitute adults were factors which gradually made native Americans more tolerant. To be sure, these attributes were not monopolized by Italians. Blacks venerated family, church, and hard work as much as any minority group. But the Italians were white, and this played no small role in their ability to integrate into Denver's mainstream.

Denver's Jewish experience was similar to that of the Italians. Neither Jews nor Italians were welcomed into elite circles such as the Denver Club or the "Sacred 36," yet they did find potential which far surpassed that realized by blacks. Professed Jews were more factionalized than the Italians. It is true that prejudice existed between northern and southern Italians, but southerners so far outnumbered northerners that the issue assumed little importance beyond the occasional arrogance displayed by immigrants from northern Italy toward their poorer, agrarian countrymen. National and regional differences were much more divisive among Jews. Of the estimated 4,000 in Denver in the late nineteenth century, the majority claimed German origins. By the end of World War I, at least 11,000 people comprised Denver Jewry, with over half of that total representing new arrivals from eastern Europe.

Country of origin, indeed one's native city or town, took on importance within Jewish society. Non-Jews paid little attention to such precise distinctions, yet they did join the German Jewish community in viewing east Europeans in general as inferior to northern and western European immigrants. When Jews from eastern Europe fled the widespread outbreaks of anti-Semitism in the 1880s, many of them came to the United States. Only a few went West in that decade, congregating instead in the large cities on the eastern seaboard. Some of these impoverished immigrants had enough money to make the trip to Colorado (it cost over $400 in the 1880s), but most could not afford to escape the sweatshops and congested slums of northeastern cities until the 1890s and after.

At first, few Coloradans welcomed the east Europeans. Gentiles saw no merit in encouraging east European settlement in the Rocky Mountains, and the German-Jewish population viewed the migration with misgivings or hostility. Non-Jews opposed the arrival of these newcomers because they were prejudiced against Jews in particular, and east Europeans in general. And German Jews, who were finding comfortable niches in Denver society—they were distinguishing themselves in business and the professions and living almost anywhere they could afford property—viewed the newcomers as threats to their own positions. The older Jewish community grew up with the city. Anti-Semitism posed few stumbling blocks to opportunity, for Denver's Jews not only realized monetary security, they became successful in politics as well. Wolf Londoner became mayor, and Otto Mears and Simon Guggenheim became powerful figures in the Republican party. Members of the established Jewish community feared that a new wave of Jewish immigrants, made up of people who spoke little or no English, and who were assumed to be less educated and sophisticated, would kindle that latent, omnipresent anti-Semitism.

There was also another problem. Denver's Jews, according to evidence presented by Ida Uchill, had successfully shouldered the burden of caring for their own poor and infirm. They not only had the problem of caring for orphans, burying indigents, and relieving the usual quota of poor found in any burgeoning city, they had the additional strain of providing medical care for the swelling numbers of Jews who made their way to Denver in search of a cure for pulmonary diseases. In brief, the thought of adding thousands more to the community conjured up visions of demands on their welfare programs which were already stretched to the limit.

Ultimately, concern for the poor and suffering brought changing attitudes. Rabbi William S. Friedman, who at first opposed the

177

coming of eastern European Jews, did an about-face. He assumed an active role in accommodating the Yiddish-speaking people who made their way to Denver in large numbers each year until World War I, but he did not labor alone. Many Jews gave generously of their time and money, and scores of people joined the rabbi in trying to make Denver a comfortable haven.

Despite the determination of Jewish leaders to accommodate the immigrants, the newcomers were not accepted warmly. B'nai B'rith, the lodge controlled by the *Deutsche Yehudim*, did not exclude east European Jews. Nevertheless, as Ida Uchill explains, only

Rabbi William S. Friedman. *Courtesy Western History Department, Denver Public Library*

a dozen were members by 1900, not one ascended to the presidency, and most who never joined either feared being snubbed by the Germans or could not afford the dues.

Eastern Jews, like non-Jewish immigrants from eastern Europe, were made unwelcome in most quarters of the city. It is true they wanted their own neighborhoods where Old World culture and traditions could be preserved and nurtured. They even segregated themselves along lines of national origin. Nevertheless, West Denver and West Colfax evolved into predominantly Jewish ghettos in part, at least, because those Jews were excluded from other neighborhoods. The area known as West Denver, bounded by Cherry Creek on the east and the South Platte on the west, was a lower economic class neighborhood when east European Jews first settled there in the 1880s. As they moved into West Denver, older settlers, among them German and Irish immigrants, moved out as quickly as possible. By the early twentieth century, West Denver became predominantly Jewish, and, gradually, eastern European immigrants spread west across the South Platte on both sides of Colfax. There they built homes, and by the 1920s that neighborhood, called West Colfax, was what many observers called the most unique Jewish ghetto in America. Ida Uchill quoted Maurice Fishberg, who described the community in the early years of the century:

A walk in this neighborhood reveals a most peculiar condition of affairs. It is the most curious "Ghetto" I have ever seen in the U.S. or Europe. All the houses are of brick, are mostly of one story. . . . Although not paved the streets are fairly clean. They are not obstructed by stands, pushcarts, wagons and other paraphernalia, which we want to associate with Ghetto streets. The homes of the poor living here are as a rule tidy and clean, nothing like the overcrowding seen in Jewish quarters in New York or Chicago. The environment here looks more like that of the average small western town than like a Jewish district of Europe or America.

Economic opportunities came slowly for these people, but they did come. Most of the West Colfax and West Denver dwellers made their livings as peddlers, first scavenging for rags and bottles and selling them to small recycling companies downtown. Gradually, they purchased horses and wagons and sold merchandise in nearby mining and agricultural communities. One-time peddlers eventually bought small jewelry, tailor, butcher, and grocery businesses, while others became active in wholesale merchandising, and warehousing.

A few became successful manufacturers, but the greatest success stories came to their children in the next generation.

None of these strides was made without difficulty. As the ubiquitous peddlers started their rounds from the West Side each day, they were frequently taunted by passersby. Occasionally the abuse was physical rather than verbal. Sometimes peddlers were pelted with rocks, and in 1905 two men were beaten so severely by anti-Semitic hoodlums that they died. Robert Speer helped ease the vendors' plight. Jews were appointed to the police force, and all patrolmen were instructed to protect the street traders.

By World War I most of the violence passed because Denverites were more accustomed to seeing bearded, strangely dressed, Yiddish-speaking peddlers, and because, for better or worse, an increasing number of eastern European Jews were becoming Americanized. Another factor that accounts for the end of this violence (besides the watchful eyes of the police) was the appearance of a new group for the nativists to hate—the Germans.

Ironically, no sooner had Colorado's Jewish and gentile Germans finished gloating about their presumed superiority over the poorer, less urbane eastern European immigrants than they found themselves subject to widespread criticism, discrimination, and physical abuse. Despite President Woodrow Wilson's plea for all Americans to be "neutral" toward the belligerents in the World War, many Americans quickly sided with the British. As propaganda depicting German soldiers as raping and pillaging beasts flooded this country from England, more Americans shifted from a neutral view of the conflict. Once Germany launched its unrestricted submarine warfare on the high seas and the news arrived that Americans died on British passenger liners, opinion became overwhelmingly anti-German.

When the United States declared war on Germany in April 1917, neutral voices were silenced. Anti-German sentiment reached frantic proportions. German-Americans in Colorado, as in other states, became victims of unaggravated attacks. Aliens residing in Denver were herded off to internment camps in Utah, and naturalized German-Americans, even native-born Americans with German names, became subjects of widespread maligning. Leaders of the German-American community in Denver, including the German language press, pledged unswerving loyalty to the president and the war effort. A delegation met with Governor Julius Gunter and offered the services of Denver's German-American community to help in any way possible in furthering the war effort.

Pledges and pleas accomplished nothing. The entire state

witnessed an anti-German binge which civic and political leaders (with the exception of Mayor Speer) did little to discourage. German-Americans were thrown in jail merely on the suspicion of being spies. Homes were desecrated, men were brutally beaten, and the names of every German alien woman residing in Denver, complete with home addresses, were printed in *the Post*. Continuing its inflammatory and irresponsible journalism, *the Post* cautioned citizens to avoid buying soaps, patent medicines, and food from German salespeople, suggesting that these items surely had been contaminated with deadly poisons or germs. *The Post* assailed the characters of German-born state and local officials, and the newspaper helped create fears that the water system would be sabotaged by German conspirators.

In the drive to protect Denver's citizens from everything German, Teutonic names were dropped from business establishments, German language instruction was taken from the public school curriculum, books in German or on Germany were purged from libraries; and the allegedly pro-German faculty was dismissed from the University of Denver and the University of Colorado. Teachers and businessmen were forced to publicly kiss the American flag as an expression of loyalty, and churches were pressured into dropping their German language services. In essence, Germans were coerced into "Americanizing" with a vengeance unprecedented in Colorado history.

By the close of the Speer era, other self-appointed guardians of civilization legislated "reform" measures which had been pursued by small groups since the 1870s. A *Rocky Mountain News* crusade to lock up the gambling houses prompted Governor Henry Buchtel, in 1907, to declare the end of one of Denver's oldest, most colorful, and lucrative business fields. Seven years later, Edward P. Costigan and Ben Lindsey helped organize disparate WCTU and Anti-Saloon League supporters in bringing prohibition to Colorado. There was not enough oppostion to demon rum to win the victory for teetotalers, but once Costigan and Lindsey convinced voters that Speer's organization could never have reached such heights or power without the saloon element behind it, they succeeded in bringing idealistic political reformers into the antiliquor crusade.

The next year those who saw virtue in enforced morality celebrated their third victory in the long-waged war against evil. The lowly cribs and the elegant pleasure palaces were closed on Market Street. By 1915 the satanic trinity of gambling, drinking, and prostitution was outlawed in the city that had made a significant part of its national reputation on wide open entertainment. To the dismay of the purists, though, laws had little impact on human nature. Local sinners and traveling transgressors found an ample array of women entertainers, stimulating beverages, and games of chance. Most certainly the recreation centers were underground after 1915, but any taxi driver, hotel clerk, or worldly policeman could direct a prospective customer to a "safe" establishment.

If Denver had not totally abolished vice by the early 1920s, it had realized tangible gains in other areas. The city was aesthetically and functionally improved thanks to Speer's beautification program. Poverty was not eradicated, but those ubiquitous tents and shanties—the symbols of the most abject poverty—disappeared as the lowest economic class made the first steps toward life's decencies and necessities. Child labor was not halted, yet the worst abuses were corrected. Equality of economic opportunity was not all-embracing, but every minority group realized gains beyond those existing a generation earlier. Although educational opportunities were far from unlimited, they far exceeded those available in the late nineteenth century.

Quite plainly, Denver's activists identified many ills of their community and took meaningful steps to correct them. If they fell short of eradicating every problem in the Queen City, they effectively fashioned Denver into one of the most attractive and liveable municipalities of its size in the nation. These accomplishments notwithstanding, no sooner did they begin to solve the problems that grew out of the prodigious growth of the late nineteenth century than they faced a new set of problems related to the onward pace of urbanization. The automobile, originally viewed as a plaything for the rich, quickly became accessible to thousands of ordinary citizens. As this anticipated change became reality, unprecedented problems confronted civic leaders. No sooner had the hostilities endemic to southern and eastern European immigration been eased than thousands of immigrants from Mexico entered the city's border, complete with new demands and problems. A fifteen-year drouth and a devastating depression imposed still greater difficulties, promising the next generation of Denver leadership an agenda of challenges just as burdensome as anything their predecessors had faced.

Part IV

Queen City,

1923-World War II

Chapter 7

On Thursday evening, August 5, 1920, mob violence erupted. Several hundred demonstrators, displaying their sympathy for over one thousand Tramway Company workers who had gone on strike for higher wages, overturned and set fire to streetcars manned by armed strikebreakers. After destroying the company's vehicles, the unruly mob, buoyed by the easy victory over the armed guards, invaded *The Post* building on Champa Street. Because the newspaper had endorsed Mayor Dewey C. Bailey's support of the company's use of armed strikebreakers, the vengeful army occupied the building and destroyed as much property as it could lay hands on. In his colorful history of *The Post*, *Thunder in the Rockies*, Bill Hosokawa writes that "In less than an hour the mob was gone. Damage estimated at twenty five thousand dollars had been done." The mayor called in 2,500 federal troops from Fort Logan and Camp Funston, Kansas, and continues Hosokawa, "before peace was restored seven persons died and more than fifty were wounded."

This needless anarchy symbolized Denver's chaotic existence after Mayor Speer's death. Sixty-year-old Dewey Bailey was an honest, well-intentioned man, but he was no leader. It would have been out of character for Speer, who had been able to pull Denver's opposing factions together—including the Tramway Company and its antagonists—to allow events to reach crisis proportions. The Tramway Company insisted that if it could not raise fares from six to seven cents, it would cut wages from fifty-eight to forty-eight cents an hour. At the same time, the union was demanding hourly wage increases to seventy-five cents. Ultimately, fares were increased to eight cents, and wages were reduced to fifty-two cents. Only the Tramway Company prospered from this development. Certainly an agreement could have been arranged before the costly strike and violence, but effective leadership was not forthcoming.

Members of Denver's business community had been conditioned to spending most of their time on private enterprise while leaving the running of the city to Speer's responsible direction. Unfortunately, they now had no choice but to put up with the inept, largely aimless approach to city management offered by Bailey until his term expired in 1923. Behind the scenes, though, the angry and embarrassed power structure was diligently seeking a new man for the mayor's office who could once again bring direction and a spirit of compromise to the Queen City.

The group that comprised the power elite by the 1920s reflected a new spirit which would dominate the mountain metropolis for a generation. Both Republicans and Democrats in national party affiliation, they showed little concern for party loyalty at the local level. Unlike the previous decision makers, there were few self-made men in the group. Inheriting their positions in local business and finance, they were raised in Colorado, educated in expensive preparatory schools, and sent on to Ivy League universities for the best educations money could buy. Never experiencing poverty, and never having gone to work at an early age, they went from infancy to college, and on into the Denver Club and handsomely furnished Seventeenth Street offices without questioning a life-style laid out for them by their successful and ambitious fathers. With inherited and established wealth at their disposal, they were conservative men who carefully protected and nurtured their legacies rather than taking the great risks of their predecessors who gambled to build fortunes and security in a tumultous and speculative mining and industrial revolution.

The era of the carpetbagger was only a colorful memory by the 1920s. There were no more instant fortunes to be made in the mines, no more public utilities to be pioneered, and the railroad network (except for the long-pursued Moffat Road) was complete. As a consequence, no more rags-to-riches dreamers such as Moffat drifted into town, and no more well-heeled speculators such as Duff and Wolcott, flush with eastern capital, arrived to win the overnight veneration of the builders of a new western emporium. The age of high-stakes gambling was gone. The gateway to power, status, and wealth was a narrow one by the 1920s, and those who passed through it usually did so by circumstances of birth or clever marriages.

One of the more prominent of the group was Claude Boettcher. Born in Boulder, Boettcher's father, Charles, came to Colorado from

Germany in 1869. In the 1870s Charles Boettcher moved to Leadville and made a fortune in hardware, utilities, banking, and mining before moving to Denver in 1890. The senior Boettcher quickly entered the Queen City's power structure, investing in real estate, banks, and the Tramway Company. In 1901 with John Campion, William Page, and J.R. McKinnie, Charles Boettcher and his son Claude organized the Great Western Sugar Company. Soon thereafter Mahlon Thatcher and Chester Morey joined them. By 1905 they merged with Henry Havermeyer's American Sugar Refining Company, creating what was generally referred to as the "Great Western Sugar Trust."

The interlocking of families and businesses soon became the natural order of Denver's economy. As Geraldine Bean shows in her biography of Charles Boettcher, first the fathers and then the sons united in business until the nucleus of the region's economy was controlled by a few families. Gerald Hughes, John Porter, Chester Morey and his son John, and both Boettchers became directors of Great Western Sugar Company. But that was only one industry. A.V. Hunter, John C. Mitchell, Charles Boettcher, George Trimble, and John Campion were involved with Leadville banks and then became directors or officers in the Denver National and First National banks in Denver.

Besides the vital banking businesses and the lucrative sugar industry (it soared from a $100,000 business in 1899 to over $3.6 million by 1901), the same men controlled the utilities. Charles Boettcher had been a major investor in Leadville's gas and electric utilities with Dennis Sullivan and A.V. Hunter. In 1906 the Leadville stockholders merged with the Central Colorado Power Company. Then in 1923 one of H.L. Doherty's holding companies, Cities Service Company, incorporated the Public Service Company of Colorado, of which Claude Boettcher became president in 1943.

Most of Denver's prominent families not only held large blocks of stock in the Public Service Company, the great banks, and the sugar industry, they had their hands in the Denver Stockyards Association, Colorado Fuel and Iron, and a host of other businesses. The investment business reflected the same inter-family relationships. In 1910 Gerald Hughes became a silent partner with his friends and former schoolmates Claude Boettcher and John Porter in the investment firm of Boettcher, Porter and Company. All three young men had attended Dr. Holbrook's exclusive school in New York and stayed East for college. Porter and Hughes went to Yale, while Boettcher selected Harvard. But the trio returned to the security and

Charles Boettcher

Claude Boettcher

comforts of Capitol Hill and the Denver Club after graduation and assumed prominent roles in their fathers' enterprises.

At the center of this predestined elite was Gerald Hughes. An unquestionably able man in his own right, he always admitted that he "was born into a charmed circle" and had the opportunity to put his talents to effective use without hardship or struggle. Hughes' father was Charles J. Hughes, Jr., a well-born Missourian who was sent to law school so he could follow in his father's footsteps. When Charles Hughes, Jr. was twenty-six years old, well equipped with a law degree, one year's college teaching experience, and two year's postgraduate legal training in his father's law office, he moved his family (including four-year-old Gerald) to Denver. There Charles Hughes began a meteoric rise in politics and law. His legal talents were purchased by most of the great corporations, among them several railroads, Great Western Sugar Company, the First National Bank, International Trust Company, Coors, the Tramway Company, and the Denver Union Water Company. Charles Hughes, Jr. was also active in Democratic politics. A Speer supporter, he shunned public office until 1909, when the party persuaded him to represent Colorado in the United States Senate. When Senator Hughes went to Washington, he turned the prestigious law firm over to his thirty-four-year-old son.

Gerald Hughes was well trained to assume the directorship. A graduate of the University of Denver's law school, young Hughes went directly into practice with his father. He became active in Democratic party politics, too, serving in the State Senate from 1901 to 1905. By the time his father went on to the national Senate, Gerald Hughes was a power in local politics and intimate with the family's legal clients, who represented many of the wealthiest and most powerful men in the region.

Within two years fate placed awesome responsibilities on the young lawyer, who was still almost one-half decade away from his fortieth birthday. Two deaths in 1911 conspired to vault Gerald Hughes into the center of Denver's circle of power. Senator Hughes died in January, leaving his son in complete charge of the law pactice. Hughes was offered his father's seat in the Senate, but declined it because of the demands of his newly inherited legal practice. The decision proved to be a wise one, because two months later David Moffat died while on a business trip in New York, leaving his complicated estate for Hughes to oversee. With these added pressures, Hughes immediately brought Clayton C. Dorsey, four years his senior and another Yale graduate, into the firm.

Gerald Hughes

Few people realized that the formation of Hughes and Dorsey in 1911 was, in effect, the establishment of a command post which would direct the economy and polity of Colorado for another generation. Dorsey was as influential in Republican circles as Hughes was in the Democracy, and both men were viewed by clients and competitors alike as "legal geniuses." The two men made fortunes in their profession and wisely invested their money in sound business ventures, using their wealth and status to enhance their influence in the respective political parties.

Dorsey was an important complement to Hughes. He was tall, smiling, and affable, and he made friends easily. Hughes, on the other hand, a short (5'6"), slender and quiet, private person, was viewed as a brilliant eccentric and virtually unapproachable. Only his closest friends saw beyond the hard-shell facade he displayed to the public. Montgomery Dorsey, C.C. Dorsey's son and a member of the law firm beginning in 1927, remembers Hughes as a warm, sensitive man who maintained a delightful sense of humor—a gentle person who studied the holy Bible he kept in his desk and generously (although unostentatiously) gave his money to needy causes. Hughes married

Mabel Nagel in 1908. The couple could never have children, but they loved young Montgomery Dorsey as their own son. The sentimental nature of Gerald Hughes surfaced—in private—as he wept when Montgomery Dorsey told him goodbye upon entering the Air Corps during World War II.

This tender side of Gerald Hughes seldom appeared as he and Dorsey labored incessantly to represent their influential clients. The biggest challenge Gerald Hughes and his associates faced came when Moffat died in 1911. For several years before his death, Moffat had been involved in building the Denver, Northwestern and Pacific Railroad from Denver to Utah. This enterprise was the last great project promoted by the empire builder as he hoped to give Denver a place on a direct transcontinental rail route. With the assistance of William Gray Evans, Moffat raised enough money to get a temporary road over the continental divide from Denver, while hoping ultimately to cut a tunnel through the mountains for a more direct line to Salt Lake City. From the beginning, though, Moffat's grand design was thwarted by financial difficulties. The panic of 1907

Clayton C. Dorsey.
Courtesy Montgomery Dorsey

shrunk credit sources, and Belgian investors who were counted on to back the project retreated at the last moment. Because the Denver, Northwestern and Pacific railroad was as much a matter of prestige to Moffat as it was a source of personal profit or an asset to the region, the vain old promoter recklessly gambled every resource at his disposal. According to an excellent history of the *First of Denver* written by Robert S. Pulcipher and based on original bank records, Moffat selfishly and carelessly used his bank's assets to keep his pet project alive. In 1911, $4 million worth of notes were due on the road's construction company, and much more money was needed to salvage the entire project. In an eleventh hour move of desperation, Moffat and Evans went to New York to find capital. Failing to raise the necessary funds, some insiders say Moffat committed suicide in his New York hotel room. Whether the seventy-one-year-old financier took his own life, or the pressure merely took its toll on the aging, overworked body, will never be known. Nevertheless, as Pulcipher described him, the man who "had been the First National Bank since 1866" was dead, "and the officials of the organization feared that an announcement during banking hours might have disastrous results."

Deaths of bank officials seldom cause financial panics, but in this case the fears of Gerald Hughes and his fellow bankers were well founded. The First National Bank, despite warnings by its examiner as early as 1908, was in financial trouble. Moffat, who owned 72% of the stock, had mortgaged almost everything he controlled to underwrite the railroad. Further, he had funneled the bank's loan portfolio into his Denver, Northwestern and Pacific scheme way beyond the point of sound banking practice.

When Hughes, who was already suspicious of Moffat's devious financial manipulations, learned of the financier's death on Saturday morning March 18, he withheld the news from the press until banking hours ended that evening. Finally announcing that the Denver pioneer died with his "house in order," Hughes moved swiftly to make that false statement truthful. Among Hughes' efforts which saved the bank from ruin was, in Pulcipher's words, "a night letter [sent] to Leadville requesting that the president of the Carbonate National Bank come down to Denver to run The First National. Absalom V. Hunter responded to Hughes' request by arriving in Denver on the first train. A.V. Hunter already in his sixties," Pulcipher continues, "was a revered and respected banker throughout the region. Someone of his caliber was needed in order to minimize speculation and rumor about the condition of the Bank." Besides Hunter, who was elevated to the bank presidency and board chairmanship in return for his monetary and good will contributions, Mahlon D. Thatcher from Pueblo's First National Bank and E.B. Field, the telephone magnate, were among the best known financial angels brought in by Hughes to save the bank. Saving The First National Bank was only the first step in a series of power plays directed by Hughes. With the support of several other men who now recognized his influence and sagacity, Hughes channeled his energies in many directions.

Hughes, Porter, and Boettcher also put money into the Denver and Salt Lake Railroad (Denver, Northwestern and Pacific until 1913), as did William G. Evans, John Campion, and Lawrence C. Phipps. And it was the leadership of these men, Hughes and Evans in particular, who prepared the legislation for the completion of the Moffat Tunnel, molded favorable public opinion, and raised most of the funds to complete that project. Their efforts saved the road from financial collapse and placed Denver on a direct western transcontinental line through Utah.

Although William Gray Evans made many public appearances to win favor for the Moffat Road and Tunnel, and served as chairman of the state railroad commission which was created to promote the project, insiders realized that it was the legal talent of Gerald Hughes which brought the plan of nearly twenty years to fruition. Hughes' sagacity salvaged Moffat's mishandled transportation dream like it rescued the First National Bank. In brief, the senior partner of Hughes and Dorsey saved Denver's wealthiest families from great financial losses.

Out of gratitude and respect for his judgement, the heirs to the Porter, Morey, Boettcher, and Evans legacies usually listened to Gerald Hughes when major questions arose regarding Denver's future. To be sure, there were differences of opinion. Indeed, Claude Boettcher and Gerald Hughes had a falling out when the former sold Moffat Road stock to the Missouri Pacific and the Denver and Rio Grande. Nevertheless, Montgomery Dorsey, the son of the junior partner in the law firm, was able to bridge the wedge between the warring factions and keep the power structure united when necessary. Embraced by Hughes as a son, young Dorsey also maintained a close personal and business relationship with Claude Boettcher.

The extent to which these inheritors of power and money worked in unison is evident in many ways. In politics they all agreed that Lawrence C. Phipps could best serve their interests in the United States Senate. Phipps was born into especially fortunate circumstances. Completing high school in his home state of Pennsylvania,

195

Mahlon D. Thatcher

Lawrence C. Phipps, Sr.

he went to work as a weigh clerk in a Pittsburgh steel mill. The popular mythology suggests that because of his own inner qualities of hard work, efficiency, and dedication, he worked his way up from clerkship in 1879 to vice president and treasurer of the Carnegie Corporation by the time it merged with United States Steel in 1901. The chronology and the upward mobility are true, but more than hard work and superior talent explain the success story. In fact, Phipps' uncle Henry owned the steel mill that merged with Carnegie's corporation in the nineteenth century, giving young Lawrence a privileged edge in consideration for promotions.

In the early twentieth century, while still in his late thirties, Phipps moved to Denver for his wife's health. Well endowed with a steel industry fortune, he arrived in Colorado with short, neatly trimmed hair, a well-groomed moustache, and a slightly discernible double chin which betrayed a life of well-fed opulence. His money and his reputation as a power in the Republican party gave him immediate access to the Denver Club and the city's inner power circle. Soon he became friends with Gerald Hughes and retained him as his attorney.

In 1918 Democrat Gerald Hughes deserted Senator John Shafroth in his bid for re-election, joining his partner Dorsey, as well as the Evanses, in elevating Phipps to the Senate. For two terms from 1919 to 1931, Phipps untiringly worked in the Senate to aid his friends who wanted to develop Colorado. While the Pennsylvania-born senator staunchly opposed excessive federal spending and government involvement in the "free enterprise system" where it might aid workers or the poor, he saw no contradiction in his successful drives to appropriate federal money to be used in exploring Colorado's oil shale resources and in building highways to the mountain parks to promote tourism. He defended the right of stock raisers to use the national forests for grazing, and he successfully lobbied for government aid in irrigating Colorado's dry farming regions. While he paid lip service to the virtues of competition, he enthusiastically voted for the Fordney-McCumber Tariff designed to protect such industries as Colorado's mines from foreign competition.

Those who listened to Gerald Hughes' counsel on the virtues of electing Lawrence Phipps to the United States Senate apparently saw the wisdom in his judgement. The attorney who revitalized an abused bank almost overnight, who piloted the Moffat Road and Tunnel through a legal and political morass, and who urged them to elect a senator who, as predicted, faithfully worked for their economic interests, must be worthy of confidence. Thus, in 1923, when Hughes was debating which mayoralty candidate could save Denver from the chaos of Dewey Bailey's administration, the local men of means deferred to the lawyer's judgement.

The kind of man Gerald Hughes hoped to see in the highest city office needed specific qualifications. The position, as Hughes envisioned it, required experience in local politics and the diplomatic agility to communicate with business leaders and other interest groups. The candidate should have a broad base of political appeal, yet not be overexposed and identified with unpopular issues of the past. The next mayor should be able to listen to counsel of others, but be independent and capable of administering the affairs of the city on his own so that business leaders could be free to pursue their own demanding enterprises. Furthermore, any mayor Hughes could endorse must be progressive within conservative lines. That is, he must conserve the traditional relationship of cooperation between business and local government. He must be sensitive to the demands of noncapitalists without altering the political-economic system, and he must improve the overall quality of urban life without reckless spending or radical reforms.

To Hughes and his associates, local government, in harmony with business, should strive to conserve, consolidate, and improve city institutions without radically altering the status quo. The power structure, comprised of native Coloradans, or residents since childhood (only Phipps could be classified as an outsider), frowned upon wild schemes of empire building and promotion so typical of their predecessors. Native born, Protestant in religion, and financially secure, they were satisfied with a future of self-propelled economic activity augmented by modest growth based on tourism and development of natural resources and agriculture. They opposed turning Denver into a booming industrial city. Such promotional ventures, as one member of the group phrased it, would only "bring low brows, foreigners and dirt into a respectable city."

These leaders did more than shun campaigns designed to attract wealthy outside investors who would upset the town's equilibrium. For a generation they throttled economic policies that would cause unbridled growth. Although outsiders would destroy the concept of controlled community development after World War II, the power elite's regulations of both the financial and the political structures of Denver precluded changes from the early 1920s through the late 1940s.

In finance, this regulated growth policy can be seen in the loan-to-deposit ratio maintained by the major banks. Today the normal ratio is composed of loans amounting to between 60 and 70% of deposits. But during the decades between the wars, the average was 15 to 18%. Gerald Hughes maintained that this fiscal conservatism was so vital that if the First National's ratio ever exceeded 32%, he would liquidate the bank. Such constriction of capital was intentionally designed to slow speculation in real estate, housing construction, and business expansion.

Gerald Hughes believed that this same philosophy should underpin Denver politics, and the man he endorsed to administer the local government in 1923 was Benjamin Franklin Stapleton. Once Hughes had made his decision, it was tantamount to election. For as Gene Cervi, the editor of the *Rocky Mountain Journal*, once phrased it, "Hughes never lost an election regardless of what party was in power." To understand the truth in that statement is to recognize that "party" per se was unimportant to these men. What they wanted was protection of their own economic interests. Democrat Hughes endorsed Republican Phipps just as eagerly as he backed Democrat Stapleton; and Hughes' Republican partner, C.C. Dorsey, entered the campaigns with no qualms either. The important thing to these men was to elect the right kind of man—that man's party affiliation was irrelevant.

Hughes could usually swing a substantial part of the Democratic organization behind any candidate, and Dorsey, Phipps, and the father and son Evans (William Gray and John) could convince a large number of Republicans to listen to them. As Montgomery Dorsey recalled, "Dad got most of the Republicans to back Stapleton," and Hughes brought the Democrats into line.

Benjamin F. Stapleton turned out to be an ideal candidate and precisely the kind of mayor Hughes and his associates wanted. With the exception of one four-year term (1931-1935), Stapleton directed Denver's government from 1923 to 1947—and he did so in a conservative, constructive, and efficient manner. Independent, responsible, and a good administrator, he instinctively served the interests of the power elite, freeing them to tend to business. Like Robert Speer, Stapleton was sensitive to the needs of other groups. He struck a balance between a variety of factions with quite different aspirations.

Stapleton certainly had shortcomings, which his critics were quick to point out. Nevertheless, he steered Denver through one of its most troublesome periods. Because Denver was a service center to the agricultural hinterland, it suffered for fifteen years as farmers struggled to survive drouth conditions which prevailed from 1925 to

1940. The crash in farm prices in the 1920's, plus the devastating depression of the 1930's, further added to the Queen City's woes. In the face of these crises, Stapleton offered wise and balanced leadership. Refusing to succumb to pressures for excessive spending which would bankrupt the city, he still managed to find ways to improve the transportation network, locate more water for the parched metropolitan area, and beautify the community. Although he shunned all plans to attract industries which he believed would destroy Denver's quality of life, he did cooperate with the Chamber of Commerce in developing the agricultural hinterland, attracting tourists, and enticing federal agencies to the mountain metropolis. Despite the difficult times, Stapleton pulled Denverites through with a minimum of hardship. Indeed, the city was a superior place in which to live after his tenure in office.

Mayor Stapleton alone did not move Denver forward between the mid-Twenties and World War II, but his leadership and the able advisors he chose set the tone for the community's progress. Critics who charge that he allowed the city to stagnate during those years are wrong. Denver was no boom city, but the population increased at a gradual and controlled pace of approximately 12% each decade. The population was just over 260,000 when Stapleton took office, and it was nearly 380,000 when he vacated the executive's desk in 1947. Controlled growth—where construction programs and the problem-solving machinery of government could effectively cope with development—was precisely what the mayor and the business leaders planned. Helter-skelter growth was not part of their master plan. On the contrary, they hoped to consolidate and improve what they already had within a context of manageable expansion. This dream was achieved admirably. About 120,000 newcomers settled the one-time miners-outfitting post between 1925 and 1947. Annexations encompassed less than five square miles, increasing the urban area from 58.75 to 63.69 square miles by 1947.

Seldom have mayors left a monumental impact on their city. On rare occasions men of ability and force have made positive, substantive, and lasting changes in their communities. Denver has had two such chief executives—Robert Speer and Benjamin Stapleton. It is to the credit of Gerald Hughes and his fellow power brokers that they urged the election of Stapleton from the ensemble of contenders in 1923. To ignore, however, the assets Stapleton possessed at the time he was picked is to misunderstand the political process and to overlook the talents he had which ultimately made him so effective.

Born in a small eastern Kentucky town in 1873, Stapleton was

Benjamin F. Stapleton

nearing his fiftieth birthday when he was elected mayor in 1923. Coming from a family of modest means, he managed to study law in Lebanon, Ohio, and was admitted to the Ohio bar in 1896. Soon thereafter he moved to Denver, joined the First Colorado Volunteers, and served in the Philippines during the Spanish-American War. When the veteran sergeant returned to Denver in 1899, he became active in the Democratic party. Between 1900 and 1904 he held patronage jobs in the treasurer's and recorder's offices. Robert Speer, who appreciated Stapleton's talent and loyalty to the organization, elevated him to the post of police magistrate in 1904. That office he held until 1915, when President Woodrow Wilson, upon the recommendation of Democratic Senators Charles S. Thomas and John F. Shafroth, appointed him Postmaster of Denver, a federal spoils job he kept until the Republicans put him out in 1921.

For the next two years he invested in oil companies in Kansas and Oklahoma but kept active in local politics. Described by George V. Kelly in *The Old Gray Mayors of Denver,* Stapleton was of average height, yet "he appeared tall because he was lean. Ben had a scholarly, almost ascetic appearance, accentuated by thin hair and metal-rimmed glasses, mod today, that gave him better than 20-20 vision when he focused on matter important to him." Always, independent, candid, and serious, he was an inner-directed man who seldom let others establish or influence his standards and values. According to one of his closest friends, George Cranmer, Stapleton was thoroughly imbued with a Victorian sense of morality. He probably learned those values from his Baptist parents, but certainly had them challenged by the United States Army and the local Democratic organization. Peer group pressures to drink never swayed him from total abstinence, and he viewed spending money on tobacco and the theater as wasteful, if not immoral. Always frugal, he earned a comfortable income from his political appointments and oil investments, but making money was not high on his list of priorities. Never driven by the challenge to build a fortune or a business empire—a mania which kept the lights burning late at night on Seventeenth Street—Benjamin Stapleton found fulfillment in politics. He genuinely enjoyed the company of men. Not the poker-playing, beer-drinking, backslapping variety; rather, the purposeful organization of men who wanted to contribute something meaningful—as they viewed it at least—to society.

Out of this need for camaraderie, coupled with his own sense of worthy goals, Stapleton became an active Mason and a member of Rotary International. Consistent with his concept of service, fellowship, and patriotism, he organized the first Veterans of Foreign Wars post in Denver. In addition to these interests, he was active in the Democratic party and labored faithfully to keep Robert Speer's organization in power.

Stapleton saw nothing inconsistent with his involvement in the Speer organization and his other societal activities. On the contrary, he believed nothing could be more patriotic than serving the party of Andrew Jackson; and he never wavered from his conviction that Robert Speer was an honorable public servant who improved his city by serving a variety of interest groups. Evidently Stapleton's wife, Mabel, whom he married in 1917, felt the same way. She worked for many years as a volunteer sewing instructor in the North Side Neighborhood House, an institution the Speer organization had always supported.

When the Seventeenth Street financiers decided to back Stapleton in 1923, the ex-soldier was a veteran politician, too. The Ohio-trained lawyer had as much to offer the businessmen as they had to give him, which enabled him to accept their support, yet still remain independent. What the future mayor had on the asset column of his balance sheet was a list of things that made him electable. He had the blessings of the old Speer organization, and he had friends in the Masons and VFW. Additionally, he knew his city extremely well from the underside up. Having spent over a decade as police magistrate, he had friends in the legal profession and police department. Furthermore, he knew the criminal element in Denver, and he recognized the crucial difference between vicious criminals who perpetrated serious crimes against persons and property and those who were unfortunate members of society's flotsam and jetsam who had to resort to minor crimes for survival. Such people he knew well, and he treated them with sympathy rather than harshness.

Stapleton's years as police magistrate also had schooled him in understanding human nature. While he refrained from consuming alcoholic beverages, gambling, or consorting with loose women, he refused to launch a lofty crusade to destroy that which could never be abolished in a city. As long as prostitutes, professional gamblers, and illegal drinking establishments maintained low profiles, segregated themselves in unobtrusive sections of town, and refrained from abusing the customers, they would be tolerated.

Not only did Stapleton have this wide-based constituency which had served as the nucleus of Speer's organization, he had financial backing from Speer's old friend, Vaso Chucovich. Besides these voters, he was offered the aid of a new force in Denver's polity and society—the Ku Klux Klan. Stapleton himself was no bigot. Throughout his life he maintained a close personal friendship with A.B. Hirschfeld, the Jewish owner of Hirschfeld Press. Likewise, his enthusiasm for his wife's work in the heavily immigrant North Side, his friendship with Chucovich, and his close cooperation with black leader Benjamin Hooper, as well as his support for Judge Ben Lindsey in helping hundreds of Jewish, Catholic, and black children, reflected sincere convictions. Still, he was offered Klan backing in 1923 if he would endorse their organization. With over thirty thousand formal members, and thousands of other Denverites who sympathized with the Ku Klux Klan, he did what seemed politically advantageous.

The Ku Klux Klan, a superpatriotic, nativistic society, similar to the post-Civil War organization of the same name, was revitalized in Georgia in 1915. At first the Klan was slow in attracting followers. Its fortunes improved when the Bolsheviks took over Russia and promised to export their revolution to the world. The formation of the Workers' (later the Communist) party in the United States in 1919, followed by a series of anarchist-inspired bombings and threats, led to widespread fear and hatred of all minority groups viewed as menaces to 100% Americanism. By the early 1920s, the KKK found eager supporters all over the United States, in cities as well as small towns and rural areas. Membership was estimated to be almost two million by 1925. Millions more sympathized with the Klan even though they never donned hoods and robes or burned crosses in yards of the "enemies."

The Klan collapsed by 1926 when cases of brutality and murder and evidence of misused funds were exposed. Its size declined to less than 10,000 that year, never again to reach the height of popularity enjoyed during the early 1920s.

In 1923, though, Klan backing was an obvious asset in Denver politics. In later years Stapleton regretted his association with "the invisible empire," and he was disgusted by their violence. He expended much effort in the future trying to convince minorities and principled liberals that his Klan affiliation was an egregious error stemming from political expediency rather than heart-felt conviction. Many Ku Klux Klan opponents accepted Stapleton's hat-in-hand apology. Lawyer Philip Hornbein, an organization Democrat who encouraged the eastern European Jews in West Colfax to support Speer, and campaigned for Stapleton in 1923, led the petition drive to recall the mayor in 1924. Although he was outraged by Stapleton's appointment of several Klan members to city jobs, he continued working for the Democratic party in the 1930s and 1940s and eventually endorsed Stapleton in subsequent mayoralty races. A.B. Hirschfeld never chastised Stapleton for his brief alliance with the Klan, and he remained the mayor's personal friend. Furthermore, Edward Costigan and other whites in the liberal circles, black community leader Ben Hooper, and many influential Italians supported the mayor over the years. They allowed the Ku Klux Klan issue to die, and in return reaped benefits of patronage and favors from city hall.

That Ben Stapleton was eminently qualified to govern Denver's polity was not always obvious. During the first year there was little time to get on with business as usual. Anti-Klan forces, disturbed by the mayor's appointment of several alleged Klansmen (among them William Candlish, chief of police), circulated a petition for the recall of Stapleton. Kenneth T. Jackson's study *The Ku Klux Klan in the City* reveals that the petition drive yielded over 26,000 signatures, necessitating a special mayoral election in August 1924. Dewey C. Bailey was tapped to oppose Stapleton, and the former mayor campaigned all over Denver pointing out the immoral and unconstitutional underpinnings of the Ku Klux Klan ideology. While the Klan fell into disrepute by 1926, there was little doubt about the community's pro-Klan sentiments in 1924. With the "invisible empire" as the front and center issue, nearly 80,000 voters marched to the polls. Stapleton carried all sixteen election districts and was retained by an overwhelming margin of 55,635 to 24,277. The anti-Klan organization even failed to win as many votes as it had signatures on the recall petition.

The Ku Klux Klan issue went to the voters again the following November as the "hooded Americans" endorsed Lawrence C. Phipps and Rice W. Means for the United States Senate and Clarence J. Morley for governor. All three won in elections "fought almost entirely along Klan and anti-Klan lines." The Klan's halcyon days, however, were nearly over when they began. In the off-year elections in 1926 Senator Means, who had been elected to finish two years of a regular term, was defeated, as was Governor Morley. While Mayor Stapleton was reelected in 1927, he openly repudiated his former allies.

The divisive Klan issue in the early 1920s consumed precious time and energy and detracted from Mayor Stapleton's long-range plans relating to water, transportation, and city beautification. But even more disconcerting to him was the four-year period when George D. Begole slipped into the mayor's office. In 1931 a charter revision was used which allowed voters to cast ballots for first, second, and third choice for mayor and other elective candidates. The new system, as George V. Kelly described it, "was based on the assumption that if no candidate won a clear majority on the first or second choices, the person with the largest number of first, second, and third-place ballots would somehow truly represent the people." The Stapleton organization, overly confident in 1931, failed to see the implications of this balloting with six other candidates in the mayoralty race. The mayor and his ward workers determined that they would only campaign for first choice votes. Ignoring what would happen if their own supporters cast numerous second or third choice votes for stronger candidates such as George Begole and Otto Bock, they neglected to circulate sample ballots with instructions to give second and third choice votes to the lesser-known candidates. This oversight resulted in Stapleton far outdistancing Begole and Bock on the first choice, but not winning a majority of all first place votes. Because Begole had so many second and third choice votes, his totals for first, second, and third bettered Stapleton's totals. Even though Begole's margin was less than 1,000, he was the winner.

The confusing and cumbersome three choice ballot is no longer used in Denver, but it was still used when Stapleton sought to recover his office in 1935. With superior tactical use of sample ballots, door-to-door campaigning by old, faithful city employees who wanted their jobs back, yeoman aid from the gambling, saloon, and red-light proprietors, as well as public endorsements, arm-twisting, and large sums of money from Seventeenth Street, Stapleton was easily elected.

"Interminable Ben," as he came to be known, was reelected twice after 1935. One of his most significant achievements was acquiring more water for Denver and the parched farmlands in eastern Colorado. From the late nineteenth century, inadequate water resources have bothered Denver. Unlike most major cities, Colorado's capital does not have an adequate supply of water from natural sources. Local rivers scarcely provided for the needs of Denver and its semiarid agricultural hinterland in the 1880s and 1890s, and by 1900 the Denver Union Water Company started construction of the Cheesman dam on the eastern slope of the mountains to direct water into the Denver region. No sooner had the dam been finished than farsighted observers questioned its capacity to provide for future needs.

Thoughtful community leaders argued that in time of prolonged drouth, water from the eastern side of the watershed would fail to meet the requirements of the growing metropolis. Prior to World War I, inquiries were made about the feasibility of securing western slope water for the east. In 1920, Mayor Dewey Bailey had engineers explore the possibility of rechanneling Fraser River water to Denver by way of the Moffat Tunnel. The thought was to use the pioneer bore (the narrow tunnel cut first for exploration purposes) of the railroad tunnel as a diversion channel. But Bailey could not act unilaterally. He needed the cooperation of the nonpartisan, five-man board of water commissioners which was created in 1918 at the time the city purchased the water company. Although the mayor could appoint the water commissioners, they served set terms which were staggered, and there was no way to replace all five members at once. Bailey's problem was that his commissioners were myopic and showed little interest in the Moffat Tunnel idea.

By the time Stapleton took office, the water diversion project was in limbo, and the wood support structure used to shore up the pioneer bore was rotting and threatening to collapse. Gerald Hughes for sometime had been convinced that the water tunnel was as vital to Denver's future as the railroad passageway, and he immediately brought the issue to Mayor Stapleton's attention. The lethargic water board still showed no interest in the plan, so Stapleton moved on his own. He persuaded the city council to appropriate $200,000 for re-enforcing the pioneer bore, recognizing that if the opening collapsed it would cost a fortune to re-bore.

When George Begole was elected in 1931, Stapleton's water project was still in progress, and half of the money was spent. Mayor Begole demonstrated unusual irresponsibility. He ignored the pioneer bore and spent the remaining $100,000 on other programs. When Stapleton got his office back in 1935, he made the water tunnel top priority. He gradually appointed new members to the water board. With their assistance, the pioneer bore was lined with concrete, and the rights to it were acquired by the city on a long-term lease. In 1936 western slope water reached Denver's treatment plant for the first time.

Stapleton did not stop here on finding water for the Denver region. He surrounded himself with able advisors. George Bull and George Cranmer studied water resources, City Attorney Malcolm Lindsey and his astute assistant, Glenn Saunders, handled the legal problems related to securing water rights. Besides the Moffat Tunnel, other plans were inaugurated. Under Stapleton's direction, the Jones Pass Tunnel was constructed, and work was started on the West Portal of the Roberts Tunnel. By the time Stapleton left office, Denver had three channels to bring in western slope water, and the city possessed legal rights to Colorado's most vital resource.

Another future-oriented program unveiled by Stapleton in the 1920s was the municipal airport. When he first took office in 1923, the prophetic—some said visionary—mayor began searching for an airfield site. Stapleton was confident that air travel would grow increasingly important, and he did not want to see Denver bypassed by air carriers as it had been by transcontinental railroads. Not every citizen shared the mayor's belief that airways would ultimately surpass trains as the most important part of the nation's transportation network. Indeed, *The Post*, under the editorship of F.G. Bonfils, unmercifully and almost libelously attacked the mayor. Sometimes arrogant and aggressive, the short, wiry, sharp-eyed, and moustached little dynamo launched a major assault against Stapleton's airport scheme. Bonfils was seldom thoughtful, and he was frequently blinded by his jaundiced view of people he disliked or could not dominate. Consequently, he labeled the mayor's purchase of 640 acres located nearly ten miles from the central business district as "Stapleton's Folly" and "Simpleton's Sand Dunes." Bonfils even charged that the mayor purchased the square mile from a political associate, Brown Cannon, as a payoff for his support rather than as a municipal asset.

Despite the criticisms, and they came from many people besides Bonfils, Stapleton had faith in the plan. In October 1929, the little airport with two dirt runways, one small hangar, a garage, wind sock, and small terminal was dedicated. On that day, just before the stock market crash, only the most sanguine dreamed that within forty years it would encompass nearly 4,700 acres and become the tenth busiest airport in the United States, served by sixteen scheduled airlines.

If few people shared Stapleton's dedication to making Denver the air transport hub of the Rocky Mountains, still fewer foresaw, as he did, the possibilities for improving and beautifying Denver. This was especially true once the depression spread its social and economic woes across the country. Fortuitously, Mayor Stapleton appointed George E. Cranmer as manager of improvements and parks in 1935. In Cranmer, Stapleton found an able administrator who was creative, optimistic, and sympathetic to his fiscal conservatism.

George Cranmer was born in Denver in 1884. His father, who died when young George was seven years old, had earned more than a comfortable income from cattle and real estate investments. George Cranmer liked to refer to himself as a "self-made man"—a habit acquired by Lawrence Phipps and many other members of Denver's business and social elite—perhaps because it was a way to justify their comforts in a society full of so many who were less fortunate. Like most of Denver's so-called "rags to riches" men, Cranmer's story hardly fits the pattern immortalized by Horatio Alger. His father left the family well fixed. Indeed, they lived off of the income from such properties as the Ernst and Cranmer Building, never having to appreciably alter their life-style after the senior Cranmer's death. To be sure, George Cranmer worked summers on his uncle's Wyoming ranch, and when he went to Princeton, he upholstered furniture to secure spending money. Nevertheless, his mother's income provided for transportation and tuition, and poverty was never a problem the family had to overcome.

Cranmer graduated from Princeton in 1907, and five years later he married Jean Chappell, the heiress to a fortune made in Colorado utilities and real estate. Miss Chappell spent the summers of her youth on the family's ranch near the Evans property. There she became a close friend of Margaret Evans, William Gray Evans' daughter. The young women in this top sphere of Denver society lived in city and mountain homes, attended private schools, and went to Europe to study languages and music. When Margaret Evans went to Paris for several years, Jean Chappell preceded her to Europe to study languages and fine arts in Germany's culture capital, Dresden.

When the young Princeton graduate began courting Miss Chappell, he was still undecided about his own future. Although he pondered going into the cattle business, his future father-in-law urged him to avoid that risky enterprise and become a stock broker. The advice was wise. Cranmer went to work for a leading Denver broker and learned the business. Before long he started his own establishment, and, thanks to his wife's social connections, soon numbered many of the city's wealthiest citizens among his clients.

The talented and hard-working businessman had made a fortune in stocks when lady luck smiled on him once again. In 1928 he had a dispute with his business partner over company policy. The feud ended with Cranmer's exit from the business. Before he could make up his mind about opening a new firm, the market crashed in 1929, leaving him wealthy and secure outside of the prostrate world of stock speculation.

In 1935 Cranmer was fifty years old, full of energy and ambition, and unburdened by financial woes. It was then that Gerald Hughes asked him to help manage Stapleton's campaign with the promise of a blank check from Seventeenth Street. After the successful election campaign, Stapleton offered the former stockbrocker any position he wanted in the city administration. Cranmer wanted to oversee the system of parks and improvements. Years later Cranmer reflected on that choice, remembering that he wanted to pursue some of the ideas which Robert Speer had put into motion over twenty years earlier; many of which had been stalled by Speer's shortsighted successors.

Cranmer was commited to the city functional and beautiful, admitting that his aesthetic tastes were acquired ones, given to him by his wife. His Princeton education, he recalled, did little to stimulate his sensitive nature. It was not until his wife dragged him around Europe and consciously labored to file off his rough edges that he learned to appreciate literature, art, music, and the texture of Europe's most beautiful towns and cities. Inspired by what he learned, George Cranmer wanted to become manager of improvements and parks so that he could put some of his dreams to work.

Cranmer's many accomplishments are remarkable because they are enjoyed by Denver's residents today. But they are even more noteworthy because of the skill required to bring them to fruition. Cranmer assumed his city office in the midst of the Great Depression, when money was scarce and taxpayers rebelled at the mention of higher assessments. In addition, Mayor Stapleton, while sympathetic to Cranmer's concept of the city beautiful, was a most frugal man. His fiscal conservatism was as natural as eating and sleeping. However, he was even more careful about authorizing superfluous new programs because of the criticism he recieved for spending on the Moffat Tunnel and airport projects.

Efficiency became an obsession with the mayor. Cranmer recalled that "he kept a private detective at work all the time, keeping him informed about what was going on." Besides the data gathered by the detective, Stapleton dropped into the various departments, offices, or the city hospital unannounced and studied the efficiency of city employees. "He might appear in any office at any time at City Hall," according to Cranmer, "as he frequently walked around. He personally was the city's employment department, and he never permitted any money to be spent for supplies that he was not informed about."

The mayor applauded Cranmer's goals for improving Denver, but as the manager of improvements and parks phrased it, "the last place I looked for money was the Denver city treasury." Instead, Cranmer's philosophy was that "any really good plan could be financed if I was sufficiently resourceful and persistent. The money would come from somewhere. The U.S. Government, the State, big business, the railroads, public utilities, and private citizens were all sources, if you went about it in the right way."

His clever program of improvements began immediately after he took office in 1935. Almost simultaneously with Stapleton's inauguration came one of Denver's most devastating floods. On the afternoon of May 30, heavy rains filled the headwaters of Cherry Creek. Upstream, the Castlewood Dam broke, and the flood broke out of the channels of Cherry Creek and the Platte in several sections of Denver. Between Colorado and University boulevards, the narrow embankments were washed away, flooding a large section of south Denver. Downtown, Wazee, Blake, and Market streets were flooded, and Union Station was inundated with water. Cranmer quickly set out to widen the channels of Cherry Creek and the Platte wherever they were too narrow to carry water during unusually heavy rains. Cherry Creek between University and Colorado was widened, and roadways were constructed on both sides of the waterway. The Platte, where it coursed downtown and for several miles north and south of the city limits, was widened and re-enforced. New streets were also constructed on both sides of the river.

To finance the flood control project, Cranmer unveiled a scheme to save city money which he would employ many times. Within the city limits were numerous acres of tax-delinquent property. Cranmer sold the properties to raise funds, or he used the property itself for beautification or improvement purposes. There was, for instance, some tax-delinquent land along the riverbanks. This property could be used for improvements. When he needed to purchase land, he merely sold or traded other tax-delinquent properties to acquire access ways.

Cranmer took advantage of the depression to do more than acquire useful or saleable property. Democratic Senators Edward P. Costigan and Alva B. Adams had appointed local relief administrators through Harry Hopkins in Washington. Mayor Stapleton's influence with his Democratic colleagues, plus Gerald Hughes' immense power in the Colorado Democracy, assured cooperation of the Public Works Administration and Works Project Administration with Cranmer's plans. The WPA opened a quarry which provided the bulk of the raw materials for construction, and PWA and WPA employees provided most of the manpower.

Cranmer found help from other federal agencies, too. During the 1920s, Stapleton had purchased 700 acres, including an area called Red Rocks, in the mountains west of Denver to expand the mountain park program which Speer had initiated earlier. Cranmer, influenced by outdoor theaters he had visited in Sicily, decided to convert a part of the Red Rocks into a similar setting. With what Cranmer described as "political pull" through the senators and the mayor, he got the WPA to build roads and a parking lot. Through the National Park Service came 300 young workers from the Civilian Conservation Corps, plus all the necessary construction materials. All that Denver's treasury contributed was the land and a small salary for architect Burnam Hoyt, who planned the seating and toilets. "The stage," as the manager of improvements and parks phrased it, "was created by nature."

The outdoor theater in Red Rocks Park was opened in 1941, but acoustical problems plagued concert goers. Finally, several years later, Cranmer went at his own expense to Germany, and persuaded Wolfgang Wagner, the son of famous composer Richard Wagner, to go to Red Rocks and suggest improvements so that Wagnerian operas could be performed effectively. Cranmer offered to pay Wagner's expenses and fee out of his own pocket. Wagner went to Red

Rocks with his own acoustical engineer, but he refused to take any money—even for his expenses—for what he described as so "worthy a cause."

Germans and federal agencies were not alone in contributing to Cranmer's plan for Denver. As he set out to modernize traffic ways which had been built for horse-and-buggy transports rather than automobiles, he sought contributions from businessmen. Denver needed a new transportation artery to carry automobile traffic from the center of the city to the growing southern region around the University of Denver. Cranmer's solution to this problem was to build Buchtel Boulevard from Logan to University, using both sides of the Colorado and Southern's railroad track. The C. and S., which was controlled by the Burlington, owned a right-of-way of 100 feet along the tracks. Ralph Budd and Robert Rice, presidents of the Burlington and C. and S. respectively, agreed to give their right-of-way to Denver so that a tree-lined boulevard could be constructed.

Land donated by the railroads and tax delinquent land were used to build major traffic arteries south of Alameda to Hampden and north of Alameda to Colfax, as well as a route from the Denargo Market to Thirty-Eighth Street. With a PWA grant to supplement the property acquisitions, versatile Cranmer improved conditions for automobile drivers, brought applause to the city administration, and scarcely touched Denver's tax dollars so carefully guarded by the prudent mayor.

George Cranmer surveying his dream, Red Rocks Theater

WPA labor was employed to build many miles of streets during the Stapleton administration and develop the beauty of the city. Both Stapleton and Cranmer admired Robert Speer's comprehensive park program. Unequivocally, they agreed that everything possible should be done to expand the former mayor's grand design of Denver as an attractive city planned for people. Because Stapleton and Cranmer believed as strongly as Speer that people need places to play, the park movement resumed the vigor it had achieved during the heyday of Speer's regime.

Once again Cranmer was instructed by the cost-conscious chief executive to avoid dipping into city funds whenever possible. Stapleton did, on the other hand, assure his city beautifier that the recreational areas were so high on his list of priorities that local money could be found for worthy projects if alternative sources were unavailable.

The short, slightly rotund, and sharp-eyed park and improvements manager took Stapleton's cue with unbounded enthusiasm. Exuding self-confidence—some say to the point of arrogance—Cranmer assured his boss that he could significantly expand Denver's system of playgrounds at relatively little expense to the city. Unlike Stapleton, who maintained his lower economic class contacts through the city payroll patronage system and socialized in the middle class circles of the VFW and Rotary, Cranmer found his friends and acquaintances on Seventeenth Street, in the Denver Club, and the Denver Country Club. Among these associates, he knew he could find help for a beautification campaign.

Viewed as an eccentric by many people, Cranmer prided himself on being distinctive. He wore bat-wing collars and bow ties even when they were not fashionable. He enjoyed exercising his enormous, singular dog in public parks, where both the remarkable canine and the gregarious master would be observed. If he was not going to city hall in his chauffeur-driven sedan, he might be seen horseback riding in undeveloped sections of southern and eastern Denver. Unique among many of his colleagues, Cranmer found time to read widely in archeology, history, and the arts. Business and politics consumed much of his life, yet he made time for reading and travel.

George Cranmer might have appeared rather peculiar and sometimes patronizing to his associates, but they found him fascinating nevertheless. He lacked the charisma of Robert Speer, and his flamboyant style robbed him of Stapleton's dignity. Regardless, he knew many people of wealth and position, he understood their

George Cranmer in 1971. *A gift to the author from George Cranmer*

natures, and he instinctively recognized how to flatter and employ them to his own ends. Cranmer said that he and the mayor adorned the Queen City with many new public gardens—at little expense to the taxpayers—"by putting tax-delinquent land into park ownership and persuading people to make gifts." The developers of University Hills donated the land for a city park. In return, they received planning aid from Cranmer, as well as valuable publicity for their beneficent act. One of Cranmer's associates, William Geddes, handed over ten acres at Sixth Avenue and Federal. A physician contributed a valuable piece of real estate at Colorado and Alameda. Florence Martin gave 1,000 acres for a mountain park, and Stapleton's friend, Martin O'Fallon, helped expand the system with a donation of several hundred acres below Evergreen in Bear Creek Canyon.

Sometimes civic benefactors became philanthropists reluctantly. The owner of a local brick company gave the city the ground at Third Avenue and Fairfax only after Cranmer found a way to reach his civic spirit. When the businessman was approached to donate this piece of property, he refused—offering to sell it to the city instead. The wily park builder expected this reply, and he was prepared. Several months earlier, while horseback riding one morning, Cranmer discovered that tons of clay had been removed from an isolated piece of land owned by the city. Upon investigation, the sporting city administrator learned that the brick company was quietly helping itself to the municipally owned natural resource. Having measured the stripped terrain, Cranmer had prepared a bill for the thrifty industrialist. Happening to have it in his pocket during the land donation negotiations, the park manager assured the manufacturer that the city would happily purchase the real estate, but only after this outstanding debt was paid. Ultimately, Denver got a new park, and the large hole in the ground was forgotten.

While tax delinquent property and gifts from private landowners became the nucleus of Stapleton's park expansions, the mayor was willing to use city funds to build playgrounds. When the Wellshire Golf Club along Hampden Avenue fell into financial difficulty, Stapleton persuaded the council to appropriate $60,000 to purchase it for the city. This municipal golf course was only one segment of the administration's program to make golfing facilities available in all parts of Denver. The master plan improved old facilities and acquired new property. Ultimately, there were golf courses in every section of the city: City Park was centrally located; Case was northwest; Park Hill was northeast; Overland Park, southwest; Wellshire, southeast; and one eighteen-hole course was located in the mountain parks.

The massive improvement and beautification programs pleased the citizens. The administration gave residents a more attractive and comfortable city without substantial tax increases. A majority of the big businessmen were delighted with Stapleton's regime, too. The mayor held their taxes down, enhanced the image of the community, and his programs increased property values. Lower economic classes were gratified by the emphasis Stapleton put on free places to play. Also, men and women, black and white, irrespective of ethnic background or religion, many of whom possessed few skills and limited educations, were given equal access to the thousands of city jobs at the mayor's disposal.

The relative ease by which Stapleton was re-elected in 1939 and 1943 testified to his popularity, but Denver was not a completely unified and harmonious community throughout his tenure. An important source of opposition came from the Chamber of Commerce and the real estate, construction, and small business interests which governed that organization by the 1920s. In the late nineteenth century, Denver's business community dominated the Chamber of Commerce and its forerunner, the Board of Trade. By the early twentieth century, the booster organization was managed by full-time professionals who reflected those interests. During this period, the power elite, comprised of big businessmen and financiers, gradually lost interest in the chamber. Their own enterprises demanded more attention. With the city securely established as the dominant regional metropolis, it was no longer essential to continually boost the city to protect their investments. Until the first years of the new century, promotional activities seemed to be necessary. Unless investors, settlers, and businesses were attracted to Denver, the city might wither.

Gerald Hughes, Claude Boettcher, John Evans, and the other young members of Denver's power structure felt little compulsion to spend time or money for promotion. As they saw it, a population explosion would add little to their businesses. The banks already had many more requests for home and small business loans than they were willing to lend. In fact, to their view, unbridled growth would bring nothing but chaos and woe. Mayor Stapleton and most of his administration, in particular George Cranmer, agreed with that point of view.

Hundreds of small merchandisers, warehousers, real estate and construction companies disagreed with that philosophy. They yearned for vast expansion and the opportunity to make fortunes like those already enjoyed by the affluent members of the private clubs. They were willing to suffer growing pains as long as they made enormous returns on their investments.

These leaner, hungrier, and less cautious entrepreneurs far outnumbered the established elite by the 1920s. Paying the same dues and having an equal voice in the Chamber of Commerce, they set its tone and direction. To the chagrin of Seventeenth Street and the city administration, the chamber was willing to sacrifice quality of life for growth and profits. The boosters, desirous of attracting industries and settlers—a campaign which Cranmer warned would flood Denver with "low brows"—sought factories throughout the period between the wars. Booklets such as *Denver the Industrial City* (1922) were printed and distributed all over the United States. Thousands of dollars were spent publishing and circulating pamphlets on Denver's advantages as an industrial center, and advertising space was bought in magazines and newspapers.

The promoters were not very successful. They did boast of attracting eight new factories by 1928, among them Ralston Purina and National Lumber and Creosoting Company. The public relations men blamed conservative politicians and bankers for a poor outside response during the 1930s, charging that loan restrictions discouraged prospective investors. Coupled with this criticism was the accusation that Stapleton counseled against diverting western slope water for industrial use. The mayor maintained that eastern Colorado would never have an overabundance of this precious resource, and what could be diverted should be conserved for drinking, beautification, and agriculture.

Although the depression was probably a significant factor during the 1930s, the city administration and the bankers certainly played a key role in directing Denver through a long period of controlled growth. This wise and guarded posture remained constant until right after World War II, when forces beyond the control of the power elite would topple the power structure, change the city's direction, and leave prodigious problems for future generations.

The Chamber of Commerce was not without influence, but it is indicative of the strength wielded by Stapleton and the bankers that only when they agreed with the booster organization did it realize much success. Chamber spokesmen were as dedicated to attracting tourists as factories, and here the mayor, Cranmer, Hughes, and associates had no quarrel. Tourism was clean. It generated income, rarely attracted "low brows," and the participants seldom stayed around after the season demanding higher wages, housing, services, or welfare.

Despite the depression, tourism grew in the 1930s. Numbers of tourists increased almost every year, reaching nearly 1,400,000 who spent $80 million by 1936. The chamber advertised Colorado as a "Year Round Playground" and sponsored "good will tours" of recreation areas for influential out-of-staters. Such programs helped, yet several other factors aided the boom, too. Robert G. Athearn's history of the Denver and Rio Grande Western Railroad, *Rebel of the Rockies*, explains the complex legal and business transactions that brought the Moffat Road to the Denver and Rio Grande line via the Dotsero Cutoff in 1934. This connection placed Denver on a direct line to the Pacific Coast through Salt Lake City. For the first time, West Coast tourists could go to Colorado with little effort.

Another boom to tourism was the airport. Thanks to Stapleton's and Cranmer's dogged efforts to expand the municipal airport and their use of federal aid to pave runways, Denver inaugurated transcontinental air service in 1937. Federal grants also helped Colorado's highway construction program. Old highways were improved and new ones were built.

Immensely important to attracting tourists were the efforts made by the Stapleton administration to provide winter playgrounds. The bulk of tourists prior to the 1930s came in the summer months to enjoy the national parks, trout streams, and lakes. Cranmer, however, envisioned added possibilities. "One of our greatest natural resources. . . I'm not referring to gold, or silver, or water," he remarked, "is ready for taking. . .—an area for a wonderful winter playground."

To be sure, winter sports were popular in Colorado long before Cranmer uttered his views in the 1930s. From early in the century, skiers had congregated at Hot Sulphur Springs and Steamboat Springs, and more travelled to those winter pleasure spots in the years just before World War I to participate in the Winter Carnivals, which featured ski racing and jumping. By the early 1930s, skiers found modest facilities—even a crude tow lift—at Crested Butte. By the late 1930s, a rope tow had been installed on the south side of the summit of Berthoud Pass, and downhill ski enthusiasts flocked there by the thousands because they could reach the area by automobile from Denver without much difficulty.

In 1937 the *Rocky Mountain News*, with support from the Chamber of Commerce, civic leaders, and local ski zealots, organized the Colorado Winter Sports Council. That group wanted to install a new tow at Berthoud Pass and design a program to open new slopes near Berthoud with the goal of relieving already overcrowded

Winter Park

conditions. Several thousand acres of land near the West Portal of the Moffat Tunnel were first leased and later purchased from the United States Forest Service by Denver. It became Winter Park—the showplace of the city's mountain park system. With $14,000 donated by local businessmen, a PWA grant of $38,000, secured through Senator Alva Adams, and volunteer labor, George Cranmer oversaw the creation of runs, lifts, and shelters.

One problem arose which threatened to stall the ski lift project. When the tow was finished and activated for its first test run, the system worked well until people mounted the seats. Then it stalled. There was not enough power to pull the weight. Resourceful George Cranmer came to the rescue. He decided that if the heavy metal plates used for seats could be removed, the system would function. Quickly Cranmer came up with a solution. He went home and collected a number of wine kegs from his prohibition era wine cellar. Construction workers removed the metal seats and replaced them with keg staves. The next test run proved the wine connoisseur's genius. A local newspaper celebrated the event by announcing that "Cranmer rolls out the barrel and saves Winter Park."

As soon as the work was completed, the Denver and Salt Lake Railroad introduced special "snow trains" to West Portal in 1938, and by the following year, the new "capital" of winter sports and Denver's mountain park system was formally christened "Winter Park."

Expanded ski facilities easily accessible by train, plus new highway, rail and air routes in Colorado's "Year-Round Sports Paradise" all conspired to make the Centennial State a tourist mecca. The Chamber of Commerce took full credit for the prewar tourist boom, but nothing so dramatic could have been accomplished without the wholehearted backing of city hall and Seventeenth Street.

Denver's Chamber of Commerce devoted considerable resources to one other promotional venture during the 1930s. The "Little Capital of the United States" campaign, like the plan to develop tourism, was successful because the power structure approved it. Sometimes called the Second Capital program, Denver's leaders hoped to benefit from the trend to expand federal bureaucracies. Beginning in the first decade of the twentieth century and increasing almost every year, federal bureaus and agencies of all kinds were created. Presidents Theodore Roosevelt and Woodrow Wilson did more than any of their predecessors to inflate the system. Their successors, particularly Herbert Hoover and Franklin Roosevelt, not only preserved myriad departments designed to regulate America's society and economy, they joined the Congress in creating more. Along with the extension of governmental control into an ever-widening circle of American life came the creation of regional offices for major branches of the government.

By 1930 over two thousand federal employees were headquartered in Denver to oversee various government enterprises in the Rocky Mountain region. Before the depression, about four hundred people worked for the Department of Agriculture, with over three hundred of these serving a six-state division of the Forest Service. Three hundred more people worked at desks in Denver for the Bureau of Reclamation, and over two hundred directed operations of the General Land Office. More than one thousand people had been hired by Fitzsimons General Hospital, and scores of civilians worked for the War Department at Ft. Logan and Lowry Aviation Field or found their way into the Post Office Department and the Departments of Commerce, Justice, Navy, and Treasury.

Occasional misgivings about spending and big government were expressed in Denver during Franklin Roosevelt's administration. Rhetoric aside, however, the Chamber of Commerce, in unison with the mayor and Seventeenth Street, waxed ecstatic at the thought of enticing new agencies. Members of the power elite endorsed the "Little Capital" booster campaign because, unlike the "industrial city" drive, it was going to offer "clean enterprise." Smog, dirt, and noise did not accompany federal offices, the employees were not interested in unionizing, and they were relatively well paid. Government payrolls stimulated Denver's economy, and so did the extensive purchases of supplies by the various agencies.

The Chamber of Commerce estimated that in 1921 alone the federal government purchased approximately $3.5 million worth of supplies locally, and that figure increased annually. George Cranmer expressed why Denver wanted to become a regional center when he said, "we had good experiences with Lowry, Ft. Logan and Fitzsimons. National agencies grow and pay their bills. And they don't leave you." Ronald Reagan, in his 1976 bid for the Republican presidential nomination, expressed disdain when he said that "federal agencies represent the closest thing to immortality that we know on this earth." Cranmer and his colleagues knew this in the early 1930s, and they counted it as an asset for Denver.

During the 1930s and early 1940s, community leaders made frequent trips to Washington, D.C. There they huddled with senators and congressmen and lobbied in decisionmakers' offices to get new federal installations for Denver and its hinterland. They met with more than modest success. By 1941, nearly 6,500 Denver area people were employed by the United States govenment, and in June 1946, a survey showed 16,456 federal civilian employees in the Denver metropolitan area.

To be sure, some of this bureaucracy would have come Denver's way if no one had gone after it. But it is naive to assume that Denver would have attracted all the permanent agencies and installations it did without active lobbying in Washington. Other cities, after all, were soliciting federal bureaus, too. In truth, the competition was, and still is, keen for communities seeking a share of the nation's budget. An example of how Denver's power structure worked to win prize facilities occurred while war was raging in Europe, but before the United States had entered the conflict. As soon as the government announced that it was going to open an Air Corps training center, Denver put in a bid for the facility. The city offered a piece of real estate to enlarge the Lowry Aviation Field, which had opened in the mid-1920s.

When the Military Affairs Committee, led by Congressman Lister Hill of Alabama, arrived in Denver to inspect the proposed site and listen to local boosters, George Cranmer was asked by Colorado Congressman Lawrence Lewis to help receive the Washington contingent. Realizing that Denver was the last stop for these men who had just examined thirty-nine other prospective locations, the manager of improvements and parks decided to entertain the tired investigators rather than regale them with facts and figures which they would promptly forget. Cranmer recalled the visit of the congressional group in this way:

> After looking at so many places, I believed more acres of flat land and statistics would not be impressive or remembered. I proposed a trip to the mountain parks with stops for refreshments at Echo Lake and at Eddy Ott's Tavern by the lake at Evergreen, followed in the evening by a real party at my house. [Congressman] Lawrence [Lewis] was an ultra-conservative person and very serious. He thought they would not have time for such frivolity. Then the pilot of their plane became ill, and they had to stay here a day longer than planned; and that was my opportunity. We carried out the plan I had proposed. Mrs. Cranmer was out of town, so I asked my sister, Mrs. Coors, to round up a group of good looking girls in the social crowd, to help give the air crowd a good time. I hired a small orchestra, took the furniture and rugs out of our living room, and after returning from the mountain trip we all enjoyed a gay dancing party until well toward morning. My sister picked the girls with judgement so the party was a big success.
>
> The final decision came soon after this and Denver was chosen as the site of the air school. . . .

Cranmer helped engineer more than the location of the Army Air Corps Technical School in Denver. When the government decided in 1940 to purchase a facility (to be owned by the government but managed by Remington Arms Company) for manufacturing small arms, Cranmer received a phone call from Jess Hough, a Union Pacific executive headquartered in Omaha. Hough informed Cranmer that Omaha would not get the plant but that Denver still had a chance. Hoping to see the plant located on a Union Pacific line, Hough offered to meet Cranmer in Washington the following week to urge General George Marshall, Army Chief of Staff, to give Denver serious consideration.

Ultimately, Hough, Cranmer, Stapleton, John Evans, and Lawrence Lewis descended upon army officers and Remington officials in the nation's capital. Prevailing opinion on the part of the decision makers was that the plant should be located near the East Coast to keep shipping costs down when arms were transported to Europe. Stapleton and Cranmer hammered away at the idea that soon the United States would be at war in the Pacific, too, thereby making a more central location desirable. To what extent the reasoning was considered by the military and business leaders is impossible to say, but the Denver site was selected in late 1940. The following year a $24 million cartridge plant was opened.

Once the decision was made to locate along the Green Mountain foothills west of Denver, Cranmer urged federal architects to purchase an additional strip of land one quarter mile wide on the eastern edge of the plant. The idea behind this was to assure the government's regulation of the neighborhood, in Cranmer's words, "so they could control the neighborhood and prevent anything being built there that might harbor saboteurs."

The long-range effects of this additional land purchase were significant. After the war, because the federal government already owned so much Denver real estate, it was deemed economical to build a massive regional center there. Today the Federal Center west of downtown employs thousands of civilians, houses numerous regional agencies, and represents the acme of "clean industry"—the goal behind the "little capital" plan unveiled in the early 1930s.

What no one apparently foresaw during the late 1930s and early 1940s was the overwhelming impact of the "second capital" program. The promotional campaign, ironically, was too successful to suit Denver's power structure. A tidal wave of change was unleashed— one that inundated Denver's "controlled growth" power elite, left a new group of leaders in its wake, materially altered the city, and left it burdened with new problems.

Chapter 8

In 1927 a young and perceptive writer named Carey McWilliams wrote a small piece on Denver for *Overland Monthly and Out West Magazine*. Naming his essay "A Requiem for Denver," McWilliams bemoaned the fact that the mountain metropolis "has dozed blissfully on, unaware of its own identity, and perhaps ignorant that it has personality." When he was writing, there was truth to the charge. During the early 1920s, Robert Speer's coalition collapsed, labor strife was rampant, and thousands of insecure citizens looked for an anchor in the Ku Klux Klan. In 1926 the Chamber of Commerce summarized the immediate post-World War I period in a booster book entitled *The Long Pull*: "Denver was in the throes of reaction for some years. Tramway trouble, agitation of all sorts, a sense of insecurity—these were the symptoms evident in the Denver body politic."

Many groups contributed to those tensions. After the Russian Revolution, the local press continually stirred up fears of a Communist menace. According to Robert Athearn's *The Coloradans*, *The Denver Post* attacked "foreign labor leaders," and the *Catholic Register* charged that "open Bolsheviks," many who did not "speak English," were plotting changes for the community. Bigotry was manifested in more ways than attacks on east European immigrants. Whites, both Jews and Gentiles, in the Five Points district were angry about the black migration to their neighborhood. Ben Stapleton, during his first term as mayor, added to the divisiveness by proclaiming his ties with the Ku Klux Klan and then appointing leaders of that nativist organization to major city offices.

Great Western Sugar Company, directed by the powerful Boettcher, Morey, Porter, Mitchell, Hughes, Coors, and Porter families, indirectly brought tension. Until World War I they found laborers from eastern Europe—particularly Germans from Russia— to cultivate their sugar beets. The war disrupted communications and halted immigration, so the corporation executives turned to Mexico for inexpensive farm workers. With their brown skins, Spanish language, Catholic religion, and unfamiliar customs, these impoverished Mexicans were greeted by Coloradans in the same way Chinese, Italian, and east European immigrants had been previously received.

By 1920 the majority population protested importation of Mexican labor. But trucks crowded to capacity with Mexican nationals continued their journeys to Colorado's beet fields. Anglo farmhands resented foreign competition, but the sugar growers and processors continued glutting the market to keep costs down. The sugar interests paid the lowest possible wages, leaving the workers without enough money to return home. Sometimes the growers withheld wages, deliberately forcing the Mexicans to remain in Colorado so they would be available for next season's harvest.

When harvesting ended, the migrant workers drifted into cities and towns seeking work. Penniless and unable to return home, they had no source of livelihood until beet harvesting time arrived the following year. Because Denver had more employment opportunities for unskilled workers than smaller towns, plus a city hospital and a welfare program for the destitute, Mexicans found their way there by the thousands. In 1920, 1,390 Mexicans lived in the Queen City. Nearly 7,000 resided there by 1930.

The depression caused Coloradans to demand the removal of Mexican aliens. In 1936, Governor Edwin C. Johnson oversaw the deportation of 100,000 Mexicans to their homeland, and he sent the National Guard to Colorado's southern border to block the entry of anyone who tried to return. Despite these efforts, an estimated 22,000 Mexicans entered Colorado. Their admittance was abetted by the sugar growers and processors who were determined to have inexpensive labor regardless of public sentiment and official policy. As a consequence, over 12,000 Mexicans were living in Denver on the eve of World War II. Forced into the worst housing once inhabited by blacks and poor whites, a ghetto, or barrio, of Spanish-speaking people developed along Cherokee, Delaware, and Elati, not far south and west of the Civic Center, while some families moved to Five Points.

Wartime economic needs in factories and farms eased the plight of these exploited people for a few years. Indeed, jobs were so abundant that Hispano-American farmers and ranchers who had lived in southern Colorado years before gold was discovered along Cherry Creek moved to Denver to take advantage of the boom.

Social conflict dominated Denver from the Red Scare days after World War I right through the peak Ku Klux Klan years. Bigoted attacks and counterattacks were directed to and from most quarters of the city until it seemed that most community resources were harnessed for unproductive purposes. But Denver was not paralyzed for long. By 1926 the fear of Communist revolution in America subsided, and the Ku Klux Klan was devastated by exposes of abject corruption among its depraved leaders.

In 1926 Mayor Stapleton provided the leadership which helped bind warring social factions and turned community energy toward constructive unity. Stapleton's goal was to inspire pride in the city— not the haughtiness found in rapid growth, rather, self-esteem firmly grounded in beauty and recreation. From the late 1920s until the end of World War II, an ethos of civic pride evolved. Led by the mayor, the Chamber of Commerce, newspapers, and business leaders, this spirit gradually permeated all walks of life. Denverites developed an esprit de corps about their city. Taking a cue from the slogan started by *The Denver Post* on its front page weather forecast, " 'Tis a Privilege to Live in Colorado," citizens began to boost their community with the fervor of Sinclair Lewis' George Babbitt.

Quality became the key to the good life. Denver must provide a splendid environment for its people—one aesthetically pleasing, clean, comfortable, and offering an abundance of healthful, outdoor recreational facilities—all designed to foster interaction and tranquility. A sense of community that all people could share was the goal.

In the nineteenth century, Denver's leaders frequently compared their town to Boston, St. Louis, and New York. Imitating those major cities was fashionable. With each well-established urban facility and style that Denver acquired, so it was assumed, the more respectable the frontier town would become. By the late 1920s, however, Denver was secure. Most influential leaders and the public at large showed no interest in patterning their city after the giant metropolises.

An important commitment to quality of life, as opposed to growth for the sake of growth, was made in 1925. Charles C. Gates, Sr., the forty-eight-year-old founder and president of the Gates Rubber Company, proposed that the University of Denver's School of Commerce do a study of local industry. As Denver's leading industrialist, Gates had started the Colorado Tire and Leather Company in 1911. Adapting his horse halter and leather tire cover factory to changing times, the ambitious and hard-working manufacturer invented the rubber V-Belt for automobiles and developed several lines of tires and retreads for motor-powered vehicles. By 1925, Gates, with his business renamed Gates Rubber Company, wanted the university's business faculty to measure the impact of his industry on human relationships. Further, he wanted to know what effect new industries would have on Denver.

His self-interest notwithstanding, Gates was one of the first to warn Denver of the dangers of indiscriminately attracting industries. His own factory demonstrated that economic advantages would be accompanied by social problems. Besides such issues as housing and labor relations, there was the problem of air pollution.

The study conducted by the University of Denver inspired the Stapleton administration to do more than take a jaundiced view toward soliciting industries. It became an incentive to clean up the foul air which had shrouded the city from its infancy. A 1917 smoke ordinance had not been enforced, but the new administration made extensive efforts to bring the mountains back into view. Pressure, backed by threat of prosecution, was used by the government to force companies to extend flues, repair defective ones, and reset boilers to required specifications. Also, factory and home owners alike were encouraged to convert from coal to natural gas. The results were astounding. One year before Stapleton took office, Denver ranked thirty-seventh among 150 cities in a federal clean air survey. By 1927, the Queen City had risen to eighteenth.

Simultaneously with steps taken to reduce smoke, Stapleton created the Denver Planning Commission. Under the direction of John S. Flower, this city and county body symbolized a dedication to excellence of life rather than unbridled expansion. Organized in 1926, the Denver Planning Commission published its first report in late 1929. Consisting of recommendations for the mayor, the report eschewed copying the development of eastern cities. New York City "is throttling itself to death with its sky-reaching magnitudes," wrote the commissioners. Happily reporting that Denver had a population density of only 6.73 persons per acre (New York, Boston, St. Louis, and Philadelphia had from three to five times as many per acre), the planners urged that Denver continue its "present policy and build a city of spacious beauty and high utility, avoiding forever the evils of tremendous congestion and vile overcrowding, which make impossible any decent orderly living."

The Planning Commission did more than warn against excessive growth, it made three specific proposals—all relative to making Denver a more pleasant place in which to live. Major streets should be widened to avoid traffic congestion because, as the commissioners predicted, more automobiles would be used in the future. Boulevards, reserved for passenger traffic, must be designed to connect an even larger park system. "The main reason," the authors argued, "is that the proper sort of park system makes the city more liveable, adding vastly to the health, happiness, and enjoyment of the citizens." Finally, the Planning Commission urged the use of city land such as parks and school property for the construction of recreational facilities.

They advocated the creation of a broad range of programs and facilities, to be spread widely and equitably across the community. "The ideal center" should provide something for all ages. Small children need wading pools, swings, sandboxes, and merry-go-rounds, whereas older youth and adults want swimming pools, athletic fields, tennis and handball courts, and indoor gym equipment. Rooms should be available for a variety of activities such as story reading, crafts, art exhibits, and music and drama programs. The rationale for the recreation centers was presented as follows:

To a degree recreation is a new problem for our cities. It did not exist a few decades ago when children could still play in the streets and the adults had fewer leisure hours for recreation. The greater complexity of our present-day, machine civilization with its intensely developed urban areas has robbed the children of their space for play while it has been giving the adults more time, and as it has been necessary to accompany this change with more thorough education, it now becomes essential to provide comprehensive and systematic recreational opportunities.

In many cities, lofty ideals articulated in planning reports never came to fruition. But in Denver the goals became reality. National-circulation magazines in the late 1920s and the 1930s frequently featured stories on Denver's beauty and utility. Urban planners, tourists, and travel writers were as awed as local residents by Denver's unique advantages. The expanded zoo was a major attraction. A model of its kind (the animals were in barless enclosures made to look like natural habitats), it became the inspiration for St. Louis' renowned Forest Park zoo. Celebrated, too, were the mountain parks, where people could enjoy the splendor of the Rocky Mountains while hiking, picnicking, or golfing. Red Rocks

Theater won national acclaim because nothing like it existed anywhere else in the United States. An Urban Land Institute spokesman at the Massachusetts Institute of Technology singled out Denver's street-widening program as a most impressive example of planning which should be followed by other cities.

Dozens of magazine articles praising Denver appeared during the Stapleton era, and this alone helped nurture a sense of community. Recognition was not the only thing that helped Denverites develop unity through identity with their town. Virtually everyone was involved in the revitalization program. Each project required materials, and this stimulated local business. Hundreds of additional laborers were hired, and the overseers made certain that the blacks, Mexican-Americans, and other minorities had their fair share of jobs. Schools, clubs, and a variety of organizations were recruited to lend support. *Industrial Education Magazine* marveled at the number of volunteers involved in planting trees each year from 1926 to 1929. Junior and senior high school classes planted pine seedlings in the mountain parks and along the roads to parks, as did the Boy Scouts and the Order of DeMolay. The Forest Service furnished the infant trees, and the Kiwanis Club and Chamber of Commerce provided the transportation.

The extent to which civic leaders sought to embrace all classes and ethnic groups was apparent in the 1930 park and recreation district plan. Denver's forty-four parks and over sixteen hundred acres of land were carefully sectioned into thirty-three districts. As R.S. DeBoer, the city planner and landscape architect, explained it, "one district is meant to serve a largely Italian population, another a Jewish section, one a Negro section, and still another a district becoming Mexican in character. In these racially different centers the ideal list of equipment will be varied to fit the needs of the particular nationality served." The city planners consulted with representatives of each minority and sought their advice on facilities and equipment.

By design, from planning construction and use, Denver was remodeled as a city for participants. No class, club, group, or organization was excluded. To be sure, blacks were segregated. They could only use the public swimming pools on designated days of the week. By recent standards, such discrimination was immoral and unconstitutional. By the standards of the pre-World War II era, on the other hand, Denver extended equality beyond the national norm. Indeed, when swimming facilities were built in neighboring Kansas City and St. Louis, blacks were not restricted to certain days, they were totally excluded.

Having a *more* equal life than blacks in other cities but still being treated as inferior was not acceptable to everyone. In 1939 a few blacks and whites demonstrated to protest discriminatory pool regulations. The demonstration was unsuccessful because the insensitive majority population believed blacks had no legitimate complaint; furthermore, Denver's black people failed to unite on the issue. Many blacks, especially those who were successful in business or secure on the city payroll, refused to risk their security by demanding equal rights. They feared reprisals if they were identified with demonstrators—whom *The Denver Post* labelled Communists.

Racial demonstrations in 1939 neither awakened people's sense of injustice nor disturbed the spirit of pride residents shared for their city. Denverites could ignore the black minority because it was small and rarely vocal. That token reminders of racial discrimination failed to disturb the city's sense of well being is not surprising. Not even the great depression caused significant divisiveness. On the contrary, because most people came through that troubled time with a minimum of hardship, enthusiasm was generated for the community which surpassed anything since the townspeople rallied to build the Denver Pacific Railroad in the late 1860s.

A number of factors account for Denver's relatively smooth journey through the depression. The healthy social climate of the late 1920s cushioned tensions in the 1930s. Habits of working toward common goals made cooperation easier when survival was the issue. Besides, Denver was not as industrialized as most eastern cities. Consequently, the massive layoffs which followed manufacturing curtailment affected Denver less severely.

This does not mean that no suffering or conflict occurred in the Rocky Mountain metropolis during the 1930s. The early years were particularly difficult. Local relief rolls were strained while President Herbert Hoover sat in Washington prohibiting use of federal money for emergency relief. Conditions did not improve measurably during the early phase of Franklin Roosevelt's New Deal. A large share of the blame goes to an indolent state legislature. That body, goaded by callous and inflexible Governor Edwin C. Johnson, and the equally obtuse new editor of *The Denver Post*, William C. Shepherd, did everything in its power to cripple New Deal programs. In January 1934, for example, federal emergency relief officials stopped payments to Colorado because the general assembly refused to appropriate matching funds. *The Christian Century* magazine reported that "40,000 people in Denver alone are affected, many of them having the government doles of salt pork, beans, flour, and eggs as their only food for weeks." But the assembly remained adamant. Members did not move until violence was imminent. Four hundred men with trucks threatened to raid chain grocery stores, and a retired carpenter announced on the floor of the legislature that "I helped to build this capitol 52 years ago and I can help tear it down."

During these difficult years, people did what little they could for themselves when federal aid was not available. One of the most successful black businessmen in Five Points, Ben Hooper, recalled that his people were critically affected by the first years of the depression. The owner of a saloon and dance hall called the Casino and the Ex-Servicemen's Club, Hooper was one of the most respected and influential men in Five Points. Known as the "Mayor of Five Points," he was a staunch Democrat. Ben Stapleton helped Hooper secure business property at 2626 Welton in the 1920s when whites tried to block the black businessman's purchase. In return, Hooper campaigned for the Democratic mayor. He even prevailed upon a leading black Republican, Dr. Clarence Holmes, to allow him to place a "Stapleton for Mayor" sign in Holmes' front yard. No wonder the "Mayor of Five Points" was persuasive. He won the hearts of his fellow citizens by preparing free lamb and pigs feet stews for the destitute during the depression, and he held Christmas parties for poor children at the Casino.

Times were difficult in neighborhoods other than Five Points. In 1933 over 10,000 families—9,300 white, over 600 black, and nearly 400 Mexican-American—qualified for assistance. When federal aid was not forthcoming, these unfortunates went hungry, suffered from malnutrition, and a few were forced to place out their children to farms or ranches. Some indigent citizens found succor through the Unemployed Citizens' League of Denver. Founded in 1932 by unemployed professional men and led by architect Charles D. Strong, the UCL opened its headquarters in an old downtown warehouse. Strong's organization was similar to but more extensive than the Citizens' Employment Committee organized by Mayor Begole in 1931. The UCL reached every Denver neighborhood with its twenty-five local branches. Companies were asked to register jobs. When regular employment could not be found, able-bodied members were taken out to harvest crops for a percentage of the yield. Sometimes they cut firewood and mined coal. Fuel and food were distributed from the league's warehouse. At the headquarters, activities were coordinated and 500 loaves of bread were baked daily. Needy persons were given used clothing, food, and fuel. In return, they were expected to help harvest, mine, cut timber, or work at the warehouse baking bread, repairing old shoes and clothes, barbering, or teaching English to aliens.

The Unemployed Citizens League also gave food simply on the basis of need. Frequently there was more need than available work at the warehouse. Once in awhile a boon came to the depleted larder when generous farmers donated loads of fresh produce. In August 1932, the local press applauded a truck gardener for his generous gift. Manuel Din, a Hispano from the San Luis Valley, drove a load of green beans to the Denver market. The most he was offered for his beans on Commission House Row was fifteen dollars. Rather than accept such paltry pay, he dropped the entire load off at the league's warehouse, where eager workers cleaned and packaged the beans for hungry families.

By 1935 these citizens' voluntary projects were supplemented by New Deal programs. Although the militantly anti-New Deal governor, Edwin Johnson, was in the executive office until he went to the Senate in 1937, Senators Edward P. Costigan and Alva Adams secured Colorado's fair share of federal funding. Johnson did everything imaginable to block Colorado's rightful portion of federal aid from reaching the people. The National Archives contain files which reveal that Johnson continually attacked Paul D. Shriver, the federal relief administrator for Colorado. Shriver, who headquartered in Denver, was appointed by Harry Hopkins on the recommendation of Democratic Senators Costigan and Adams. Johnson was a Democrat, too, but he represented the most conservative faction of the party, and he spent much of his time crusading against "radicals" like Roosevelt and Costigan.

Because Shriver was a New Dealer recommended by the liberal wing of Colorado's Democracy, Governor Johnson was relentless in his attacks. Johnson was unimpressed by the meritorious way Shriver managed New Deal programs. Colorado's work relief administration was a model of efficiency and fairness. It was the opposite of states such as New York, New Jersey, Missouri, Massachusetts, and Illinois, where waste left deserving people unassisted and politicians coerced relief recipients to support machine candidates at election time. Harry Hopkins' field investigators found Colorado's relief programs free of politics and equitably dispersed among all groups regardless of race, religion, sex, or political affiliation. Furthermore, except for anti-New Dealers like Johnson and *The Post* editor, Shepherd, Coloradans generally were pleased with the way federal agencies were directed. Inquiring specifically about morale in Denver, Hopkins was told by Shriver that "we have very little complaint here as far as relief people are concerned. . . I would welcome anybody coming from your office. We have been getting along all right. We have had very few complaints."

Despite Shriver's ability to keep man-cost hours below the national average, and concurrently keeping almost all employable people off the direct dole, Edwin Johnson continued his criticisms. In 1935 he wrote to Shriver: "On behalf of Colorado taxpayers, our unemployed citizens, patriotic organizations and good citizens generally, I most respectfully demand that no alien and no person not a citizen of the State be given employment in the Public Works Program. . . ." Shriver countered with a curt reply: "Have you considered that if aliens are excluded from employment with this Administration, they must of necessity be classed as unemployables and become the responsibility of the counties? . . . Hunger, unfortunately, is no respecter of persons or of citizenship. I cannot believe that your solution to the alien problem, even it were possible to determine who are aliens and who are not, is that such unfortunate people are to be allowed to starve within the boundaries of a State which justly boasts of its friendliness and hospitality."

Paul Shriver adhered to his principles even after the governor went public with the issue in hopes of appealing to those who shared his anti-Mexican prejudice. What Shriver did was to go to Harry Hopkins and request more help so that they could find work for all of the unemployed in Colorado. Resident aliens, however, never posed as great a problem as transients. Denver's reputation for weathering the depression better than industrialized cities, its salubrious climate, and its location on a transcontinental railroad, all conspired to attract eight hundred to one thousand sojourners to Denver each month by the mid 1930s.

Mayor Stapleton appointed banker Thomas A. Dines to head the advisory board of the city and county Bureau of Public Welfare. His task was to solve the transient problem. Dines was a remarkably able and versatile man who crowded as much into his busy schedule as any Denver entrepreneur. Born in Springfield, Illinois, in 1880, Dines went to Denver in 1903 with a few years of experience as a bookkeeper in a Puget Sound lumber company. Eventually working his way up on Seventeenth Street, the ambitious and talented financier became president of the United States National Bank in 1936. Like most of his banking colleagues, he delved into assorted enterprises, serving on the boards of Midwest Refining Company, Utah Oil Refining Company, Colorado and Southern Railway,

Denver Union Stockyards Company, and Daniels and Fisher Store Company. Unlike many of his associates, Dines found time to actively develop the arts in Denver. Always giving more than his check and name to cultural programs, the banker worked closely with Jean Chappell Cranmer in promoting the undersubscribed Civic Symphony in the 1920s and 1930s. He served as director of the Symphony Society during those years, was the director of the Art Museum, and served on the University of Denver Board of Trustees.

Thomas A. Dines invariably took more than a perfunctory interest in community affairs. He helped the mayor solve the transient problem with energy and resourcefulness. Using public and private funds, the temporary residents were fed and housed one night. If they had a permanent residence, they were given a one-way ticket back home. Both Dines and Stapleton admitted that such an answer was imperfect. It merely passed the unemployment problem on to another county. Nevertheless, they recognized that if Denver offered long-term relief to transients, the word would spread throughout the land. Denver would be inundated with paupers. Soon the Queen City would be overcrowded and bankrupt.

At least half of the rail-riding, hitchhiking vagrants had no permanent residences. Ordering them to leave the city was futile. Jail, with its shelter and daily rations, was preferable to walking the streets, sleeping in alleys, begging door to door, and rooting through restaurant garbage cans. Dines understood the situation, and he was able to persuade Washington to find money for bringing relief to the army of vagabonds.

At least one act of God brought temporary positions to able-bodied indigents. On September 27, 1936, an early snowstorm—one of the worst in Denver's history—blanketed the city. A heavy, wet snow, it brought down power lines, trees, and shrubs. Over $4 million in damage was done to park vegetation. Streets and boulevards were blocked with trees. Over 6,500 men were mobilized to put up warning signs, open streets, repair broken power lines, and haul away the debris. In seven days, $210,000 was spent to return the city to normal. The only thing that saved Denver from insolvency was the massive injection of federal money which paid most of the bills.

The New Deal did not end the depression, but its relief and recovery programs benefitted the people. Despite predictions by Governor Johnson and editor Shepherd, makeshift projects did not erode the character of those who found jobs with the Works Projects Administration or the Civilian Conservation Corps. Instead, federal agencies enabled the unemployed to work for the sustenance and

WPA workers laying concrete pipe for city improvement

simultaneously improve the beauty and utility of the community. Thanks to men like Stapleton, Shriver, Cranmer, and Dines, efficient and thoughtful use was made of federal emergency funds.

Johnson, Shepherd, and other venomous anti-New Dealers failed to destroy the atmosphere of unity and civic pride which grew out of the trials of the 1930s. This was so because local leaders saw that all people—men and women, blacks and whites, aliens and citizens—had access to relief, and no one was coerced to support incumbent politicians. Also, these civic leaders continually pointed to the improved quality of life which was left in the wake of every federal grant. Rather than the insidious monster described by *The Post*, the New Deal not only fed thousands, it poured millions of dollars into trans-mountain water diversion for Denver, expanded and improved mountain and local parks, built golf courses, boulevards, and flood control systems, and converted the infant airstrip into a first-class municipal airport.

By late 1942, when the last of the relief and recovery agencies were phased out, Denver was one of the most attractive and least crowded cities in the United States. Tourists who went in and out of Colorado's capital marvelled at the clean, dry air, mountain view, tree-lined boulevards, and ubiquitous parks and recreation centers. The pride that Denver's residents expressed in their town was not based on hollow, lofty expectations for the future, it was firmly grounded in hard-earned reality.

236

But cities, like the people who inhabit them, never remain the same. While the depression brought lasting alterations to Colorado's showplace city, World War II left a wake of change as profound as anything since the silver boom of the 1870s and 1880s. Before Pearl Harbor was attacked, the repercussions of the European conflict reached the city. Denver's economy, like the nation's business system, perked up in 1940 and 1941. Each month less New Deal money was pumped into Colorado. By 1942 so many opportunities existed in private enterprise that Paul Shriver closed his office permanently.

Beginning in 1940, and growing throughout the war, an electric-like enthusiasm permeated the community. People were off relief, and high-paying jobs were available for ordinary people. Opportunities to get ahead were legion as Denver and its hinterland boomed to meet wartime needs. Denver's grain mills, sugar refineries, and meat-packing plants strained to capacity. The fifteen-year drouth ended just as the war started, and America's allies needed as much food as farmers and processors could supply.

The war stimulated extractive industries just as it encouraged agriculture and food processing. According to Robert Athearn, a $600,000 state road-building project opened the Naturita and Uravan region in Western Colorado for vanadium mining. By 1942 over 600 tons per day of this steel-hardening element were produced. The Leadville area, once an important silver-producing part of Denver's hinterland, found renewed life in molybdenum mining. Early in the war Colorado became the world's leading supplier of elements to be alloyed with steel. Indeed, vanadium and molybdenum worth $100 million were extracted from Colorado by 1942.

Total income payments for the state were down to $447 million in 1935. In 1940 the figure grew to $617 million and by 1945 it had soared to $1,317,000,000. A large share of this revenue was earned in the Denver region as concrete, brick, rubber, and steel fabricators expanded and converted to meet the demands of war. Old foundries, for example, originally designed to manufacture mining and later sugar refining gear, plunged into oil equipment and various war materials production, creating jobs for engineers and thousands of skilled and semiskilled workers.

Denver's population had increased slowly during the 1920s and 1930s, but during the war it jumped approximately 20%. People from small towns and rural communities rushed to the metropolis to take advantage of new opportunities. Some went on the payroll of established companies. Others went to work for the new facilities

Expanding facilities at Lowry Field in 1940

created by war needs. The government employed approximately 6,500 nonmilitary personnel in 1941. At the end of the war the figure was nearly 17,000. The Fitzsimons Hospital staff grew, and a medical supply depot was built. Lowry Field expanded, absorbing much of Ft. Logan's staff and opening clerical, photography, bombing, and gunnery training programs in the Army Air Corps Technical School. Many civilians were hired at Lowry, and hundreds more found positions at Buckley Naval Air Station, which was constructed east of Lowry Field in 1942.

Private enterprise came to Denver, too, providing thousands of additional war-production jobs. Remington Arms Company hired nearly 20,000 people (50% men and 50% women) by 1943, comprising 40% of Denver's factory personnel to manufacture small caliber ammunition. Kaiser Company, Incorporated opened a plant to finish rough cast artillery shells. It hired 1,000 persons. The Rocky Mountain Arsenal made chemicals for the war effort and engaged 14,000 people.

Denver's economy was stimulated still more by the military personnel who moved through the metropolitan area with a frequency reminiscent of miners during the gold rush days. Besides the soldiers at Lowry Air Base and the naval trainees at Buckley Field, army men from nearby military installations went to Denver whenever they could get a free night or weekend liberty. They came from Camp Hale in the mountains west of the city, where special mountain warfare training was held in the Holy Cross National Forest. Almost 170,000 men were trained for combat at Camp Carson near Colorado Springs between 1941 and 1945, and most of these soldiers made pilgrimages to the Queen City before they went overseas.

For many American communities, the visitation of thousands of servicemen for rest and recreation was disastrous. Neither the military nor the civilian population fared well. When too many servicemen got drunk and disorderly, contracted venereal disease, or landed in jail, the community was declared "off limits" by post commanders. Denver, however, adjusted well to the onslaught. The visitors were good for business, and the community was kind to its guests. So singular was the Denver experience that in July 1943 *Business Week* dubbed the Colorado capital the "Good Neighbor." According to the news magazine, Denver had "done spadework in showing how a city and an Army camp can get on peacefully and profitably."

The city administration was primarily responsible for the excellent relations which existed. To be sure, local citizens developed a reputation for being warm and generous to soldiers, but thoughtful programs were designed to prevent tension and clashes. Robert E. Harvey was appointed to coordinate relations, and he did an

A recruiting caravan at Lowry Field during World War II

outstanding job. MPs were assigned to Denver police cars, When a soldier got in trouble, the military policeman took the GI in tow and escorted him to an Army facility. Harvey discovered that drinking-related problems usually occurred after midnight, so he asked all tavern keepers to close at that hour. Some refused, but most saloon owners cooperated with Harvey's request. Likewise, concerted efforts were made to track down women with venereal infections. When found, they were hurried to Denver General Hospital for free treatment.

Robert Harvey also smoothed difficulties related to civilian construction of military sites. He arranged for local trucking firms to haul materials to bases but then assumed responsibility for preventing slowdowns. Because speed and efficiency were top priorities, Harvey had investigators alert him to unnecessary delays. Once, when truckers slowed down on a site, the troubleshooter held up gas and ration coupons until work resumed to normal.

Mayor Stapleton personally intervened to improve community-military relations. Ben Hooper had no license to use the upstairs of his Ex-Servicemen's Club for sleeping rooms. When the police discovered that Hooper was renting lodging space to black soldiers, they ordered him to stop. One call to the mayor from Hooper ended the problem. Stapleton realized that black soldiers were not welcome in many hotels and rooming houses. Hooper's facility was clean and orderly, so the police were ordered to leave it alone.

The war brought profits to everyone, from the stockholders of Gates Rubber Company and General Iron Works to Louis Ballast, who created and patented the "Cheeseburger" at his Humpty Dumpty Drive-In Restaurant on Speer Boulevard. But the war boom also made problems. The housing shortage was most serious. Those who suffered far more than anyone else were the Mexicans who had been seeking refuge in Denver from the beet fields and the northern New Mexicans and southern Coloradans of Spanish descent who ventured northward to the city in search of war-industry employment.

Prejudice which had been directed toward Italians and east-European immigrants subsided after the Ku Klux Klan frenzy in the early 1920s. While these groups still tended to congregate together in their own colonies, the hatred poured on them was redirected toward the Spanish-speaking people who comprised the bulk of the lower economic class newcomers. If Spanish-surnamed settlers recognized important cultural differences between the immigrants from Mexico and the long-time residents of the American southwest, whose ties to

Entertainment for the troops: The Lowry Field Revue

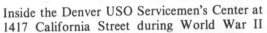
Inside the Denver USO Servicemen's Center at 1417 California Street during World War II

North America preceeded the Anglo, the majority population lumped them all together. Like the minorities who came before them, they were viewed as ignorant, inferior people. They were denied access to all but the most menial jobs, and they were discriminated against when they searched for housing. The few apartments, rooms, and houses available to rent were closed to these recent arrivals. They could find lodging only in the barrio near the business district.

Absentee landlords took advantage of the Hispanos by converting one- and two-family dwelling units into facilities that could accommodate more. In some of these slum houses there were no toilets or running water, and at times only one water closet served as many as a dozen families. Most of these dwellings were inadequately heated and ventilated, and they were often infested with vermin. A Works Projects Administration study completed in 1941, as well as a local survey conducted during the war, concluded that most Spanish-Americans lived in substandard housing and that their per capita income was the lowest in Denver.

Blacks were also well below the majority population in per capita income, and much of their housing failed to measure up to decent standards. Nevertheless, they were measurably better off than Hispanos. This fact was apparent to anyone who travelled through Five Points. Relatively crowded by the early 1940s, this predominantly black neighborhood reflected a standard of living superior to that found in the barrio. In addition, the more affluent black business people were finding new, more spacious housing east of Five Points years before VJ Day.

White Denver fared much better during the war years. Few new homes were built during the world-wide conflict, so some white newcomers were unable to find living quarters which suited them. But most middle and upper class Denverites were comfortably situated away from the central business district before 1940. Major population shifts took place between the world wars. Many families of the social elite deserted Capitol Hill and built new homes south of Cheesman Park and then in the district near the Denver Country Club. Less affluent, but comfortable, people in the middle and upper middle classes moved to newer subdivisions in eastern and southern parts of the city.

The automobile enabled thousands of people to escape the high taxes and real estate values in Denver County during the two decades preceding the war. Toys for rich people, they were expensive and impractical. By 1920, though, the automobile was obviously an innovation that would bring major changes. That year approximately 30,000 vehicles were owned by local citizens. On the eve of the depression the number had more than doubled. When the Second World War began, over 100,000 cars and trucks were in use around Denver on the traffic ways, roads, boulevards, and highways which had been widened and improved by federal works programs.

Two developments symbolized the growing impact of the automobile on the metropolitan area. In 1926 the Colorado and Southern Railway Company ran the Denver and Interurban commuter train for the last time. The electrically powered railway started its service between Boulder and Denver in 1908, making the one-way trip in just over an hour. Advertised as the route which carried commuters "along the foothills and into the mountains," it made stops at Globeville, Standley Lake, Louisville, Eldorado Springs, and several other little communities between Denver and Boulder. For eighteen years the Interurban carried farmers, miners, and small-town residents to Denver and back for an evening or weekend, and it took the big city folks to the university at Boulder or to outings at Eldorado Springs. But by 1926 so many people owned motor vehicles that the line was closed because it could not make a profit.

The second sign of the automobile's effect on the region was the growth of suburbs surrounding Denver City and County. Denver's Planning Commission expressed alarm in 1940 over census figures which showed that suburbs in Jefferson and Arapahoe counties were "outstripping Denver proper," as the planners phrased it, "in rate of population growth by nearly five to one." The mayor and his planning commissioners feared decentralization. The problem was endemic in most large cities. Many were not only losing population, the downtown areas were decaying and the tax base was slipping away to towns and counties on the outside.

Denver was not suffering like most eastern cities, but business and political leaders hoped to halt the trend before it became more serious. The war helped curtail the trend because gasoline and tires were rationed, housing construction slowed, and automobiles were not manufactured for civilian use. The Stapleton administration played a role in slowing decentralization, too. The beautification program was pursued with that object in mind. Also, the mayor and his associates did everything possible to provide good services without increasing taxes.

To stem the predicted rush to the suburbs once the war ended, city officials devised a housing code for improving substandard dwellings. When the law was enacted in 1944, *American City* magazine praised Denver's leadership for joining "the small list of local governments with comprehensive ordinances regulating existing housing. The ordinance," according to the editor of *American City*, "defines substandard dwelling units and empowers the building inspector to compel correction."

Noble effort that it was, the 1944 Housing Code was not enough to block the postwar forces of change. Eventually, the automobile would bring more smog to Denver than the coal-powered industries and heating systems of a generation earlier. Almost 150,000 cars would be registered in Denver alone by 1950, and their availability would hasten decentralization and concommitant urban decay.

At the end of the war, however, these problems were incipient rather than apparent. Denver was blessed with cleaner air than it had during the early 1920s. Its schools, as judged by educational journal writers, were on a par with, if not superior to, other cities. Denver had outstanding parks and recreation areas— superior to any metropolis in the nation. Culturally, the Queen City was not as advanced as San Francisco, Boston, or New York. The Symphony was not as well supported as those in St. Louis or Cleveland. The Art Museum was less distinguished than the one in Kansas City.

Such shortcomings notwithstanding, Denver was one of the most beautiful, healthful, and liveable cities in the United States. That this view was shared by others than the Chamber of Commerce was evident when thousands of veterans returned permanently to the Rocky Mountain municipality once the war ended.

Part V

Vertical City,

Since World War II

Chapter 9

Within a few months after VJ Day, long-time residents and frequent visitors noticed a significant change in the Queen City. A special liveliness pervaded the capital. People's faces emanated sparkle, and there was vivacity in their movement. Buoyed by the victory over Germany and Japan, they felt confident in America's military-industrial might; they exuded boundless hope for the future. In autumn 1946, an aging Mayor Stapleton looked out his office window at what George V. Kelly described as a traffic-cluttered Bannock Street and Broadway. "Civic Center was alive with scores of persons converting the mall into a park. The trolley cars were jammed, because the autombile industry was still retooling from war production. These activities, visible from the mayor's office, were symptoms of a boom that would transform Denver from a quiet, conservative, fairly large city into a burgeoning metropolis with mushrooming suburbs and with seemingly unsolvable problems, not at all attuned to Mayor Stapleton's idea of what the community should be." Stapleton was asked how Denver would solve the problems which the newcomers would create. "If these people would just go back where they came from," he answered, "we wouldn't have any problems here."

But there was no turning the people around. World War II had brought servicemen and industries. With them came growth and prosperity unlike anything Denver had experienced since the 1880s. Newcomers were caught up by the same mania to build an empire that had engulfed citizens two generations earlier. The postwar desire to foster growth, make fortunes, and encourage change for the sake of change spread like a contagious disease. By 1947 a majority of Denverites were ready for bold, new directorship. The controlled

Quigg Newton

conservatism of Hughes and Stapleton failed to satisfy new appetites. In the municipal election that year, Denver's citizens said goodbye to their seventy-three-year-old leader, overwhelmingly defeating him at the polls.

The new mayor was J. Quigg Newton, Jr., a vigorous young Navy veteran who symbolized a fresh era for Denver—one dominated by youthful optimism and growth.

Mayor Newton and his successor, Will Faust Nicholson, helped bring profound changes. Hardworking and well-meaning men, they joined the postwar generation of bankers, real estate brokers, merchants, and small industrialists who, in concert with the Chamber of Commerce, sought growth at any price. Both Newton and Nicholson devoted major shares of their time seeking more western slope water for Denver. There was enough of the precious resource to meet the needs of the population for the time being. What these mayors wanted was ample water to serve the thousands of people and industries which they hoped to attract to the Rocky Mountain metropolis in the future.

Quigg Newton tirelessly worked with the Water Board to secure Blue River water for Denver, while western Coloradans lobbied to preserve the rights to what nature poured into their valleys and communities. Newton's efforts obtained only half as much Blue River water as he and the board sought, but Nicholson's administration fared better. With an able city attorney, Harold Roberts, a dedicated Water Board, and Nicholson's influence with President Dwight D. Eisenhower and Attorney General Herbert Brownell, the federal court gave Denver what it wanted from the Blue River. In 1964 the twenty-three-mile Roberts Tunnel (named for Harold Roberts) was finished. As George V. Kelly phrased it, "Through it flows, when needed, water that has made Denver metropolitan expansion possible."

Greater Denver's expansion in the postwar years was phenomenal. The city and county comprised only 322,412 people in 1940. By 1950 it grew 29% to 415,786, then climbed another 18% to almost 500,000 in 1960. The total population for the City and County of Denver was approximately 515,000 by 1970, but much of the increase was the result of a voracious annexation program. The city limits encompassed 63.6 square miles when Stapleton left office. By 1970 the total was nearly 102. The metropolitan area grew prodigiously compared to the city and county. What the census compilers defined as the Standard Metropolitan Area (Denver, Adams, Arapahoe, Jefferson, and Boulder counties) numbered 445,206 in 1940, with Denver com-

Will F. Nicholson. *Courtesy Denver Public Library, Western History Department*

prising 72% of the total. By 1970 the Standard Metropolitan Area embraced 1,227,529 people, and Denver represented less than 42% of the total.

Without Newton's and Nicholson's successful efforts to bring more water, the 750,000 people who settled the area between 1940 and 1970 never could have been accommodated. The role that these mayors played in creating this regional disaster was significant, but they did not act alone. Citizens of the City and County of Denver overwhelmingly endorsed the expansion crusade, even if it meant going down in their own pockets. In 1955, for example, local residents answered Mayor Nicholson's call for a $75 million water bond issue, voting fourteen-to-one in favor of financing water projects for the metropolitan area.

While elected officials and voters did their part by bringing more water to the exploding metropolis, bankers did an about-face which made Denver even more attractive to prospective industrialists and settlers. Before World War I and until the late 1940s, Denver's banking policies were as conservative as any in the nation. Gerald Hughes, the chairman of the board at the First National Bank, and John Evans (son of William Gray Evans), the president of the First, usually held the loan-to-deposit ratio down to 15 to 18%—never letting it exceed 32%. Harold Kountze of the Colorado National Bank and John C. Mitchell and Roblin Davis at the Denver National Bank maintained similarly conservative fiscal policies. The "Big Three" dominated Denver banking, essentially divided most of the financial business among themselves, and refused to solicit customers from each other. Even the smaller banks, such as the United States National (it eventually merged with the Denver National Bank) with Thomas A. Dines as president, followed the ultrasafe example set by the larger institutions.

Proponents of growth criticized the tight-money philosophy espoused on Seventeenth Street. Numerous industrialists searching for plant locations overlooked Denver because loans were difficult to get; and the Queen City gained a well-deserved reputation as a community where home mortgages were more scarce than strawberries in January. One of the most outspoken critics of local banks was Eugene Cervi. Born in Illinois in 1906 into a family of northern Italian immigrants, Cervi came up the hard way. His father, a coal miner, bequeathed him a good mind, a strong body, unbounded energy, lofty ambition, but no money. When young Cervi was nine, his father moved them to Colorado. Within a few years, Gene Cervi had to go to work to help support the nine-member family. He

253

Gene Cervi

worked at a variety of jobs, and when he could afford it, he attended Colorado College. Eventually, he had to give up his studies. He worked on an automobile assembly line in Michigan, in an Ohio steel mill, and on road gangs in Colorado's mountains.

Cervi found the break he was looking for in 1929. He secured a position on the reporting staff of the *Rocky Mountain News* that year and then moved to *The Denver Post* in 1935. His newspaper experience earned him the regional directorship of the Office of War Information during World War II. When the global conflict ended, he opened a public relations business and simultaneously published a weekly financial newsletter. In 1949 Cervi, who in four years had become known as "the stormy petrel of Denver commerce and finance," commenced publication of *Cervi's Rocky Mountain Journal. Cervi's Journal*, like the newsletter, was devoted to reporting and editorializing business news of the Rockies.

In 1959 the bespectacled and slightly balding journalist, with a reputation for the hottest temper in town, wrote an article titled "My War with 17th St.—And Who Won It" for the 100th anniversary edition of the *Rocky Mountain News*. He recalled that in the 1940s, while trying to start his newspaper, "I tried to borrow $1,500 from the U.S. National Bank, and Tom Dines said no. But that was the situation all over town . . . [because] less than 30 percent of Denver bank deposits were out on loan as against 40 to 50 percent in other financial centers." Cervi was so angered by this "repressive banking" that between 1945 and 1949, he said, "we hardly ever went to press without a blast at the restrictiveness of Denver's 17th St."

In 1943 a well-groomed man in his mid-fifties arrived in Denver. Dressed stylishly but conservatively, with gold-rimmed glasses and shortly trimmed, sparse hair, Elwood Brooks assumed control of the Central Savings Bank and Trust Company. No one, not even Gene Cervi, saw anything in this man's background or demeanor to suggest that he was about to start a revolution in Colorado's capital. A prudent bank executive from Kansas, Brooks had most recently distinguished himself as the Sunflower State's banking commissioner.

Quietly, yet deliberately, Elwood Brooks unveiled policies from the Central Bank which ultimately revolutionized banking in Denver. His offices on Fifteenth Street symbolized his aloofness from the financiers two blocks away, and he reenforced his independence by refusing to seek membership in the clearinghouse dominated by his Seventeenth Street colleagues. With initiative and foresight, Brooks seized the opportunity to place the struggling Central Bank in the vanguard of modern banking practices in Colorado. Cervi recalled

Elwood M. Brooks. *Courtesy Denver Public Library, Western History Department*

Gerald Hughes late in his career. *Courtesy Montgomery Dorsey*

Cris Dobbins

that "In sharp and effective contrast to the status quo of 17th St., the Brooks bank began to lend money." According to the editor, "nobody will ever know how many thousands of prospective borrowers, turned down all along 17th St., trudged over to 15th St., and got a sympathetic hearing from Elwood Brooks, who personally met many of his new customers at the front door himself."

Brooks decided to rebuild the Central Bank by offering consumer loans. He even provided loans so that people could buy automobiles—a practice unheard of in Denver before the war. By the late 1940s, the former Kansas banker had not only placed his institution on a sound financial foundation, he had raised the eyebrows of the clearinghouse conservatives and spirited them into liberalizing their own lending procedures.

By the early 1950s, an aging Gerald Hughes, the man Gene Cervi once said "is 17th street," saw broken his inviolable rule of never allowing loans to go beyond 32% of deposits. When Hughes died in 1956 at the age of eighty-one, not only the First National Bank, but most of the institutions along Seventeenth Street were lending approximately 60% of their deposits.

A decade and a half after World War II, the *Rocky Mountain News* boasted of the new posture in Denver banking: "Money for a million people"—"Banks for the business boom." In the same booster tradition, Cecil Puckett, the director of the Denver branch of the Federal Reserve Bank of Kansas City, declared that "the banks are set up now for a long time to come. The present facilities are adequate to take care of a million population, and the industry and business that will follow the people." Puckett noted that the merger of the First National Bank and the International Trust Company enabled that combine to make a single loan of at least $1.75 million without seeking outside capital; and the consolidation of the Denver U.S. National Bank put its single loan potential even higher at $1.8 million.

While bankers were making more capital available and politicians were diverting water to the eastern slope, other members of the power structure were seeking more businesses and governmental agencies and all the new settlers such installations would attract. The Chamber of Commerce became increasingly aggressive after World War II. In the late 1940s and early 1950s, under the leadership of banker Thomas A. Dines and Cris Dobbins, who was directing the various Boettcher enterprises, the chamber expanded its membership, increased the number of full-time employees, and established a long list of promotional committees.

The chamber pursued old campaigns with more vigor. It promoted tourism, devoting more money to advertising Colorado's winter attractions. The staff continued to promote the livestock hinterland by sponsoring farm and ranch meetings and the annual stock show. Boosting Denver as the ideal convention center was part of an ongoing program, too, culminating in a drive in 1964 to build a modern convention center and exhibition hall. With the guidance of mayor Thomas G. Currigan, the facility which bears his name was built downtown, overlooking Cherry Creek, a few years later.

Top on the chamber's list of priorities, however, was commercial and industrial expansion. By the mid-1950s, new businesses were spending over $100 million annually in the metropolitan area. Some companies came on their own, but the booster organization played an important role in attracting many. The Chamber of Commerce was particularly effective in developing Colorado's oil industry. The association sponsored an "Oil Progress Luncheon" in 1954, hosting over 700 oil and related businessmen. Civic leaders encouraged oil exploration in eastern Colorado and promised to work for favorable tax laws for oil companies. The chamber also advertised Colorado's advantages in petroleum trade journals and urged companies to establish offices in Denver.

These efforts were extremely successful. Crude oil production was only five million barrels in 1945. By 1950 production exceeded twenty-three million barrels a year climbing to over forty-seven million per annum in 1960, with a slight downward trend over the next decade. The state's refining capacity soared from about ninety million barrels per day in 1963 to 130 million in 1970. Oil exploration, drilling and refining companies moved into the mountain state in large numbers during the 1950s and 1960s and many opened offices in Denver.

The Chamber of Commerce went after federal agencies with the same resolution that it recruited oil companies. Mushrooming federal bureaus after World War II caused the United States government to build massive regional centers in several sections of the nation. Because Denver already housed most regional offices for the Rocky Mountains, it became a convenient location for expansion. Just in case the federal decision makers might consider other communities for their bureaucratic offices, the boosters lobbied in Washington, D.C. They reminded agency chiefs that the nation already owned a large piece of real estate—complete with buildings—where the World War II Denver Arms Plant was located.

The arms plant was gradually converted into the Denver Federal

Center, and agency after agency opened regional branches there. In 1948 only 10,000 federal civilian employees worked in the metropolitan area. By 1951, 14,000 civilians were on the federal payroll. Ten years later the figure was over 23,000—and growing. In 1975, 31,500 nonmilitary personnel worked for Uncle Sam in the Denver area.

Runaway federal bureaucracy was a significant boon to postwar growth, but nothing stimulated population and industrial expansion like the Cold War. When the world learned that the Soviet Union had the atomic bomb in 1949, fear for the safety of the nation's capital became an obsession. *Newsweek*, in its December 11, 1950 issue, capsulized what military strategists and defense industrialists were doing about the apparent crisis facing America's defense:

If an atom bomb should wipe out Washington, or any other major city, what then? That grim possibility has sent top government officials on nationwide tours. Officials of large corporations are also busy investigating the possibility of new plant sites.

Recently, the search for safety has centered on one largely undeveloped region—the Denver metropolitan area. Its advantages are obvious: A thousand miles of mountain protect it on the west; great distances separate it from the Canadian border, the Atlantic Ocean, and the Gulf of Mexico.

Boosters were capitalizing on the Truman administration's drive for decentralization. The Chamber of Commerce had helped pave the way for the Air Force's relocation of its Air Defense Command headquarters from New York to the Rocky Mountains; and the professional promoters were lobbying for the Air Force Academy (it was in the planning stage in 1949) to be built in Colorado near Lowry Air Force Base and Buckley Field.

Late in 1950 several manufacturers of defense-related precision tools, chemicals, and electronic equipment were enticed to the beautiful and "safe" metropolitan area. Thomas M. Dines announced that "We feel we fit very effectively into the current mobilization pattern." To underline his contention, Dine's bank hired the Econometric Institute of New York City to compile and publish a 200-page statistical survey of the area. That book was the largest piece of booster literature ever published on Denver. It elaborated on the region's beautiful climate, inexpensive land, abundant resources, low cost of living, and contented labor force.

The United States National Bank boasted that it had $90 million in assets to help new industrialists. Its book was rushed to businessmen all over the country, and the contents included detailed lists of investment possibilities. The dry air was noted to be ideal for the location of research and engineering laboratories, as well as precision equipment manufacturing. Because Colorado possessed 15% of the nation's coal reserves, Denver was an ideal site for the chemical industry. Among other opportunities, the booming ski and tourist businesses made the metropolitan area a logical spot for the manufacture of ski and other outdoor equipment and clothing.

Dines' blueprint, combined with the state's attractive climate and the efforts of other booster agencies, produced the desired results. In each of the industrial fields singled out by Dines, development was prodigious. During the 1950s and 1960s, new companies mushroomed along the front range between Boulder and Denver. Hundreds of laboratories devoted to medical and dental research and service opened in the metropolitan area, along with geological and aerospace development. Ball Brothers Research Corporation, Martin Marietta Aerospace Corporation, and Beech Aircraft Corporation were just three of the companies which gained international reputations in the aerospace field, just like the National Center for Atmospheric Research and the National Oceanic and Atmospheric Administration did in environmental research.

When IBM, Hewlett-Packard, Johns-Manville, Sunstrand, Honeywell, and a host of other engineering-technology companies moved into the five-county area, so did the chemical industry. The two largest facilities were Rocky Flats, operated by Dow Chemical and the Atomic Energy Commission, and the Rocky Mountain Arsenal under the direction of the Army Chemical Corps.

Catering to the ever-growing popularity of skiing—there were over thirty major ski areas in Colorado by 1975—nearly three dozen skiing equipment wholesalers and manufacturers moved into Denver's standard metropolitan area. Lange and Head have become two of the best known companies and their merchandise has been marketed in hundreds of retail sporting goods stores and outdoor speciality shops. Camping and hiking gear manufacturing and sales companies have become just as important to the economic growth of the region, with Holubar Mountaineering and Gerry among the more popular.

Natural advantages have done more than stimulate outdoor sports industries, they have promoted tourism in general. Tourist spending in Colorado increased almost every year after 1945, reaching a peak of $700 million in 1975. But that revenue represented only half of what the military spent in the state. The Pentagon decided to make the Colorado Springs-Denver area a defense center in response to the Cold War, and billions of dollars have been pumped into the economy since 1950. Indeed, by the early 1970s, over 21,000 military personnel were stationed in the Denver metro area alone (the majority was assigned to Lowry Air Force Base), and military spending for the state reached $1.36 billion in 1975.

A downtown construction binge of unprecedented proportions accompanied the business boom. Erection of large buildings was not a new experience for the core city, but the construction of skyscrapers certainly was an innovation. The absence of high-rise buildings marked Denver as a unique and attractive city. During the Speer administration, an ordinance was passed prohibiting the construction of buildings over twelve stories so that workers and shoppers downtown would always have a view of the mountains. Thanks to Speer's efforts, Denver was blessed with no skyscrapers, save the D and F Tower, until the repeal of the high-rise ordinance in the postwar period.

In lockstep with the mania to grow as large and as fast as possible came the madness to emulate other cities in their haste to pile people on top of one another just as fast as derricks and cranes could raise scaffoldings and girders. The inspiration for Denver's skyline came from three outsiders—William Zeckendorf and John and Clint Murchison. Zeckendorf was a New Yorker. The Murchison brothers were from Texas. They were reminiscent of men like Henry R. Wolcott and James Duff, who went to Denver during the great expansion period of the late nineteenth century to invest their money and that of their associates in urban development.

At first, Denver's Seventeenth Street magnates were as reluctant to see their city grow vertically as they were to loosen credit. But once Zeckendorf and the Murchisons initiated the trend, all the monied interests tried to outdo each other with the tallest building. Zeckendorf's corporation, Webb and Knapp, led the way by purchasing the old Court House Square between Fifteenth and Sixteenth and Court Place and Tremont. On that site and one he purchased across the street, Zeckendorf eventually built the May-D&F and Hilton Hotel structures, which are joined by an elevated pedestrian bridge. While he was making plans and unraveling the legal problems, Zeckendorf also underwrote the Mile High Center (later named the United Bank Center) at Seventeenth and Broadway.

The Murchison brothers, millionaire Texas oilmen, bought the Denver Club at Seventeenth and Glenarm. They tore down the old club building and replaced it with a twenty-story unit. Then they surpassed that effort by erecting a new First National Bank Tower,

William Zeckendorf. *Courtesy Denver Public Library, Western History Department*

twenty-eight floors high. Other Texas oilmen, plus some oil-rich Oklahoma investors, raised the massive Petroleum Club and Continental Oil Building in the heart of downtown.

Other buildings followed in rapid pursuit. Elwood Brooks' Central Bank, the Denver and Rio Grande Industries, and Leavell Enterprises put up a $23 million edifice named Park Central. The First National joined Brooks in underwriting a high-rise apartment complex, Brooks Towers. Insurance companies also entered the furor. Two of their contributions are Prudential Plaza and the Security Life Building. More towering apartment and office structures followed in the wake of those developments, and by 1976, no slack appeared in the postwar building trend.

The Skyline Urban Renewal project—an apt name given to much of the post-1965 construction program—was only part of the effort expended by civic leaders to make the Mile High City blend into the garish landscape that pervades urban America. Governor Ed Johnson, Mayor Will Nicholson, and dozens of other men of influence labored in the 1950s to secure major transportation arteries for the Denver area. When the federally sponsored, massive interstate highway system was almost ready for President Dwight D. Eisenhower's signature in 1956, I-70 was part of the total 40,000-mile network. That route, however, was to go no farther west than Denver. Mayor Nicholson did not want to see Denver bypassed on the federal transcontinental highway network, so he went to Governor Johnson to see what could be done to get the road extended westward as far as Utah.

Johnson and Nicholson ultimately went to Washington and conferred with President Eisenhower, who was always interested in pleasing Coloradans. Colorado, after all, was Mamie's childhood home and one of Ike's favorite golfing and fishing resorts. The president sympathetically listened to the plea of the Rocky Mountain politicos. Before he signed the bill, he saw to it that an additional 1,000 miles were added, with nearly 300 of those additional miles earmarked to extend I-70 west from Denver into Utah.

Beginning in the 1950s, construction began on many miles of federal and state divided highways which now converge on Denver. Today I-70 is the major east-west route. I-25 runs north and south. I-80 angles into Denver from the northeast, and Highway 36 goes northwest from Denver up to Boulder and beyond. These expressways have encouraged the postwar economic and population explosion. They are the lifelines of commerce which have brought tourists into the state via Denver. These highways are also the routes that transport

265

Clinton W. Murchison. *Courtesy Denver Public Library, Western History Department*

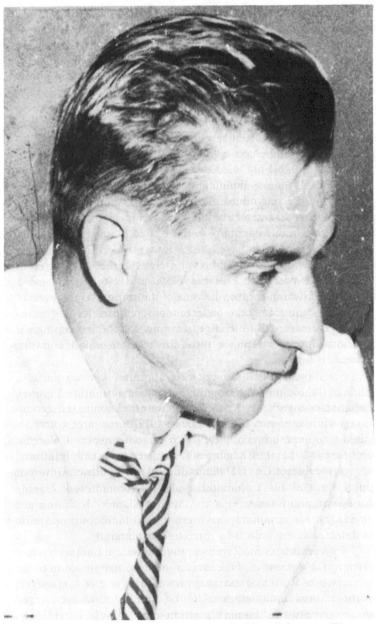

John Murchison. *Courtesy Denver Public Library, Western History Department*

the region's products to consumers across the nation. The network of divided traffic ways has enabled the real estate developers to construct an ever-widening ring of suburbs around the core county, with commuters being assured access ways to their places of employment. Until the 1970s, community leaders unquestioningly assumed the automobile to be the superior mode of transportation. Previously, no one with the influence to change conditions gave a thought to an efficient mass transit system. Consequently, most metropolitan area residents have been forced to rely on cars for all transportation needs. Vehicle registrations have climbed even more alarmingly than population. In 1946, only 153,000 vehicles were registered in the five-county area. Over one-half million were licensed in 1960. By 1974, the figure had more than doubled. Almost 1,150,000 motor vehicles were registered that year, and metropolitan Denver had more automobiles per capita than any community in the United States.

Partisans of growth have ruled Denver since 1947. But like the businessmen who made decisions for Denver in the late nineteenth century, the power elite of the 1950s and 1960s has created a community it cannot control. Because of the above-average levels of education required in the high-technology industries and governmental agencies, the Mile High metropolis has the second highest educational level per capita in the United States—only Huntsville, Alabama, is higher.

Since the early 1970s, signs have appeared which point to a decline in the old power structure. Opponents of unbridled growth became increasingly vocal. Many citizens were questioning the conventional wisdom espoused by boosters. In 1972, metro area voters organized to oppose bringing the 1976 Winter Olympics to Colorado. Despite the fact that the Chamber of Commerce, the usually influential and highly respected Cris Dobbins of Ideal Basic Industries, Governor John Love and his Committee of 76 (a committee of leading businessmen and financiers), and Mayor William McNichols urged bringing the international sports event to Colorado, the proposition was defeated at the polls by a three-to-two margin.

Two years later State Representative Richard Lamm was elected governor. He was one of the leaders in organizing opposition to the Olympics because that extravaganza would have cost taxpayers a fortune, caused mountain sites to be torn up, and encouraged unnecessary growth. Lamm's election in 1974 was heralded by journalists across the land as a major victory for environmentalists and antigrowth partisans.

Lamm campaigned on a controlled growth platform. He never

went on record against growth per se, although some of his supporters hoped he would adopt that posture once inaugurated. Nevertheless, the voters did have a choice in 1974. Governor John Vanderhoof, the incumbent and Lamm's Republican opponent, was a progrowth candidate with backing from Seventeenth Street and most of the big business community.

But once again the local Babbits were defeated. With strong grass roots support in the Denver area, Lamm was elected. Once in office, he disappointed hard-core antigrowth people when he hired James A. Michener, the famous novelist and author of best-selling *Centennial*, to write a promotional piece on Colorado for *Business Week*. The article did make clear Lamm's opposition to widespread extractive mining in Colorado, as well as his opposition to growth at any price. Still, the article let the national business community know that the governor welcomed more "clean" industry, even along the crowded eastern slope.

Governor Lamm and his co-workers have incurred the wrath of industrialists and expansionists with several policies. Totally out of step with his recent predecessors in the executive mansion, Lamm tried to block construction of a new interstate highway in the Denver metropolitan area. Although he ultimately failed, the governor fought valiantly to stop that paved incentive to more suburban development and dependency on the automobile.

Lamm, in opposition to the postwar tradition of granting governmental favoritism to any industries desiring to exploit Colorado's natural resources, has worked to repeal the state sales tax on food. To make up for the lost revenue, he has proposed a new tax on large extractive industries. Mining corporations have grown increasingly unpopular among urban dwellers who resent destruction of the state's environment.

In 1975, Cris Dobbins admitted that he and his associates who comprised Denver's decisionmakers in the 1950s and 1960s are losing their hold on Denver. No longer can they make decisions and count on implementing them with influence and money. The directors of Denver's recent past, however, are not abdicating without a struggle. The Forward Metro Group and the Denver Chamber of Commerce are working just as diligently for growth as at anytime. To be sure, the blatant expansionism is toned down when presented to area residents. Typical of the boosters' local propaganda was a large advertisement placed in the *Now* section of the *Rocky Mountain News* on April 20, 1975. Hoping to placate the numerous citizens who view development with a jaundiced eye, the chamber and Forward Metro noted, "We have made some wrong turns here in Colorado. There've been periods when growth overran planning . . . it's time for a change of direction: To growth that helps us all and harms no one. Careful, managed growth . . . ."

Precisely where the "careful, managed growth" fits into the February 23, 1976 advertisement in *Business Week* purchased by the Forward Metro Denver Group and the Denver Chamber of Commerce is difficult to discern. After praising Denver's educational level, airport, and scenery, the promoters asked businessmen if they were aware of "the strong growing economy of the mile high city: A boom that's been fed by a highly educated, young, hard-working population. A growing market for your products, skilled labor force for your business and a loyal pool of talent that tends to choose life style over dollars when the executive recruiters come sniffing around." The boosters continued their story by reporting the size of Denver's population, and then they took the liberty of speaking for the one and one-half million residents. "They'd like you to join them. And their scenery."

If promoters of growth have not surrendered their goals, they certainly are on the defensive. Until recent years, environmentalists and advocates of zero population were ignored. The few who did speak out were considered fools or harmless eccentrics. No one dignified such offbeats by responding to their outcries. Today, the "knockers of progress" have become a force that cannot be ignored. Indeed, when Colorado National Bank Chairman Bruce Rockwell spoke at the 1976 honors banquet for the University of Denver's College of Business Administration, he devoted part of his speech to attacking environmentalists. According to a student newspaper account, Rockwell described opponents of growth as a "threat to the economic well being of the nation."

In a similar way, Eugene H. Adams, chairman of the board of the First National Bank Corporation, Inc., felt compelled to justify his economic philosophy. When Denver's Channel 7 television staff selected and interviewed their choices for the "Ten Most Influential Men in Colorado," Adams spoke in favor of growth. The bank executive rationalized a position which was assumed, not debated, in Denver for over two decades after World War II.

Clearly there is a leadership crisis in the dominant metropolis of the Rocky Mountains. For better or for worse, the old power structure is losing its grip. Becoming more defensive each year, Seventeenth Street, industrialists, and professional promoters no longer can make decisions about the region's development with the public's enthusiastic support, or even its apathetic neutrality. On the other hand, the antigrowth forces have failed to provide leaders who inspire enough confidence to bring a sense of community and direction to the disorganized, embattled, and drifting municipality.

What the 118-year-old city apparently needs is another political broker like Robert Speer or Benjamin Stapleton—someone who can find areas of agreement among conflicting groups, generate a new community spirit, and get on with the business of improving the environment.

Chapter 10

Unquestionably, Denver's quality of life has deteriorated in several important ways since World War II. The beauty of the Rocky Mountains, the delightful climate, the growing popularity of outdoor sports, the untapped natural resources in the midst of an energy crisis, and the colossal success of booster campaigns have inspired a boom of destructive proportions.

In 1974 a *New York Times* News Service article was featured in a number of urban newspapers. The *Times* newsman suggested that with as many as 1,200 people moving into the metropolitan area per week, "Denver's Appeal May Cause Its Downfall." But the reporter's catalogue of the Queen City's ills was so long and significant that it seemed to describe a "downfall" in process rather than a possible future catastrophe.

The journalist accurately noted that Denver was "a big city with big problems." The writer described Denver with uncomplimentary matter-of-factness:

> Denver's air, for example, is polluted. Its endlessly sprawling suburbs are filled with more than enough neon, plastic and ticky-tacky to fill a baby Los Angeles. It leads the nation in both cars and rapes per capita. Traffic jams are common, downtown crime is feared and the chief topic of conversation these days is not skiing, it is bussing—schools in the city proper have been ordered desegregated.
>
> Denver's airport sits beside enough stored military nerve gas to kill off the whole town. And an Atomic Energy Commission bomb trigger factory has sprinkled a fringe of the city with radioactive plutonium and seasoned a suburban drinking water supply with radioactive hydrogen.

A smoggy day in Denver. *Photo by Dianne Kedro*

The unflattering list of problems could have been longer. There was no mention that even on smog-free days the mountain panorama is obscured from many downtown locations because of the sky-scrapers, and that billboard advertising blocks the natural wonders from view along many streets and freeways. The *Times* correspondent noted neither the smoke and stench which belch from oil refineries near Stapleton International Airport, nor the similarly nauseous effusions which rise from the asphalt product and chemical factories along the Valley Highway. The unnatural foam in Sand Creek's waters near the airport industrial district was ignored, as was the noisy and ugly steel recycling and warehousing district beneath the Speer Boulevard viaduct along the South Platte River.

Most of these problems have plagued Denver for years. Yet, newcomers arrive daily who are determined to make Colorado's capital their new home. Little wonder, however, because for every derogatory article there are numerous ones celebrating the mountain capital as one of the outstanding places in which to live in the United States. In June 1975, *The Christian Science Monitor* featured Denver as one of "America's 10 Most Livable Cities," and another publication that year cited Denver as one of the ten towns "Where the Jobs Are," despite a national economic recession.

To be sure, Denver has a multitude of problems—many more than it had thirty years ago. Nevertheless, it provides residents with a quality of life far superior to that available in most metropolises. Every major city has congested traffic ways, smog, high crime rates, and unsightly tall buildings. Few large ones, on the other hand, have over 300 days of sunshine each year, plus majestic mountains, lakes, and streams less than one hour's drive away.

But Denver is more than a pleasure seeker's "Gateway to the Rockies." Many other factors lure people to the city. The cost of living is lower than in a majority of communities. Not only are food and housing costs reasonable by national standards, medical care is of the highest quality and relatively inexpensive. Denver contains the largest medical center between the Missouri River and the Pacific Coast, boasting the University of Colorado Medical Center, Fitzsimons Army Medical Center, National Jewish Hospital, and a comprehensive cancer research and treatment facility. Among the twenty-two major hospitals in the metro area is the massive Denver General Hospital. It provides surgical, medical, and health care to city and county residents on the basis of their ability to pay.

By 1976, only 10% of Denver's citizens were chronic-disease ridden, whereas the figure was 16% for rural Colorado. The better health rate in Denver was due in part to the superior facilities, but some of the contrast was the result of physicians migrating to Denver from rural Colorado since 1945.

Throngs of Colorado's senior citizens have moved to Denver in the last three decades. They have been deprived of adequate medical care in smaller communities, especially since so many doctors have deserted rural towns. Retired Coloradans not only have access to physicians and modern medical facilities in Denver, they are assured adequate care even if they cannot pay for it.

Children, as well as the elderly, have been treated well in Denver. In 1940 voters defeated a bond issue to build a school for crippled children. When this happened, Claude and Edna Boettcher, who always had demonstrated an interest in the Children's Hospital, decided to underwrite the institution themselves. A portion of the family assets was placed in the Boettcher Foundation in 1937. On the eve of the war, their charitable organization built the Charles Boettcher School for Crippled Children across the street from Children's Hospital and connected the two institutions by tunnel.

The Boettcher family fortune has been used to improve many other aspects of community life. Under the management of Cris

275

Dobbins and John C. Mitchell, the foundation has patronized the Denver Symphony. It built the Claude K. and Edna C. Boettcher Memorial Conservatory and in 1960 gave the Boettcher home (originally the Walter Cheesman house) at Eighth and Logan to the state for the Executive Mansion. In 1971 the Boettcher Foundation unveiled an $850,000 education building for the Botanic Gardens, and in the past three and one-half decades, the benevolent organization has supported hundreds of research projects, scholarships, and other worthy causes.

Nearly a generation after Robert Speer's death, wealthy Denver families made his "civic benefactor" dream come true. Mayor Speer had always urged the community's wealthiest citizens to give some of their riches back to the city that had been so good to them. Prior to his passing, only a modest response was forthcoming. But in the more recent past the response has been overwhelming.

Local patrons who have improved the community are many. The worthy projects they have supported are too numerous to mention. Suffice it to say that trusts such as those established by Gerald Hughes, A.V. Hunter, and the Evans family have gone far to improve people's lives and make Denver an attractive city.

Mr. and Mrs. Arthur E. Johnson did much in the postwar era to upgrade greater Denver. One of the most notable projects they helped finance was the modern and expanded Denver Zoo. Among numerous enterprises underwritten by other families were the Gates Planetarium (Charles Gates family) in the Museum of Natural History and the Lawrence Phipps Auditorium in the same complex.

The Bonfils family—especially Helen G. Bonfils (Frederick G. Bonfil's daughter)—did much for Denver charities and culture. Miss Helen, as she preferred to be called, was born in 1889. She was educated at Miss Wolcott's School and the National Park Seminary in Maryland. Although she loved acting more than anything, she helped manage *The Post* after her father's death in 1933, eventually becoming chairman of the board. Miss Helen was tall, blonde, intelligent, and aggressive. She pursued a career of acting and producing concurrent with overseeing the paper and distributing millions of dollars of the family's philanthropies.

She generously supported the University of Denver and with Jean Chappell Cranmer did much to improve the arts. Both women backed the symphony and *The Denver Post* Opera Foundation, and they helped young artists get formal training which launched several important careers. Ultimately, the newspaper heiress built the Bonfils Theatre. And after her death in 1972, at her

276

Helen G. Bonfils. *Courtesy Denver Public Library, Western History Department*

request, the family's foundations were channeled into the Denver Center for the Performing Arts. The center is still being developed. Bill Hosokawa believes it will become "a cultural complex covering four square blocks in downtown Denver . . . [which] will include a concert hall, four theaters, a large parking garage, amphitheater, and administration building, all tied together with soaring glass-roofed galleries for shops and restaurants." If financial problems can be solved and the master plan finished, the Denver Center for the Performing Arts will become an important addition to Denver's postwar emphasis on the arts.

More emphasis on the community's recent commitment to its long underdeveloped cultural life can be seen in the monumental Art Museum, the new Denver Public Library, and the support given to a first-rate symphony. Likewise, the city is able to attract outstanding theater and ballet groups from New York and Europe. Devotion to the arts is reflected in the increasing numbers of avant-garde and experimental theaters. The Changing Scene, Germinal Stage, and the black performers' Nudijah Productions represent some of the alternatives available to greater Denver entertainment seekers.

Since the 1950s, a growing throng of artists and artisans has migrated to the area. A small but culturally sophisticated public is supporting sculptors, jewelry makers, potters, and painters. Today dozens of galleries dot the city. There artists can display and find markets for their creations. Scores of cooperative facilities have opened, too, where artists and craftsmen can work together in a mutually stimulating atmosphere.

The Denver area has become a center for creative writers and publishers. This trend has already surpassed a similar development in the late nineteenth century. Extremely important to this movement has been the English Department at the University of Denver. Alan Swallow first gave that department national recognition. During his brief life he set into motion a number of innovations which live on today. Swallow was born in 1915 on a Wyoming farm. He grew up there and attended the state university, where he wrote verse and started a little mimeographed literary magazine titled *Sage*. After graduation he attended Louisiana State University, where he earned a Ph.D. in 1941.

Graduate school gave Swallow more than exposure to Robert Penn Warren and Cleanth Brooks and a degree which enabled him to teach at the University of New Mexico, Western State College (Colorado), and finally the University of Denver (1946-1954). The years at Louisiana State provided him with an opportunity to try

Alan Swallow in 1966. *Courtesy of the Swallow Press*

publishing and editing—an avocation which became a career. In Baton Rouge he bought an inexpensive, used handpress. On that machine he printed *Signets: An Anthology of Beginnings*, a collection of writing done by fellow graduate students.

After an interlude in the Army, Swallow moved to Denver in 1946. There he packed teaching, writing, and publishing into the last twenty years of his life. When he died at his typewriter in 1966—he was fifty-one—he left a rich legacy. A man who unselfishly devoted his professional life to literature, he directed the underfinanced University of Denver Press throughout its life, which was even shorter than his own.

Besides the university press books, Swallow published numerous volumes of fiction, poetry, literary criticism, and western Americana under his own imprints of Big Mountain Press, Alan Swallow, Publisher, Sage Books, and Swallow Paperbacks. For a few years he was the nation's largest publisher of new poets, and he enhanced the fiction-writing careers of Janet Lewis, Vardis Fisher, and Frank Waters. Swallow also contributed his resources to "little magazine" ventures, he pioneered a singular doctoral program in creative writing, and he found time to do his own writing.

At the University of Denver, Swallow's inspiration continues under the able leadership of John Williams. One of Swallow's students, Williams founded the prestigious *Denver Quarterly* in 1966. He is director of creative writing at the university and author of two volumes of poetry and four novels, including *Augustus*, which won the National Book Award.

John Williams and his colleague, novelist Seymour Epstein, have done much to add to Denver's reputation as a center for creative writers, but they do not pursue their craft alone. Rex Burns, Warwick Downing, and John Dunning are gaining recognition as novelists. Many poets, including the remarkable Thomas Hornsby Ferril, find the metropolitan area compatible with writing verse.

Swallow's publishing company was moved to Chicago after he died, but that did not symbolize what was happening to the Rocky Mountain publishing business. Fred Rosenstock's Old West Publishing Company, specializing in western Americana, can be found in Denver. Pruett Publishing Company in Boulder has made a name for itself, producing books on regional subjects and western history. Frederick A. Praeger launched Westview Press in Boulder in 1975. The first year it boasted a list of over 140 nonfiction titles in the social sciences, history, and the arts.

Smaller publishers have multiplied dramatically in recent years.

Little presses such as Ally, Black Ace/Temple of Man/Bowery, Eggplant and Lodestar have specialized in poetry but have not devoted themselves exclusively to that subject. Most recently Great Divide Press was organized by several historians and free-lance writers. Devoted to publishing quality books on Rocky Mountain Americana, this newest addition to the growing list of companies will reprint rare, out-of-print books on the Rockies and print first editions of regional novels, poetry, and history.

The cosmopolitanism of Denver's postwar environment has been enhanced by the publication of several ethnic newpapers. Although the *Jewish News* and the Swedish *Western News* were started long before 1945, several other papers have joined them in recent years: the *Rocky Mountain Jiho* (Times), a Japanese newspaper; the *Denver Weekly News,* a publication for blacks; *Santa Fe Trail,* a Chicano community paper; and *El Gallo* published for the Crusade for Justice.

Journals, like writers, have found a home in Denver. In 1976 a new trade journal for the arts, *Ocular,* began publication Not since the turn of the century has a magazine been published and edited by women especially for women. Now *The Colorado Woman Digest* has begun publishing bi-monthly in Denver. Among the magazines edited in the city are *Denver* and *The Denver Magazine.* These monthly periodicals have featured articles on social and cultural subjects of particular interest to metro area readers.

Like the climate and mountains, Denver's coming of age intellectually and culturally served as a magnet for newcomers. To be sure, these inducements were powerful, but they were minor compared to the lure of economic opportunities. The economic boom of the past thirty years created an unusually open job market. Even during recession periods, metropolitan Denver's unemployment remained below the national average. Indeed, throughout the last quarter century the job market has been among the most favorable in the nation in the fields of accounting, agricultural-related industries, banking, energy production, health and medical service, insurance, and real estate.

Economic opportunity is not equal yet, but women and minorities fare much better now than they ever did historically. The federal government has led the movement since World War II to knock down discriminatory hiring policies. The fact that Denver houses so many federal agencies (there were over 31,000 federal nonmilitary personnel in 1976) and embraces so many industries and institutions which are supported solely or partly by government contracts insures equality of economic opportunity in a large sector of the economy.

During the war, women found government agencies and companies with government contracts to be the most fruitful avenues for economic advancement. For thirty years that trend has continued. At the state and local levels, too, women have found access to better jobs and equal pay for equal work.

The publishing field has been most receptive to women. Just as it was in the late nineteenth century, it remains one of the few areas of private enterprise in which women earn salaries comparable to those of men. They have located top editorial and administrative positions, and they have equal access to outlets for creative writing. In recent years women, for example, have edited *The Colorado Magazine* (a quarterly history journal), and over half of the members of the Colorado Authors' League—an organization of writers who receive pay for their skills—are women.

Since the late 1960s, women in greater Denver have secured an increasing number of managerial positions in private industry. Also, they have become involved in television broadcasting and in administrative offices in institutions of higher education. These advances have come about as the consequence of the nationwide women's rights movement. In Denver, as in other major cities, women have banded together, vocalized their demands, and sought, through demonstrations and legal action, to secure their constitutional rights.

That women are beyond sitting back and waiting for the male-dominated economy and polity to grow sensitive to their rights is apparent. On their own they are seeking power. Patricia Schroeder successfully campaigned for a seat in the United States House of Representatives in a metro Denver district in 1974. In 1976 a group of thirty-six women and five men were in the final stages of organizing the First Women's National Bank in Denver.

In some ways, the story of blacks is similar to that of women. Since the war, the federal government, and more recently state and local governments, have lifted barriers to their agencies. Blacks comprise just over 10% of Denver's population, yet they have acquired a higher percentage of positions on the government payroll.

There remains a larger percentage of blacks than whites in substandard housing, but that gap has grown smaller each decade since 1940. Only the poorest blacks remain in Five Points. Most of the middle class families have moved north and east of that ghetto, and blacks now have access to most neighborhoods where they can afford the housing.

282

Black Denverites have freedom to use all hospital facilities. This, plus their higher incomes (the gulf between white and black median income has dwindled every decade since 1940, too) and decent insurance plans, has virtually erased the difference between these two races on infant mortality.

However, blacks are as yet discriminated against in Denver society. They are not welcome in the exclusive clubs, and until a recent venture into bussing, the majority has attended de facto segregated elementary and high schools. The overall quality of life for them is less than what is available to whites. Nevertheless, they are increasingly prosperous.

The fortunes of two people, George Brown and Mary Berry, symbolize the possibilities now available to talented, educated blacks. In 1974 George Brown, a native of Lawrence, Kansas, became the first black man to be elected lieutenant governor in the United States. Running on Colorado's Democratic ticket with Richard Lamm, Brown's victory was not his only history-making first. A graduate of the University of Kansas School of Journalism and a veteran Air Corps officer who saw combat in World War II, Brown became the first black newsman for *The Post* in 1950. Soon the cub reporter became active in Democratic politics. In 1955 he was rewarded with an appointment to fill a vacancy in the state House of Representatives. In 1956 he surprised most political observers by winning an at-large seat in the state Senate. He was reelected four consecutive times, leaving that post in 1975 to take the lieutenant governorship.

George Brown's political successes demonstrate that able Afro-Americans have more opportunities available to them now than civil service or business careers within the black community. Another outstanding example is in higher education. In 1976 Dr. Mary Berry was lured to Colorado from the East when the chancellorship at the University of Colorado in Boulder became vacant. She was not only the first black to attain a top-level administrative post at the state university, she was the first woman to achieve such status.

Compared to the Spanish-surnamed population, women and blacks have made giant strides toward equality of opportunity. By all standards, Hispanic residents of Denver have the poorest living conditions of any group. Comprising approximately 17% of the population, they own the fewest homes, live in more substandard housing, have the lowest level of education, suffer the highest infant mortality rate, and receive the lowest per capita income.

There are several reasons why the Spanish-surnamed minority

have not found a better quality of life in the Queen City. Where education and government employment have helped blacks and women improve their lot, those ladders to success have not been available to many Hispanic people. Most of these immigrants went to Colorado from Mexico or moved to the metropolis from Spanish communities which date back to the late eighteenth and early nineteenth centuries in northern New Mexico and southern Colorado. In either case, Spanish was their native language. In Colorado's English-language schools they were always disadvantaged. By the 1940s and 1950s, many of the second generation had learned English. But even those who had a command of the dominant culture's language remained deprived. If they did seasonal migrant farmwork— and many did—the school-age children missed school, or, at best, they had their education interrupted and abbreviated by being forced to attend many different schools for short terms. Handicaps of language and inferior education meant that few native Americans of Spanish descent and Mexican-Americans qualified for the better jobs offered by equal opportunity employers.

Lack of unity within the Spanish-surnamed community has hindered their progress for thirty years, too. Members of this minority who claim Spanish rather than Mexican ancestry have set themselves apart from the Mexican-Americans. Some of the younger members of this group now identify with the larger Spanish-speaking culture, but historically the Hispanos have assumed themselves to be racially, culturally, and intellectually superior to the Chicanos or Mexican-Americans.

Hispanos have not only disparaged their neighbors from Mexico, since migrating to Denver they have accepted the Anglo-dominated system. Quietly, they have sought through education and assimilation to find their niches within the established order.

Beginning in the late 1960s, younger Hispanos and Chicanos sought new ways to find their rightful place in the economy and polity of the central Rockies. Shunning the approach taken by a majority of women and all but the younger blacks, they have rallied around Rodolfo "Corky" Gonzales. A wiry, moustached little dynamo, Gonzales was born in Denver in 1928. His father was a migrant farmer. From the time Corky was ten years old he hardened his body and hands working beside his father in Colorado's sugar beet fields. During the winter months, young Gonzales attended public schools when his family returned to Denver. Enrolled in nine schools before earning a high school diploma, Gonzales said his teachers taught him "how to forget Spanish, to forget my heritage, to forget who I was."

284

After high school, Gonzales devoted his energy to boxing. An outstanding Golden Gloves fighter, he won both the national and international amateur championships. During the late 1940s and early 1950s he fought professionally, battling his way to the number three spot in the featherweight division of the National Boxing Association.

In 1955 he gave up a professional sports career for various jobs including lumberjacking and migrant farming. For eleven more years Gonzales tried to improve his own position and that of his people by working within existing political and economic institutions. In 1957 he became the first Mexican-American district leader in Denver's Democratic party. Two years later he published *Viva*, the first barrio newspaper in the city.

Gonzales became a businessman as well as a politician and journalist. He bought a bail bond business and an automobile insurance agency, managing these while he organized the Mexican-Americans for Kennedy in 1960. The year President Kennedy was assassinated, the thirty-five-year-old Chicano organized Los Voluntarios, a group that protested the treatment of Spanish-speaking youths by the police department and lobbied for more Mexican-American representation on the police force.

From 1964 to 1966, Gonzales remained active in the Democratic party. In return, he found employment with local programs of President Lyndon Johnson's Great Society. He became director of the Neighborhood Youth Corps and chairman of the Denver War on Poverty program. His dedication to the Democratic party won him even larger responsibilities with the regional Anti-Poverty Program and the Job Opportunity Center.

By 1966, however, the personally successful Mexican-American leader became disillusioned. He felt that his work within the political system was accomplishing too little for his people. When the *Rocky Mountain News* accused him of discriminating against blacks and whites in the Neighborhood Youth Corps program, he resigned and organized the Crusade for Justice.

Since 1966 Gonzales has led this movement for civil rights within a frameword of ethnic pride and awareness. With headquarters in the barrio at 1265 Cherokee, he has begun a newspaper, *El Gallo*, and has sponsored conferences and events aimed at improving the living standards of Hispanic people while preserving their cultural identity. Gonzales and his followers have established their own political party in Colorado, La Raza Unida. They intend to use the influence of their ethnic group (the largest in the city and state) to get bilingual educational programs and the teaching of Hispanic history and culture required in the public schools.

In line with their ethnic pride and consciousness aims, Chicano activists in the mid-1970s advocated a form of separatism. They hoped to promote Chicano businesses, charter banks, and preserve their own cultural communities. Consequently, the ardent activists opposed bussing. They viewed it as just another attempt at forcing Spanish-speaking people to assimilate into the dominant Anglo culture.

Despite the apparent determination to find the good life outside of the system, many young Chicanos, like blacks and women, have taken advantage of the educational opportunities available in Denver. Until the 1960s, however, that option was sorely restricted. Accessibility to institutions of higher education—particularly for the lower economic class—is a new development. The University of Denver, Colorado Women's College, Regis College, and Loretto Heights College have been and still are expensive institutions. The University of Colorado had always been a relatively inexpensive facility for residents, but its location thirty miles from Denver made it inconvenient.

No progress was made toward extending opportunities for higher education in the 1940s and 1950s. Community leaders ignored the need. In fact, some members of the decision-making elite actually blocked hopes for widening the area's facilities. The Chamber of Commerce, for example, went on record against federal aid to education as late as 1961. The problem received serious attention only after lower and middle income taxpayers began demanding institutions for their needs.

State and local political leaders, with assistance from the federal government, finally appropriated funds for a number of colleges conveniently located and designed to fit the budgets of ordinary people. Metropolitan State College was authorized in 1963, Arapahoe Community College in 1965, and a multicampus Denver Community College in 1968. These schools support the undergraduate needs of the Queen City. Since then, the University of Colorado has opened a separate campus downtown. Originally created as an extension center, today it is a regular campus of the university, offering a variety of opportunities for students in graduate as well as under-graduate degree-granting programs.

The Community College, Metropolitan State, and the University of Colorado-Denver merged into the Auraria Higher Education Center in 1976. Local residents now have access to a large, functional, and centrally located education complex in which taxpayers from all walks of life can find an excellent faculty as well as low-cost graduate and undergraduate degree-granting programs. Students can attend classes on the 169-acre campus full or part time, day or night.

Other contemporary movements are going on which have revitalized the core city. In 1965 Dana Crawford conceived a plan to renovate one of the oldest parts of the downtown business district. Thanks to her energy and foresight, approximately thirty businesses thrive in renovated red brick buildings in Larimer Square. Tourists and residents have flocked to the shops and entertainment establishments centered along the historic 1400 block of Larimer Street. Also in the last decade, a nonprofit organization called Historic Denver, Incorporated has been valiantly fighting to save historic houses and buildings before wrecking companies raze them to make way for modern structures. Several monuments of the past have been saved already. If Historic Denver can find the money, more will be done in the future to give Denver architectural continuity with its history.

Two local banking institutions joined the preservation and beautification movement in the mid-1970s. First Federal Savings offered a membership to Historic Denver to anyone who made a minimum deposit of $500. First of Denver planted a tree at the confluence of the Platte River and Cherry Creek in the name of any person who deposited $200 in a savings account. This was their contribution to the city's attempt to reclaim this one-time blighted area into a sodded, tree-covered park.

Because Denver lost approximately 50,000 trees to Dutch elm disease, a "Think Trees" movement was started in spring 1976. The Denver Board of Realtors encouraged city home owners to buy and plant a tree on the public right-of-way adjoining their property. If the tree cost at least forty dollars and a planting permit was secured from the city, the Board of Realtors paid each participating property owner twenty dollars.

Creating a high-quality environment has never been the foremost concern of most Denver leaders and ordinary citizens. Earning profits has been the highest priority. Nevertheless, at various times and in different ways private enterprise, politicians, and taxpayers alike have shared in beautifying their community and extending opportunity to all. That they have at least been modestly successful is obvious. Despite its multitude of inequalities and problems, the Queen City of Mountain and Plain has continued to be one of the most pleasant cities left in America.

But Denver is now at the crossroads. Community leaders and

rank-and-file voters historically have sought more trans-mountain water to support future growth. Expansion, after all, stimulates the economy. Today, a debate rages over the merits of continuing that tradition. No one knows which side will win. The only certainty is that if metropolitan Denver finds the water to continue its financially profitable postwar pace of expansion, overall quality of life will deteriorate. If that happens, Denver will lose its minority status as one of the remaining liveable cities. The Mile High City will become just another sprawling metropolis.

Rudolfo "Corky" Gonzales. *Courtesy Denver Public Library, Western History Department*

Bibliographical Note

In the following pages I have made no attempt to list all of the literature available on Denver. I have not even tried to include everything that I have read on the Queen City and its hinterland. Instead, this bibliographical note contains the sources from which data, interpretations, and ideas were borrowed.

For every chapter I relied upon microfilm files of the *Rocky Mountain News*, *The Denver Post*, and *The Colorado Statesman* as well as the statistics compiled by the United States Bureau of the Census. The volumes of the *Colorado Yearbook* were indispensable to this study, as was Jerome C. Smiley's *History of Denver* (1901). The 1971 reproduction of this massive work was most useful, thanks to the detailed index compiled by Robert L. Perkin.

Besides Smiley's tome of almost 1,000 pages, I kept three other secondary works on my desk at all times: Carl Ubbelohde, Maxine Benson, and Duane A Smith, *A Colorado History* (1972, third edition); Robert Perkin, *The First Hundred Years: An Informal History of Denver and the Rocky Mountain News* (1959); Bill Hosokawa, *Thunder in the Rockies: The Incredible Denver Post* (1976).

Chapters One and Two

For material on Denver's power structure, the books by Smiley and Perkin were supplemented by Harry E. Kelsey, Jr., *Frontier Capitalist: The Life of John Evans* (1969); Thomas L. Karnes, *William Gilpin, Western Nationalist* (1970); William N. Byers,

Encyclopedia of Biography of Colorado, History of Colorado, Volume I (1901); an unpublished essay by Joan H. Beasley, "General William Larimer" (1972); Bernard Axelrod, "John Evans and the Commercial Development of Denver, 1862-1897," M.A. Thesis, U. of Denver, 1963; Jimmie Lee Frazier, "Early Stage Lines in Colorado, 1859-1865," M.A. thesis, U. of Denver, 1959; Junius E. Wharton, *History of Denver* (1866); *Record of Denver and Vicinity, Colorado: Portrait and Biography* (1898); Eugene Frank Rider, "The Denver Police Department: An Administrative, Organizational, and Operational History, 1858-1905," Ph.D. dissertation, U. of Denver, 1971; Nolie Mumey, *Pioneer Denver* (1948); and *History of the City of Denver, Arapahoe County, and Colorado* (1880).

Two articles by Deryl V. Gease were helpful on hinterland promotion and development: "William N. Byers and the Case for Federal Aid to Irrigation in the Arid Region," *Colorado Magazine* 45/4, Fall, 1968, and "William N. Byers and the Colorado Agricultural Society,' *Colorado Magazine* 48/4, Fall, 1971. I also relied upon two early issues of the *Colorado Magazine*: James F. Willard, "Spreading the News of the Early Discoveries of Gold in Colorado," 7/3, May, 1929, and LeRoy R. Hafen, "Supplies and Market Prices in Pioneer Denver," 4/4, August, 1927. A first-rate study by Thomas J. Noel, "All Hail the Denver Pacific: Denver's First Railroad, *Colorado Magazine* 50/2 spring, 1973, is the best account of that subject.

Much of the descriptive material came from travel accounts. One of the best is Lavina Honeyman Porter, *By Ox Team to California: A Narrative of Crossing the Plains in 1860* (1910). Only fifty copies of this account were published, and the few which survive are in the Bancroft Library, University of California, Berkeley. Other published travel logs and memoirs which I used are: "Across the Plains and in Denver, 1860: A Portion of the Diary of George T. Clark," *Colorado Magazine* 6/4, July 1929; "The Story of a Colorado Pioneer," *Colorado Magazine* 2/1, January, 1925; Mrs. Daniel Witter, "Pioneer Life," *Colorado Magazine* 4/5, December, 1927; Libeus Barney, *Early-Day Letters from Auraria (Now Denver), to the Bennington Banner, Bennington, Vermont, 1859-60* (n.d.); Albert Richardson, *Beyond the Mississippi* (1867); Colin B. Goodykoontz, "Colorado As Seen By a Home Missionary, 1863-1868, " *Colorado Magazine* 12/2, March, 1935; Louis L. Simonin, *The Rocky Mountain West in 1867* (1966, reprint); Albert B. Sanford, "The 'Big Flood' in Cherry Creek, 1864," *Colorado Magazine* 4/3, May, 1927; and Mrs. Mary E. Byers Robinson, "Mrs.

W. N. Byers, Pioneer Woman," *Colorado Magazine* 21/1, January, 1944.

Michael McGiffert, *The Higher Learning in Colorado: An Historical Study, 1860-1940* (1964) was central to my research on education, as were two articles in the *Colorado Magazine*: O.J. Goldrick, "The First School in Denver," 6/2, March, 1929, and Thomas F. Dawson, "Colorado's First Woman School Teacher," 6/4, July, 1929.

Sanford A. Linscome's "A History of Musical Development in Denver," D.M.A. dissertation, U. of Texas, 1970, is an important, thoughtful, and detailed history of cultural life in early Denver. An attractive complement to it is Thomas J. Noel, "The Multifunctional Frontier Saloon: Denver 1858-1876," *Colorado Magazine* 52/2, spring, 1975.

A pioneer work on poverty in Denver from the town's founding until the early 20th century is Bernard Rosen's "Welfare and Philanthropy in Denver," Ph.D. dissertation, U. of Colorado, 1976. Allen D. Breck's *A Centennial History of the Jews of Colorado, 1859-1959* (1960) has useful material on poverty as well as Denver's Jewish population.

The R.G. Dun Collection at Baker Library, Harvard University, not only proved to be extremely rich in business and economic history, it revealed much about territorial society, especially the upward mobility of blacks. The manuscript census records are on microfilm at the Federal Archives and Records Center in Denver, and they hold valuable data on Denver blacks, as does an article by Eugene H. Berwanger, "William J. Hardin: Colorado Spokesman for Racial Justice, 1863-1873," *Colorado Magazine* 52/1, winter, 1975.

The records of the United States District Court for Colorado Territory are at the Denver Federal Archives and Records Center. There I learned much about the troublesome issues which confronted people in frontier Denver. Selling whiskey to Indians, for example, was a far greater problem than saving the territory from the "sesesh" (Confederates) during the years 1861-1865.

Chapters Three and Four

For the period from 1870 to 1904, I found much on Denver's power elite in the R.G. Dun Collection, Henry B. Hyde (Equitable

Life Assurance Society of New York) Papers, and the Henry Lee Higginson (Lee, Higginson and Company, Boston) Papers at Harvard University's Baker Library.

The microfilm files of the *Denver Republican* at the State Historical Society, as well as the *Rocky Mountain News* and *The Denver Post*, were invaluable on economic development, as were issues of the *Denver Inter-Ocean*, a business magazine, and two other magazines, *Why?* and *The Mecca*, all preserved at the State Historical Society.

Articles on Denver's growth appeared in many late-nineteenth-century periodicals. Particularly helpful were essays which appeared in *The New England Magazine*, New Series, October, 1892 and in *Harper's* Volume 76, 1888 and Volume 86, 1893.

Two publications by Gunther Barth, "Metropolitanism and Urban Elites in the Far West," in Frederic C. Jaher, ed., *The Age of Industrialism in America: Essays in Social Structure and Cultural Values* (1968), and *Instant Cities: Urbanization and the Rise of San Francisco and Denver* (1975) have some good insights on the power elites.

Bibliographical data on business leaders is available in Smiley's *History of Denver*; Wilbur Stone's *History of Colorado*, 4 volumes (1918-1919); Frank Hall's *History of the State of Colorado*, 4 volumes (1889-1895); *Portrait and Biographical Record of the State of Colorado* (1899); *Representative Men of Colorado* (1902); and Byers' *Encyclopedia*. An article by Dwight Akers, "David H. Moffat and His Home Town," *Colorado Magazine* 27/3, July, 1950, has some interesting details on Moffat.

A good overview of the activities of the Chamber of Commerce is a 1966 U. of Wyoming M.A. thesis, "The Denver Chamber of Commerce and Board of Trade from 1884 to 1900," by Stephen John Leonard. For more detail, however, one must consult the "minutes" of the Denver Chamber of Commerce and the published Annual Reports beginning in 1883. A small book compiled by the chamber from its minutes, *The Long Pull* (1926), is superficial but interesting. A pamphlet, *The Artesian Wells of Denver*, is an example of the scientific-booster literature inspired by the Chamber of Commerce. An article in *Harper's Weekly*, October 30, 1897, titled "Festival of Mountain and Plain at Denver, Colorado," features photographs and details about one of the city's major promotional efforts. Literary boosterism, overlooked by historians for nearly a century, was discovered by M. James Kedro. Some of his findings are presented in an article, "Literary Boosterism," *Colorado Magazine* 53/3, summer, 1975.

Two books by Robert G. Athearn, *Rebel of the Rockies: The Denver and Rio Grande Western Railroad* (1962) and *Union Pacific Country* (1971) helped me sort out the complexities of railroad development, as did a long working paper on railroads going in and out of Denver, prepared for me by Rick Steele.

A superb study of banking, based largely upon First National Bank Archives, is *First of Denver: A History* (1971), by Robert S. Pulcipher. This work was immensely valuable to me, as were my conversations with Pulcipher and his help with my own research in the bank's archives.

Allen D. Breck's book, *William Gray Evans: Portrait of a Western Executive* (1964), is loaded with significant material on late-nineteenth-century Denver utilities corporations. Breck is much more sympathetic toward Evans and his fellow entrepreneurs than is Clyde L. King, *History of Government in Denver, With Special Reference to Its Relations with Public Service Corporations* (1911).

Three articles in the *Colorado Magazine* were useful on hinterland development: Albert E. Seep, "History of the Mine and Smelter Company," 23/3, May, 1946; Alfred P. Tischendorf, "British Investments in Colorado Mines," 30/4, October, 1953; and Ralph Blodgett, "The Colorado Territorial Board of Immigration," 46/3, summer, 1969. Among the books which helped me are: Clark Spence, *British Investments and the American Mining Frontier, 1860-1901* (1958); Duane A. Smith, *Rocky Mountain Mining Camps: The Urban Frontier* (1967); Gene M. Gressley, *Bankers and Cattlemen* (1966); and Lewis Atherton, *The Cattle Kings* (1961). One of the best Ph.D. dissertations done on Denver is by Stephen Leonard. Written at Claremont Graduate School in 1971, "Denver's Foreign Born Immigrants, 1859-1900" contains some excellent sections on British investment in Colorado. To my knowledge, Leonard is the first historian to recognize and explain James Duff's role in the growth of Denver.

I found good descriptive material on Denver in Don Etter, *Auraria, Where Denver Began* (1972); Sally Davis and Betty Baldwin, *Denver Dwellings and Descendants* (1963); Louisa Ward Arps, *Denver in Slices* (1959); and Edith Eudora Kohl, *Denver's Historic Mansions: Citadels to the Empire Builders* (1957). The *Colorado Magazine* contains four articles from which I drew local color: Robert Latta, "Denver in the 1880s," 18/4, July, 1941; "Colorado as Seen by a Visitor of 1880," Diary of Rezin H. Constant, 12/3, May, 1935; Edward Ring, "Denver Clubs of the Past," 19/4, July, 1942; and W.H. Bergtold, "Denver 50 Years Ago," 8/2, March, 1931.

I learned much about Denver's lower economic classes and minorities from the newspapers, especially the *Denver Republican* and the *Rocky Mountain News*. Extremely important for my work was Rachel Wild Peterson's autobiography, *The Long-Lost Rachel Wild, or Seeking Diamonds in the Rough* (1905). Stephen Leonard's "Denver's Foreign Born Immigrants, 1859-1900" has details on several immigrant groups, among them the Irish, Germans, Italians, Scandinavians, and Chinese, but he is unable to go into every group in as great a detail as more specialized works such as Gerald E. Rudolph, "The Chinese in Colorado, 1869-1911," M.A. thesis, U. of Denver, 1964; Breck's history of the Jews; or Ida Uchill, *Pioneers, Peddlers, and Tsadikim,* a detailed and lively history of Colorado Jewry. Likewise, Bernard Rosen presents new material in his thoroughly researched work on minorities and poverty in "Welfare and Philanthropy in Denver," and Eugene F. Rider has fresh insights on how the police related to the lower classes in his previously cited dissertation.

My material on black Denver comes from two black newspapers at the State Historical Society: *African Advocate* (only one issue survives) and *The Statesman*, a forerunner of the *Colorado Statesman*. A good biography of Barney Ford by Forbes Parkhill, *Mister Barney Ford: A Portrait in Bistre* (1963), Rider's dissertation, and an M.A. thesis done at the U. of Denver by James Rose Harvey, "Negroes in Colorado," (1941), were vital to my study.

Most of my evidence on the status of women came from the R.G. Dun Collection, newspapers, magazines such as *The Modern World* and *Business Women's Magazine*, and Martha A.B. Conine, "Women's Work in Denver," *Municipal Affairs* 2/3, September, 1898.

Chapters Five and Six

There are two published works on Robert Speer. The most recent is Charles A. Johnson, *Denver's Mayor Speer* (1969). Although more objective than Edgar C. MacMechen's, *Robert W. Speer: A City Builder* (1919), Johnson's book lacks the insights of the earlier volume. There are some good stories about Speer in Gene Fowler, *Timber Line: A Story of Bonfils and Tammen* (1933). I gathered much information on Speer from the files of *Municipal Facts*, and from the Benjamin Barr Lindsey Papers at the Library of Congress. Rivaling the Lindsey Papers for being most valuable, was

J. Paul Mitchell, "Progressivism in Denver: The Municipal Reform Movement, 1904-1916, " Ph.D. dissertation, U. of Denver, 1966.

Business, especially as it related to local politics, is the subject of Clyde Lyndon King's, *History of Government in Denver* (1911). The Edward P. Costigan Papers in the Western History Collections at the U. of Colorado cast invaluable light on this topic, and so did the Archives of the First National Bank.

The Lindsey and Costigan papers, the Mitchell dissertation, and Lindsey's book, *The Beast* (1910), told me much about the reform movement in Denver. Also valuable was an article by Elliot West, "Cleansing the Queen City: Prohibition and Urban Reform in Denver, " *Arizona and the West* 14/1, winter, 1972. Of further use were the following: Frances Anne Huber, "The Progressive Career of Ben B. Lindsey, 1900-1920," Ph.D. dissertation, U. of Michigan, 1963; Roland DeLorme, "The Shaping of a Progressive: Edward P. Costigan and Urban Reform in Denver, 1900-1911," Ph.D. dissertation, U. of Colorado, 1965; and "Turn-of-the-Century Denver: An Invitation to Reform," *Colorado Magazine* 45/1, winter, 1968, by the same author. George Creel's incredibly biased *Rebel at Large: Recollections of Fifty Crowded Years* (1947) is helpful when used with care.

Local newspapers and publications of the Chamber of Commerce were consulted for data on promotional activities and regional development. *After 50 Years: History and Biographical Sketches of the Founders and Directors of the Denver National Bank, 1884-1924* was important, as was LeRoy R. Hafen, "The Coming of the Automobile and Improved Roads to Colorado," *Colorado Magazine* 8/1, January, 1931; Roy M. Robbins, *Our Landed Heritage: The Public Domain, 1776-1936* (1942); and George S. McGovern and Leonard F. Guttridge, *The Great Coalfield War* (1972). I also relied upon statistics in the publications of the U.S. Bureau of Census and the *Colorado Year Books*.

Descriptive evidence on quality of life came from newspapers and national-circulation magazines, in particular the files of *American City* and *Architectural Record*. For the section on entertainment and Mary Elitch Long I relied upon Linscome's "A History of Musical Development in Denver," and Elinor Bluemel's *One Hundred Years of Colorado Women* (1973). Ms. Bluemel's *The Golden Opportunity: The Story of Emily Griffith Opportunity School of Denver* (1967) is the best work on that subject.

My evidence on child welfare and the larger issues of poverty and welfare came from the Lindsey Papers, Costigan Papers, the dissertations by Bernard Rosen, Eugene Rider, and Frances Anne Huber, an interview with Margaret Evans Davis (William Gray Evans' daughter), and a small book by Guy T. Justis, *Twenty-Five Years of Social Welfare, 1917-1942* (1942).

I relied upon federal census data for the statistics on minorities. A black newspaper, *Colorado Statesman*, was invaluable to my section on blacks. The thesis by James Rose Harvey, "Negroes in Colorado," was an asset again. My research was enhanced by James Atkins, "The Negro in Colorado," *Denver*, June, 1967, and by an excellent paper done in my seminar at the U. of Denver by Margaret Picher, "The Colorado Negro Business League: Its Plan For A Colony, 1905-1910" (1975).

The sources consulted on the Italians were the newspapers, and two rare books located in the State Historical Society: Giovanni Perilli, *Colorado and the Italians in Colorado* (1922), and Marcello Gandolfo, *Gli Italiani Nel Colorado Libro Dedicato agli Italiani, 1899-1900* (n.d.).

Source material on the Jews came from two previously cited works: Ida Uchill, *Pioneers, Peddlers, and Tsadikim*, and Allen Breck, *A Centennial History of the Jews*. My article, "The Ordeal of Colorado's Germans During World War I," *Colorado Magazine* 51/4 fall, 1974, is the basis for the section on the Germans.

Most of the biographical sketches included in chapters five and six came from the extensive biographical files in the State Historical Society and the Western History Department at the Denver Public Library.

Chapters Seven and Eight

The Red Scare story comes from Bill Hosokawa, *Thunder in the Rockies: The Incredible Denver Post* (1976); Philip L. Cook, "Red Scare in Denver," *Colorado Magazine* 43/4, Fall, 1966; and a manuscript copy of Robert Athearn's, *The Coloradans*.

For my interpretation of business leadership I used material from Geraldine Bean's well-researched and extremely helpful Ph.D. dissertation, "Charles Boettcher: A Study in Pioneer Western Enterprise," U. of Colorado, 1970. This history doctoral thesis (recently published by Westview Press) contains rich data on Colorado business. It is much broader than the title implies. The biographical files at the State Historical Society and Western History Department at the Denver Public Library were indispensable for this section.

I interviewed the late George Cranmer, as well as Cris Dobbins, Margaret Evans Davis, Montgomery Dorsey and Benjamin Stapleton, Jr. These people gave me details of their lives and the lives of their relatives and associates. They gave me insights, and they critically evaluated my own interpretations of people and events.

Robert S. Pulcipher's *First of Denver: A History* was useful in chapter seven like it was in earlier portions of the book. His guidance through the Archives of the First of Denver enhanced chapter seven, as did his willingness to answer my questions about contemporary banking and bank history.

Allen Breck's biography of William Gray Evans was most helpful on the railroad problem, and so was Robert Athearn's *Rebel of the Rockies: The Denver and Rio Grande Western Railroad* (1962).

Benjamin Stapleton, Jr. helped me improve the parts of the book relating to his father. Montgomery Dorsey had some fascinating things to tell me about Stapleton and the business community. These men supplemented the rich memories George Cranmer had of his close friend and colleague.

I examined the Ku Klux Klan collection at the State Historical Society. While enlightening, its value is limited because names which appear on what is purported to be a membership list do not always correspond with a record of dues-paying members. In short, great care must be used in deciphering who actually belonged to the Klan, if indeed it is even possible.

Marjorie Hornbein answered my questions about her father's attitudes toward Stapleton and the Klan. Benjamin Stapleton, Jr. helped me understand his father's viewpoint. Kenneth Jackson's *The Ku Klux Klan in the City, 1915-1930* (1967) was quite helpful.

I supplemented what I learned from interviews with Montgomery Dorsey, George Cranmer and Benjamin Stapleton, Jr., about the mayor, with George V. Kelly's *The Old Gray Mayors of Denver* (1974).

The *Reader's Guide to Periodical Literature* led me to scores of articles on Denver. Numerous issues of *The American City, The Survey, Industrial Education Magazine, Time* and *Business Week* fleshed out what I learned on local improvements from interviews, newspapers, publications of the Denver Planning Commission, and Kelly's *Old Gray Mayors*.

My stories on the New Deal were pieced together from many sources. Invaluable were the Works Project Administration records for Colorado in the National Archives. The Costigan Papers were a boon to my research, as were interviews with George Cranmer,

Benjamin Hooper and Montgomery Dorsey. Many issues of *The American City* and *The Christian Century* provided a rich yield, and I borrowed material from James F. Wickens, "Depression and the New Deal in Colorado," in John Braeman, et al, eds., *The New Deal: The State and Local Levels,* Volume II, (1975), and Bernard Mergen, "Denver and the War on Unemployment," *Colorado Magazine* 47/4, fall, 1970.

I learned about booster campaigns from the reports and publications of the Chamber of Commerce. The sources on the ski industry were George Cranmer and local newspapers.

Statistics on federal employment and installations came from records of the Chamber of Commerce, *Colorado Year Book*, and city directories.

Manufacturing and income data came from volumes of the *Colorado Year Book*. Automobile statistics were generously provided to me by the Colorado State Department of Revenue, and much of the material on decentralization came from the published volumes of the Denver Planning Commission.

Information on minority groups was gathered from several sources including newspaper and census records: Denver Planning Commission reports; James A. Atkins, *Human Relations in Colorado: A Historical Record* (1968); Ida Uchill, *Pioneers, Peddlers and Tsadikim* (1957); James Rose Harvey, "Negroes in Colorado," M.A. thesis, U. of Denver, 1941; and *The Negro Population of Denver, Colorado* (1929).

The local press, articles in *New Republic* and *Business Week,* federal censuses, and interviews with Bejamin Hooper and George Cranmer, served as the primary sources for the parts of chapters seven and eight which focus on World War II.

Chapters Nine and Ten

I relied more heavily upon newspapers, particularly the *Rocky Mountain News*, *The Denver Post*, and *Cervi's Rocky Mountain Journal*, in these concluding chapters than elsewhere in the book. Few worthwhile studies exist on postwar Denver. The handful of useful books which cover parts of the period are: Bill Barker and Jackie Lewin, *Denver!*, Bill Brenneman, *Miracle on Cherry Creek* (1973), which has much information on Elwood Brooks; George V. Kelly, *The Old Gray Mayors of Denver* (1974), which goes forward beginning with Stapleton; Elinor Bluemel, *One Hundred Years of Colorado Women* (1973); Bill Hosokawa,*Thunder in the Rockies* (1976); and Robert L. Perkin, *The First Hundred Years* (1959).

Interviews with Cris Dobbins, Robert Pulcipher, Montgomery Dorsey, and George Cranmer were crucial to what I wrote in chapters nine and ten.

Boosterism is catalogued in the reports, publications, and advertisements of the Chamber of Commerce, and the statistics cited in these chapters came from Chamber of Commerce reports, federal censuses, city directories, and the Colorado State Department of Revenue.

I am indebted to Dr. Mark S. Foster of the U. of Colorado-Denver for allowing me to use the manuscript for his article "Coloradans Reject the 1976 Winter Olympic Games: a Look Behind the Ballots," which appeared in *Colorado Magazine* 53/2, spring, 1976. Cris Dobbins gave me some insights and ideas on the Olympics controversy, too.

My observations on postwar quality of life came from major urban newspapers published outside of Denver, from national circulation magazines, and from my own observations. Barker and Lewin's *Denver!* and Hosokawa's *Thunder in the Rockies* influenced me as well.

The details of Alan Swallow's career came from two sources: Alan Swallow, "Story of a Publisher," *New Mexico Quarterly* 36/4, winter, 1966-67; and "Alan Swallow: Winter's Publisher," *The Denver Quarterly* 10/3, autumn, 1975.

Evidence for what I said about black Denver goes back to the writings of James Atkins cited previously. I also used Shelly Rhym, *Through My Eyes: The Denver Negro Community, March 1934— January 1968* (1968). The sketch on George Brown came from Hosokawa's book on *The Post*.

Beyond dozens of articles in Denver newspapers, I relied upon three sources for my outline of Spanish-surnamed Denver: Christine Marin, "Rudolfo 'Corky' Gonzales: The Mexican-American Movement Spokesman, 1966-1972," *Journal of the West* 14/4, October, 1975; *Report to the General Assembly: The Status of Spanish-Surnamed Citizens in Colorado* (1967); and U. S. Commission on Civil Rights, *Mexican-American Education Study*, Report 1, *Ethnic Isolation of Mexican-Americans in the Public Schools of the Southwest* (1971).

Index

First National Bank, 16, 22, 71, 74,
77, 79, 134, 151, 189, 191, 194,
195, 253, 259, 265, 287
First National Bank of Pueblo, 195
First National Bank Tower, 263
First Women's National Bank in
Denver, 282
Fishberg, Maurice, 179
Fisher, Vardis, 280
Fitzsimons Army Medical Center,
127, 128, 220, 221, 238, 275,
"Five Points", 104, 172-73, 225,
226, 232, 242, 282
flood of 1864, 36-38
Flower, John S., 228
food in early Denver
diet, 32-33
imported foods, 10
lack of during Indian
uprising, 40
Ford, Barney L., 53, 105
Fordney McCumber Tariff, 197
Fort Laramie, 38
Fort Logan, 127, 187, 220, 221
Fort Lyon, 40
forty-niners, xiii
Forward Metro Group, 269-70
Franciscans, 116
Frankenstein, Doctor, 90
Fraser River, 206
Friedman, William S., 117,
151, 177
"Friendly Shelter", 115, 145

gambling, 130-31, 133, 135, 172,
181, 203, 206
Gas and Electric Co.
charter agreement, 138
Lindsey, 152
money for parks, 139
& Speer, 134, 141
Gates, Charles C. Sr., 227
Gates Family, 276
Gates Planetarium, 276
Gates Rubber Co., 227-28, 240
"Gateway to the Rockies", 275
Geddes, William, 215
General Federation of Women's
Clubs, 84
General Iron Works, 240

General Land Office, 220
Germania Glee Club, 49
German Americans
German Jews, 176-80
mentioned, 179, 226
& music, 49-50, 162-63
& Speer, 122
World War I, 180-81
Germany, 180-81
Germinal Stage, 278
Gerry Co., 262
Gibson, Thomas, 5
Gilpin, William
& Chivington, 41
& Civil War, 31
first Governor of Territory, 9
mentioned, 12
replaced, 10
"Give While You Live", 144
Globe Smelting Co., 84
Globeville, 80, 243
gold, xiii, xiv, xv, 8
Golden, 4, 14, 22
golfing facilities, 215
Gonzales, Rodolpho "Corky",
281, 284-85
Good Shepherd Home, 116
Goodheart, James, 145
"Gospel Wagon", 116
Gottlieb, Joel, 52
Gould, Jay, 60
Grand Army of the Republic, 126
Grand Junction, 83
Grant, James B.
biographical sketch, 80
home, 88
& laborers, 95
& power elite, 65, 86
& University of Denver, 89
Grant, (Mrs.) James B., 116
Grant Smelter, 80
Grant, Ulysses S., 16
Gray, Fannie, 105
Great American Desert, xiii, xv
Great Depression, 209, 231-36
The Great Divide, 64, 108
Great Divide Press, 281
Great Fire, 34-35
The Great Southwest Magazine,
128

318